Job Interviewing

A Wiley Brand

Job Interviewing

by Pamela Skillings

A Wiley Brand

Job Interviewing For Dummies®

Published by: **John Wiley & Sons, Inc.,** 111 River Street, Hoboken, NJ 07030-5774, www.wiley.com

Copyright © 2024 by John Wiley & Sons, Inc., Hoboken, New Jersey

Published simultaneously in Canada

For general information on our other products and services, please contact our Customer Care Department within the U.S. at 877-762-2974, outside the U.S. at 317-572-3993, or fax 317-572-4002. For technical support, please visit https://hub.wiley.com/community/support/dummies.

Wiley publishes in a variety of print and electronic formats and by print-on-demand. Some material included with standard print versions of this book may not be included in e-books or in print-on-demand. If this book refers to media such as a CD or DVD that is not included in the version you purchased, you may download this material at http://booksupport.wiley.com. For more information about Wiley products, visit www.wiley.com.

Library of Congress Control Number: 2023947360

ISBN: 978-1-394-19291-5 (pbk); 978-1-394-19293-9 (ebk); 978-1-394-19292-2 (ebk)

SKY10057764_101823

Contents at a Glance

Table of Contents

Introduction

To win any job offer, you must first pass the intimidating test of the job interview. The good news is that anyone can learn the skills needed to ace interviews with the right preparation. This book is your guide.

About This Book

Follow the guidance in this book and you'll be fully prepared to make the most of any job interview. The advice and examples are based on my experience as a career-and-interview coach who has worked with thousands of clients over more than 15 years. I know my approach works because I have seen the proof in my clients' successes. Here's a walk-through:

1. I start in Part 1 with a big-picture overview of the world of interviewing. I walk you through the latest trends, the high-level best practices that have worked for my clients, and a field guide to the types of interviews and interviewers you're likely to encounter.

2. Next, I delve into actionable advice to kick off your preparation for your upcoming interviews (whether you have one night or several weeks to prepare). In Part 2, you start with analyzing the job description, researching the opportunity, and evaluating your fit. This will help you anticipate the most likely questions you'll face in your interviews.

3. Then it's time to get you prepared to answer those questions. Part 3 provides deep dives into all the most challenging questions. Each chapter covers a common question type, why interviewers ask it, and how to answer it effectively. I include helpful models for outlining your answers and sample answers for inspiration.

4. Once you're an expert on the questions, it's time to follow the action plan in Part 4. I guide you through applying the advice and getting ready to shine in your interview. I cover best practices for outlining your speaking points, communicating confidence with body language and eye contact, refining your presentation through practice, and reducing interview anxiety. I also outline specific advice for common interview challenges — including explaining layoffs and gaps, prepping quickly when time is limited, brushing up on skills when you're rusty, positioning yourself for career change, and more.

5. The book concludes with The Part of Tens: ten tips directly from my hiring manager friends, advice on spotting red flags at companies interviewing you, and tips to level up your job search and land more interviews.

Icons Used in This Book

Books in the *For Dummies* series highlight particularly important text by using these icons:

TIP

This book is filled with tips, but I mark particularly important or fresh ones with this icon.

REMEMBER

You may have heard these ideas before, but they're important enough to deserve a shout-out.

WARNING

Avoid these common pitfalls to ensure success.

Beyond the Book

In addition to the material in the print or ebook you're now reading, you get a free, access-anywhere Cheat Sheet with even more tips for acing your interviews. To get this Cheat Sheet, visit www.dummies.com and type **Job Interviewing For Dummies Cheat Sheet** in the Search box.

I am also offering you free trial access to my company's Big Interview training platform, a resource trusted by top universities and used by millions of job seekers. Big Interview provides video lessons, an interactive practice interview tool, AI interview and resume feedback, and more. For access and more information, go to www.dummies.com/go/bigInterview/.

Where To Go from Here

You may choose to read this book from cover to cover, or you may prefer to read just what you need when you need it — that's *just-in-time* learning. If you prefer the latter method, just review the table of contents and turn to the page you're motivated to read. In either case, I hope you find this book worthwhile and enjoyable.

1

Learning to Ace Any Job Interview

Chapter **1**

Accelerating Your Career with Interview Skills

Are you ready to learn how to ace your next job interview? I'm here to help.

I realize that you're probably not reading this book for fun. You're looking for a new job and you know you'll need to win over a series of interviewers before you can land that offer.

Demystifying the job interview is my specialty, so I'm well aware that most people dread interviewing and find the whole process exhausting.

It's true that job interviews can be challenging, but I can teach you the skills you need in order to wow any interviewer. These skills will boost your confidence and expand your career opportunities.

Mastering the Simple Techniques to Ace Any Job Interview

I'm here to give you actionable advice and real strategies, not just a lot of theory.

These are the same interview preparation techniques that I've taught to thousands of interview coaching clients over the years.

These techniques work. I've been teaching people to land their dream jobs for a long time.

I've also spent more than 15 years working as a hiring manager and human resources consultant.

I work on both sides of the interview table — so I know what interviewers are looking for and what turns them off.

Finally, I'm the founder and chief coach at Big Interview, an online interview training platform that is licensed by more than 600 schools, universities, and government agencies. Millions of users have benefited from our lessons and practice tools.

In other words, I spend all my time helping people with interviews and I want to share this knowledge with you.

Preparing for success

The most qualified candidate doesn't always get the job. In addition to the right qualifications and background, you need solid interviewing skills to compete in today's job market.

TIP

The first mantra I want you to learn is that preparation is everything.

Prepare well and you'll perform better than nine out of ten of your competitors. The trick lies in *how* you prepare.

REMEMBER

If you know how to prepare, you can anticipate the majority of the interview questions you'll face. You can plan how to answer those questions in a way that will position you as a superior hire. You can practice in a way that boosts your confidence and refines your presentation skills.

I strongly believe that anyone with the right preparation can excel at interviewing.

Projecting confidence

Another rule to live by: Convey confidence, get hired.

If you seem confident in your abilities, you'll inspire confidence in others.

Confidence comes through in your body language and how you make eye contact, but especially in how you talk about your skills and accomplishments.

Projecting confidence is where a lot of job seekers run into trouble. Most people don't have a lot of practice in the art of self-promotion, so they shy away from the idea of "selling" their qualifications in interviews.

"I'm just not good at selling myself!" This is one of the most common complaints I hear from my coaching clients.

I love hearing these words because I know I can help these clients make a dramatic improvement in their interview game pretty quickly. They tend to be people who are successful and confident and poised, but just a bit too modest when it comes to talking about themselves.

Luckily, you can learn to "sell" yourself without feeling like a sellout.

Take my client Lawrence, for example. He was an accomplished IT professional with an impressive resume and no problem standing up to speak in front of a room full of colleagues.

However, he was struggling in job interviews, and he didn't understand why. Despite his impressive resume, he was being passed over in favor of other candidates.

The issue became clear in our first practice interview. He avoided bringing up his most impressive accomplishments and then stumbled and generalized when asked about his strengths.

Lawrence was a humble guy by nature and unaccustomed to talking about himself in glowing terms. Also, for the past several years, he had been promoted based on his work and his reputation, so his interview skills were rusty. He wasn't used to interviewing with people who didn't already know him and his track record.

If you can relate to Lawrence's challenges, you're not alone. Some of my most impressive clients have suffered from this same discomfort with self-promotion.

Like Lawrence, you can learn to work through this issue and start attracting offers.

Confidence versus arrogance

In daily life, people are rarely called on to list their strengths and weaknesses or summarize their proudest accomplishments.

In fact, many people grew up with the conditioning that it's obnoxious to brag or call attention to their achievements. This is just good manners when it comes to cocktail parties, but it will hurt you in job interviews.

It's unfair, but great candidates often get passed over for people with worse qualifications but better persuasion skills.

TIP

Candidates worry too much about coming across as arrogant — I would argue that if you're worried about sounding arrogant, you aren't in danger of actually crossing that line. I've had only a few coaching clients whom I advised on toning down their self-promotion. Every other client has benefited from turning up the volume on their accomplishments.

Yes, you should aim to be polite and likable. However, the interviewer also *wants* you to communicate what makes you stand out from other candidates. That's why you're there.

Their job is to pick the best candidate. It's impossible to get a full and complete picture of any human being from a conversation that lasts only 30 or 40 minutes, so the interviewer must rely on a limited set of data points.

You must clearly convey what sets you apart and how you can benefit the organization if hired.

I'm not recommending an aggressive or dishonest approach here. I'm talking about putting your best foot forward, knowing your strengths, and communicating them in a memorable and persuasive way.

To make sure you don't cross the line into arrogance, avoid

>> Trying to hijack or "take control" of the interview

>> Interrupting or correcting your interviewer

>> Being condescending

>> Acting like you're too good for the job

In a job interview, it's *never* a good idea to make your interviewer feel stupid, defensive, or annoyed. You want to make a connection, establish rapport, and make a positive impression.

REMEMBER

Despite your expertise and impressive background, people won't want to work with you if they think you're obnoxious, demanding, confrontational, or full of hot air. Interviewers will worry that you have an attitude problem and wouldn't be a good team player.

How to sell yourself in an interview

One way to get more comfortable channeling your self-promotional side is to think about it as switching into Interview mode.

Interview mode is that version of you that's irresistible to employers. It's not a fake persona; it's just a more polished and confident and professional version of you — a version that isn't afraid to talk about how great you are.

Later in this book, I cover a number of effective ways to embrace Interview mode and "brag in a likable way." For now, here are a few big-picture recommendations to keep in mind as you read on:

» Own your strengths.

» Share your success stories.

» Make your individual contributions clear.

» Avoid self-deprecating comments.

» Practice confident, nonverbal communication (posture and eye contact, for example).

Being authentic

The good news is that you can learn to sell yourself in a way that still feels authentic. You don't have to lie, exaggerate, or act like a scam artist. You just have to do the work of understanding your key strengths and preparing to communicate them in a concise and compelling way.

REMEMBER

Never, ever lie in a job interview. Interviewers are good at sniffing out blatant dishonesty; any lies you tell are likely to come back to haunt you. I encourage you to be truthful.

I want to stress that selling yourself doesn't mean misrepresenting the facts. Interviewers are more likely to connect with you and like you if they see you as a real and authentic human being and can get a sense of your true personality and values during the interview.

Sure, honesty is the best policy, but that doesn't mean you have to reveal everything — just be strategic about what you emphasize and how you present information. When it comes to job interviews, there is such a thing as being *too* truthful. You don't have to volunteer every weakness.

Understanding the interviewer's perspective

Interviewers are not all-powerful, judgmental robots. They are humans with their own jobs to do, with their own worries and goals.

Understanding their perspective will help you customize your communication style to connect with and persuade them.

In Chapter 3, I cover the various types of interviewers you'll encounter, from recruiter to CEO, and what to expect from each.

In general, your interviewer is responsible for making a qualified hire. If they miss a red flag and hire a dud, it's a big hit to their reputation (and maybe their performance bonus).

Remember this when they ask annoying questions. They're trying to get the data they need in order to make a decision and they don't have a lot of time in a typical interview to get to know you.

That's why it's important for you to proactively "sell" your strengths and give them the information they need, even if they don't know to ask for it.

Keep it concise.

Like the rest of us, interviewers have short attention spans these days. If you bore them, you lose them. As a result, the rule of thumb here is to not go longer than two minutes on any single answer unless you're asked follow-up questions.

Aim for interview answers that are only a minute or two long. At less than 1 minute, you're probably leaving out something good. If you go much beyond 2 minutes as a monologue, you'll lose them.

Show some enthusiasm.

The interviewer will also want to see clear signs of enthusiasm about the position and the company. Nobody wants to hire a candidate who's lukewarm about the job. They want someone who's excited, who asks questions, who seems like they would be truly motivated to succeed if they were hired for the position.

So dial back the hard-to-get factor. I've seen many candidates rejected because they just didn't seem to want it enough. Maybe their answers to questions like, "Why are you interested in this role?" were too general or unconvincing, or maybe their attitude or body language made them seem too casual or unmotivated.

Showing enthusiasm also helps you establish rapport. People like to be heard and appreciated, even interviewers. They're looking for a way to connect with you, and you can bond over common interests related to the position.

Embracing Interviewing as a Life Skill

Right now, you're focused on how performing better in an interview can help you land your next job. However, you should know that interviewing is also an essential life skill. The time you invest now in strengthening your interview game will pay off throughout your career.

REMEMBER

Interviewing helps you hone your presentation and communication proficiency, your ability to think on your feet, and your talents of persuasion. These abilities will serve you in many other aspects of life and career as well.

At the same time, given the rapid changes taking place in the job market these days, you'll likely be interviewing many times as you progress in your career, consider career changes, and adapt to changing job requirements.

Let's look at the many reasons you'll benefit from the information in this book — even after you've landed your next position.

Recognizing that job change is inevitable

The average person holds 12 different jobs during their adult lives.

In fact, according to numbers from the Department of Labor's Bureau of Labor Statistics, 27 percent of the population with 4-year college degrees or better have held between eight and ten jobs between the ages of 18 and 42.

Change is a constant and the workforce keeps revolving. You never know when the perfect opportunity will appear. *Don't you want to be ready?*

REMEMBER

If you master the process of preparing for job interviews effectively, you will never have to feel trapped in a bad job.

Staying ready to seize opportunity

Sometimes opportunities arise when you're not looking for them. You want to be ready for those lucky breaks.

Looking for a new job is exhausting and time-consuming. People understandably put it off. ("I'll wait to start looking until I have time to update my resume and work on my interviewing skills.") However, that vague feeling of not being ready can hold you back. Imagine the following scenarios:

>> You're at a conference or networking event and you run into someone from your dream company who says, "We're looking for someone with your background. Can you come meet my boss tomorrow?"

>> A LinkedIn contact reaches out because you seem perfect for a suitable role that just opened up at their firm.

>> Your manager's boss approaches you about an internal move that would dramatically increase your compensation.

If you know how to interview well, you won't have to hesitate to jump at the opportunity.

Bouncing back from layoffs

Unfortunately, layoffs are now a fact of life. They happen at even the most successful companies.

Even great performers in "indispensable" roles can be laid off.

You shouldn't live in fear, but you should stay ready.

Many coaching clients have found me after getting blindsided by a layoff. They had to start from square one with their job search during a time when they were already dealing with the stress of losing their job.

The good news is that they'll never be in that situation again, because strong interview skills are easy to refresh once you have them.

Leveling the playing field

You hear a lot about people who landed great gigs because they were connected — they "knew somebody," in other words. It's a fact of life that some people (or some people's parents) are privileged enough to attend the best schools and socialize with industry leaders. They receive training and mentoring that the rest of us don't have access to.

Good interview skills can help level the playing field. You can learn what interviewers really care about and how to speak their language.

Improving your hiring and mentoring skills

Did you know that interviewing is also a critical management skill? I frequently conduct training workshops for hiring managers. I teach them what to do (and what not to do) to empower more effective hiring decisions.

Companies come to me for this because so many hiring managers have never had training in how to interview. As a result, they ask bad questions, jump to biased conclusions, and hire the wrong candidates. Sometimes, they put their companies at risk of discrimination complaints.

You can become a better interviewer and manager by understanding the nuances of the interview process. This will help you choose better questions, minimize bias, and gather more reliable data for making hiring decisions.

Mentoring is another key management skill. You'll be a better mentor if you can help people get better jobs. You can advise friends, family members, and others in your community.

I can attest to the fact that people are always looking for advice and feedback on their interview skills. In addition to my coaching clients, I have advised relatives, neighbors, former co-workers and employees, and nice people I know only through LinkedIn. I have also volunteered with organizations that help high school and college students with their interview skills.

You can pay it forward once you know the secrets.

Gaining presentation confidence

Interview prep will also make you a better presenter and public speaker.

You'll improve your verbal communications skills by learning how to persuade with your words. You'll also develop impressive nonverbal communication skills through practice and adapting your body language and delivery for different audiences.

You'll learn how to project confidence even when you don't feel it. This will serve you well in many aspects of life.

Finally, you'll gain storytelling skills by developing your STAR examples (Chapter 11 covers this useful approach to creating interview stories) and using them to make interviewers love you.

Avoiding Common Mistakes

Now let's look at the common interview mistakes that trip up even the smartest and most-qualified candidates.

Skipping preparation

This is one that has brought down many a great candidate. Good preparation includes analyzing the job description, researching the firm, thinking through your answers to key questions, and practicing your delivery.

Once you learn how to prepare properly, you'll have a major edge over the competition. Most people just do a couple of online searches for common interview questions, skim their resume, and hope for the best.

That's not enough to get hired in a competitive market.

Lacking professionalism

A failure in this area can knock you out of the running before you even open your mouth. Professionalism means showing up on time, dressing appropriately, using appropriate language, and following interview etiquette (Chapter 2 will educate you on current etiquette guidelines).

Selling yourself short

I see this one all the time. An accomplished, impressive coaching client tells me they're getting lots of interviews but no offers, and I immediately guess what the issue is.

The practice interview always confirms my suspicions. They're letting modesty hold them back from promoting their strengths and accomplishments properly.

Often, they're doing "fine" in interviews, but they're just not standing out, because they're too humble.

Boring them with generic fluff

When you don't prepare, your answers tend to be lame. They're all generalities and clichés: team player, people person, problem solver, great fit.

You'll lose your interviewer's attention quickly this way and leave no lasting impression when you leave.

Going negative

Never, ever bad-mouth your current or former managers or co-workers in an interview. Sure, maybe your manager was terrible. Plenty of terrible managers are out there.

However, you must find a way to keep it positive — or at least neutral. Otherwise, you risk raising concerns that you are a complainer or difficult to get along with.

REMEMBER

If a situation ended badly, that makes it especially important to prepare some bullet points so that you can provide just enough detail and the right words to avoid sounding defensive or unprofessional.

Rambling

Some people tend to ramble when they're nervous. They go on and on and on — without saying much of substance.

After a while, the interviewer tunes out and prays for it to end.

Preparation helps you stay focused so you don't wander off on a tangent.

Dodging questions

If you avoid answering a question, even if you think you're doing it gracefully, the interviewer will think you're hiding something.

Nobody wants to risk hiring someone they can't trust.

Knowledge Is Power

You can avoid all these common mistakes if you follow my advice.

So, let's get to it. The next few chapters cover everything you need to know about how interviews work and how they're evolving, and the interview formats and approaches you'll encounter.

Then, in Parts 2 and 3 of this book, you'll see exactly how to prepare for interviews using the methods that have worked so well for my coaching clients.

In Part 4, I show you how to turn all that knowledge into a concrete prep plan, help you perfect your delivery, and provide you with the tools you'll need to handle challenging interview scenarios.

Chapter **2**

Understanding the New World of Interviewing

The world of work is constantly evolving. New technologies emerge while old ones become obsolete. New industries heat up, creating all-new job descriptions. Old industries shift, requiring new areas of expertise and automating entire functions.

It makes sense that the world of interviewing and hiring must also evolve to keep up. If you're new to interviewing or it's been a while since your last job search, it's important to stay up to date on what's new and how you can adapt.

In this chapter, I give you an overview of the trends you need to know about and how they're changing the hiring landscape. These trends include the rise of AI and ChatGPT, the effects of remote work, and more.

I also provide a primer on your rights as a job seeker, based on the most recent anti-discrimination legislation.

Next, I zoom out to show you how interviewing fits into the overall hiring process — outlining the stages of the typical recruiting cycle from sourcing to onboarding, what happens behind the scenes, and best practices for navigating each stage.

Finally, I touch on the key rules of interview etiquette, how they have changed, and how to avoid making a mistake that could hurt you.

Keeping Up with Trends and Technology

Technology and business trends influence how people work, what skills are most in demand, and how companies recruit and hire.

Change has accelerated in recent years and will continue to keep job seekers on their toes. The COVID-19 outbreak turned the world of work upside down, fast-tracking many changes that were already in the works and creating new challenges.

Remote work became a necessary option for most positions. Video interviews replaced in-person interviews.

Now, many companies and employees are determined to return to the pre-COVID normal, while others continue to embrace new attitudes and ways of working.

Meanwhile, new technological developments, including machine learning and artificial intelligence, promise more big changes for many industries and professions.

In this chapter, I cover the recent trends that have significantly affected the hiring process and give you tips on how to adapt your approach to ensure that you stay competitive.

Looking at job market trends

The job market is always changing. These days, the pace of change is just *faster*, and everyone is expected to keep up.

The past few years have been a virtual roller-coaster ride. First, the U.S. economy saw a wave of layoffs and job losses during the COVID-19 pandemic as many companies and entire industries struggled to stay afloat. As the economy gradually reopened, companies initiated a rebound in hiring. Hiring shortages in many professions led to more power and choice for qualified candidates. Then, after a period of growth, companies began layoffs as they realized that they had expanded too quickly.

Meanwhile, new trends and technologies are creating new job titles, transforming job requirements and hiring criteria and leading to new questions to prepare for in job interviews.

Read on for brief overviews of each trend and how it's impacting hiring and interviews. I also provide recommendations to help you respond and adapt to these trends to gain an edge in the job market.

TIP

The remote work trend has played a major role in recent job market changes. I examine that trend in depth in the next section.

Artificial intelligence

Artificial intelligence (AI) and machine learning are revolutionizing business across industries. Most recently, companies have begun replacing many automated support and content-generation tasks with *ChatGPT*, an AI-powered language model that generates human-like responses based on a vast digital knowledge base.

As a result, demand is soaring for professionals who have AI experience and skills in data analysis, programming, statistics, and algorithms. Companies are hiring for new roles to support AI initiatives, including data scientists, AI developers, AI trainers and interpreters, and AI project managers.

Many of these AI initiatives involve multiple departments, so organizations are looking to add AI-related skills to job descriptions for many traditional roles as well (including customer support, product, marketing, and IT).

Meanwhile, jobs that focus on repetitive and manual tasks may be automated or replaced by AI.

In the short term, it makes sense for all professionals to educate themselves on AI and how it's being used in their industry. Even if AI doesn't affect your job now, it probably will eventually.

This educated mindset will help you identify future opportunities and determine whether additional training and/or certifications will make you more marketable. It will also prepare you for new interview questions that might come up to assess your ability to stay current.

Many job seekers have been experimenting with using ChatGPT to support their job search and to save time on repetitive tasks. For example, ChatGPT can help write cover letters, suggest resume improvements, and even advise on interview questions to expect.

REMEMBER

ChatGPT has shown great potential, but it's important to use critical thinking and not accept every ChatGPT suggestion as sacred: ChatGPT gets the facts wrong at times. Meanwhile, managers are getting better at recognizing ChatGPT-speak and questioning information that seems less than genuine.

In-demand skills

Beyond AI, trends in technology use have also increased employer demand for other skills.

Digital skills — including data analysis, programming, and digital marketing — are increasingly valuable.

With AI now automating many routine tasks, soft skills have also become more important. As companies focus on innovation, they face an increased demand for human competencies such as adaptability, critical thinking, and collaboration.

Economic factors

In the current economic environment, there's no such thing as job security. As market conditions fluctuate, companies are continually reevaluating their workforce needs, leading to cycles of growth followed by periods of layoffs and hiring freezes.

To thrive, you must be able to manage your career proactively. You never know when you will have to pivot, so it's important to prioritize lifelong learning and develop skills for adapting to change.

How job seekers can adapt to these trends

Change can be stressful, but it can also create opportunity. Let's review some strategies to help you manage your career in the face of these changes:

>> **Research your possibilities:** Expand your thinking about your career future. What is the next logical step on your current career path, and does it have future potential that excites you? If so, how is the job changing? What new knowledge and skills are required for success? Think about how you can enhance your resume to better highlight your qualifications. Then consider what new training or experience you need to pursue to stay competitive.

However, don't limit yourself to the obvious next step. Consider other possibilities and investigate future career changes. Even if you choose not to make a shift at this time, it's helpful to identify long-term options and start working toward developing new skills and connections.

>> **Customize your resume:** As I tell my clients every day, presenting a one-size-fits-all resume isn't your best strategy in the current job market. Even job descriptions with the same title can vary significantly. As new skills and competencies become more important, you must incorporate them into your resume to get yourself noticed.

These days, it's also more common for an individual to apply for multiple types of positions during a job search, exploring different career options where their transferable skills would be valued. You must customize your resume for each target path or risk being dismissed as irrelevant.

For example, I worked with a client who was simultaneously looking at more senior roles in their current specialized career track in finance while also applying to roles in other areas of finance and at tech firms as well. This person's tried-and-true resume had to be customized for each path (and their speaking points for certain interview questions had to be customized).

>> **Commit to lifelong learning:** It's more important now than ever before to commit to continuous learning. Seek opportunities to expand your knowledge and skills. Consider unconventional career moves that provide valuable learning experiences. Look for training and certifications to help you master new technologies and differentiate yourself in the job market.

Beyond the value of the learning itself, you'll expand your opportunities by showing your commitment to learning and development. Every new role has a learning curve; you can set yourself apart by communicating your adaptability and a knack for quickly mastering new abilities.

>> **Focus on in-demand skills:** Research the skills that are in high demand in your industry and take the time to develop those skills through online courses, on-the-job experience, and other methods.

TIP

Don't neglect your *soft skills.* These are areas where humans have a distinct advantage over AI algorithms. Companies are increasingly looking for people with the ability to think critically, adapt to change, build relationships, and solve problems collaboratively (among other abilities). These soft skills are valuable across industries and job titles.

REMEMBER

>> **Build your network:** Now more than ever, it's important to build a strong professional network, both online and offline. A large and diverse network will expand your reach beyond your current job and location. With nurturing, it can be a source of information, advice, recommendations, and referrals.

Your network can help alert you to new trends, advise you on how to handle them, and then support you in making a change when the time comes.

Charting the rise of remote work

The pandemic kicked the remote work trend into overdrive. Companies that were reluctant to allow employees to work from home were suddenly forced to make it work. For many companies and workers, the shift opened up exciting new possibilities.

Now, while some are eager to go back to the old routine, remote work remains a preferred option for many others. For companies, remote and hybrid work policies allow for smaller (and less expensive) office spaces and the ability to hire talent outside their local commutable area. Companies also have learned they can attract talent with flexible remote work policies.

That's because many professionals continue to prefer remote work due to its many benefits, including more autonomy, reduced commute time, greater work-life balance, and access to opportunities around the world.

In addition to fully-remote work options, many companies now offer hybrid work models with flexible scheduling and the ability to spend some days in the office.

Remote work has transformed the hiring process by popularizing virtual interviews, online assessments, and video conferencing tools, which are now used by both remote workers and traditional employees back at the office.

When hiring for remote and hybrid roles, it's necessary to evaluate a candidate's ability to work without supervision and collaborate remotely. This has led to more focus on interview questions about competencies like the ability to work independently, time management, and online collaboration.

REMEMBER

Though some companies have been pushing hard for a full-time return to the office, remote work is here to stay. Some organizations are leaning more toward hybrid models, which some employees embrace as offering the best of both worlds (the benefits of remote work with some regular team time at the office). Other companies have embraced fully remote work for the long term, seeing it as a competitive differentiator and a way to attract talent.

Interviewing for remote and hybrid positions

If you're interested in remote opportunities, be ready to demonstrate your ability to thrive in a remote work environment.

TIP

Increasingly, companies are looking for candidates with demonstrated experience working remotely. Prepare to discuss your successful stints in remote jobs and strengths that make you effective on virtual teams. You also need to be comfortable using the collaboration tools and technologies that are now common for virtual teamwork, such as Zoom, Slack, Notion, and Google Drive. Familiarize yourself with these common tools if you haven't used them, and look up any unfamiliar technologies mentioned in the job description.

Because remote work enables individuals to work for companies in various countries far from home, you'll have more opportunities, but you'll also have more competition. This makes it even more important to develop specialized skills and build a strong personal brand that helps you stand out from the crowd.

Interviews for remote positions are likely to include behavioral questions about required competencies, such as these common ones:

>> **Questions about remote work experience**

In your opinion, what is the best part about working as part of a remote team? What's the worst part?

Which tools or methods did you use to manage remote projects?

What would you change about your past remote work experience if you could?

Have you ever had a miscommunication with someone on your team? How was it resolved?

How did you handle communication across multiple time zones?

Walk me through what you would do if you had a deadline but no clear direction on how to proceed with a project.

How do you organize your workflow?

>> **Questions about remote work competencies**

Tell me about a time you had to communicate technical information to a colleague with a limited understanding of the topic.

Someone on your team won't deliver on time, causing you to miss your deadline — how do you approach this problem?

Tell me about a time you had a tough deadline.

Tell me about a time you had competing priorities. How did you handle it?

Tell me about a time you had to change your approach to an important project.

Tell me about a time you had to adapt to accommodate a new team member.

Describe a challenge you weren't sure how to approach at first but ended up succeeding with.

Tell me about a time you managed to sway a colleague or manager to your point of view.

Focusing on diversity, equity, and inclusion

Another major trend is the increased emphasis on diversity, equity, and inclusion (DEI) in talent management and hiring. Many companies have invested in diversity recruitment initiatives to create more inclusive work environments.

Studies have shown that diverse teams perform better. At the same time, a commitment to diversity is essential in attracting top talent. Surveys show that job seekers, especially younger ones, consider a company's investment in DEI a priority when considering a new job.

This push has led to more active investment in hiring individuals from different racial and ethnic backgrounds, genders, ages, sexual orientations, and abilities.

On the recruiting side, companies are actively expanding their candidate pools by leveraging job boards and platforms that reach underrepresented groups.

There is also a push to adopt interview techniques that minimize bias and put the focus squarely on qualifications. Finally, companies are putting more emphasis on nurturing an inclusive culture, which means ensuring that all new hires value DEI.

What does all of this mean for you and your job search? First, you will see that more organizations are including interview questions about diversity when hiring for all types of positions. Here are some common examples:

>> What is your experience working in a diverse team environment?

>> Tell me about a time you worked on a team with people from different backgrounds.

In interviews for leadership roles, you might hear more advanced questions such as these:

>> How have you considered diversity, equity, and inclusion when hiring?

>> How do you ensure that your direct reports feel a sense of inclusion?

>> Tell me about a time you advocated for diversity, equity, and inclusion in the workplace.

These questions are designed to evaluate your culture fit and determine whether your values align with the organization's. During your interview preparation, it's important to consider how you would address these types of questions.

TIP

If you have limited experience in working on a diverse team, don't try to fake it. Describe any experience you might have had, and sincerely express your interest in gaining more experience and learning from others in a diverse environment. Discuss what you value about working for a company with a commitment to diversity, equity, and inclusion. If you're sincere, your values will shine through. Whatever you do, avoid pretending you're an expert or using platitudes such as, "I don't see color." Read up on DEI initiatives if you're not familiar with them.

Beyond the interview questions, you may notice some organizations making other changes to minimize bias and ensure fair hiring. The ones I'm seeing most often include these:

>> Skill-based assessments to ensure that abilities and talent are properly considered and evaluations are less subjective

>> Blind resume reviews and anonymizing technology to reduce bias during screening, to prevent reviewers from making assumptions based on names, assumed gender, and other irrelevant factors

>> Training for interviewers to help them minimize bias by asking structured, consistent questions and evaluating candidates objectively

>> Diverse interview panels to ensure multiple perspectives are considered in candidate selection

Dealing with video interviews

Companies first embraced video interviews by necessity during COVID. Now, video interviews have become a permanent fixture in hiring across industries and job types.

Video interviews are essential for hiring remote candidates and for including interviewers from all locations in the process. Companies also use video interviews with local candidates at times, often in place of phone interviews during early screening rounds.

For companies, video interviews save time and allow them to reach an expanded candidate pool. In addition to live interviews via video conference, many companies now use asynchronous video interviews, in which candidates record and submit answers to prerecorded questions.

You can expect to spend a lot of time in video interviews during your job search these days. In some ways, they're easier, but they also offer challenges that can trip you up.

TIP

In Chapter 3, I walk you through the details of how video interviews are different and how to prepare to ensure that you make a great impression on video — live or prerecorded.

Evaluating AI for screening

As I discuss earlier in this chapter, AI is transforming jobs and industries. AI and automation are also revolutionizing how companies source, screen, interview, and select candidates.

This news can be positive in terms of saving time and allowing a larger group of candidates to be considered. However, it also presents risks in companies relying too heavily on flawed AI assumptions. To help you gain a better sense of the positives and negatives, let's look at the various ways organizations are using AI and gauge how it can affect your experience as a job seeker. This list is a good starting point:

» **Sourcing candidates:** AI-powered tools can analyze massive amounts of candidate data from a wide range of online platforms, job boards, and social media networks. The AI algorithms can match relevant profiles with job requirements and expand the candidate pool to reach passive candidates.

» **Resume screening:** AI-powered resume screening tools use natural language processing (NLP) algorithms to scan resumes and flag the candidates who are the best matches according to preset criteria. This saves recruiters time but can lead to qualified candidates slipping through the cracks because the wrong keywords were used.

» **Candidate communications:** Many companies use AI-powered chatbots to interact with candidates and provide real-time information and help. The chatbots can answer questions, identify relevant job openings, schedule interviews, and even ask qualifying screening questions.

>> **Interview analysis:** Some companies have used AI to analyze recorded video answers to recommend which candidates should move forward in the process. Algorithms can identify keywords in answers and assess eye contact and body language. This has raised concerns about bias — concerns that have led some to propose laws that would limit the ability to make hiring decisions based on AI alone.

TIP

My training company, Big Interview, created a video AI analysis tool that uses AI to evaluate users' answers and provide feedback on issues like eye contact and word usage. The goal is to provide immediate feedback on key issues — and also give job seekers an idea of what companies might see if they use AI to assess their answers.

On the positive side, AI may help to streamline the recruiting process and save you time and effort as a candidate. However, the use of AI also raises concerns about fairness.

As of now, the biggest consideration for job seekers relates to resume screening. Considering the increased use of automated resume screening tools, you must customize your resume to ensure that it advances past the AI gatekeepers and makes it to a human reviewer.

The key is to customize your resume for each opportunity and mirror key wording from the job description. If a nurse job description prioritizes triage experience or primary care experience, for example, be sure that your resume contains those keywords.

REMEMBER

Careful analysis of the job description will help you identify which keywords are most important. For example, include any requirements listed in the first bullet points in any section of the job description. Skills mentioned multiple times are important.

Consider repeating important keywords in your resume. In some *applicant tracking systems* (ATS), repetition helps your resume score higher.

WARNING

Don't overstuff keywords in your resume. The AI algorithms are savvy to this tactic, and it's a real turn-off to the humans who read resumes that advance past the automated screeners.

This book isn't about resumes, so I don't have room to go into more in-depth advice on customizing your resume to move past AI screeners. However, I have written many articles on this subject that are available for free on the Big Interview website at `https://resources.biginterview.com/category/resumes/`. The site also features an AI Resume tool that scans resumes and provides improvement suggestions, including advice on how well a resume is customized to match with a specific job description.

I also recommend the book *Resumes For Dummies* by Laura deCarlo (published by Wiley).

Keeping up with social media

Social media continues to transform the job search process and how companies recruit. Savvy use of social media can open up new worlds of opportunity, but oversharing can get you in trouble.

Even if you're not a fan of social media, it's smart to maintain at least a basic presence to support your career, especially (but not only) during a job search. As I'm sure you know, networking is an excellent way to move to the front of the line for job opportunities. In fact, a recent survey from LinkedIn revealed that 85 percent of new jobs were found through networking.

Social media has made networking much easier. Previously, you had to either have the privilege of existing connections or work your tail off to go to events and work the room.

In many ways, LinkedIn levels the playing field for networking. You can find and connect with people you'd never encounter in real life.

REMEMBER

Expand your networking beyond the people who already know you well. A classic sociology study indicates that you're more likely to find a job through an acquaintance than through a best friend. Your closest contacts tend to know the same people you do. However, your acquaintances, or *weak ties,* as the study called them, usually travel in different circles and can offer access to a greater variety of advice, job leads, and contacts.

Social media is also a valuable tool for finding job listings, marketing yourself to potential hiring managers, and researching opportunities.

TIP

My primary social media recommendation is to use LinkedIn to your full advantage. In addition to its networking opportunities, a lot of recruiting occurs on LinkedIn these days. The LinkedIn job board is a top choice for most companies posting job openings, and recruiters use LinkedIn as a primary way to search for and vet candidates. LinkedIn is also a fantastic resource for research and advice.

You're probably already familiar with LinkedIn, but you may not be aware of all the ways it can help you (or maybe you've been reluctant to invest too much time).

First, it's important to create a professional and compelling profile. Highlight your skills, experience, and achievements. Use relevant keywords to increase visibility to recruiters and hiring managers.

REMEMBER

Your profile is your calling card. Whether you're simply networking or actually applying to jobs, you can assume that your new contact will check your profile and you want to establish immediate credibility.

An optimized profile can also help you get found by recruiters, but don't wait around for recruiters to contact you. Search the LinkedIn job listings, set alerts, and follow your target companies.

Once your profile is set, you can also get serious about expanding your network. Connect or reconnect with former colleagues, clients, and other contacts. Beyond your closest circles, spend some time researching industry thought leaders and other interesting people, and then engage with their content and start to build relationships. Consider joining industry groups and participating in discussions.

LinkedIn is also a useful place to research companies and track down job search advice. See Chapter 4 for more about company research.

WARNING

If you're looking for a job, you *must* clean up your online presence. Adjust privacy settings and remove or hide any content that might negatively impact your job search.

It's a fact that employers review applicants' social media profiles. This can be an advantage when they check out your carefully curated professional LinkedIn account but could cause problems if your wild party pics show up in a public search for your name.

Knowing Your Rights

As part of understanding the current hiring landscape, it's important for you to be aware of your rights as a job seeker.

Though I fervently hope that you won't encounter discrimination or unfair treatment during your job search, it's important to know how to spot inappropriate behavior and how to respond.

Handling legal considerations

First, you should know a bit about the laws that protect job seekers from discriminatory and inappropriate hiring practices.

I want to be clear that I am not a lawyer, and this legislation is constantly evolving. For the latest information, please see the US Equal Employment Opportunity Commission's current guidance at www.eeoc.gov/employees-job-applicants.

The United States has equal opportunity laws that aim to ensure that candidates are evaluated based on their qualifications and not on personal qualities that are irrelevant to their ability to do the job.

At the federal level, the primary law governing equal opportunity is the Civil Rights Act of 1964. This law prohibits employment discrimination based on race, color, religion, sex, or national origin. This Act also established the Equal Employment Opportunity Commission (EEOC), which is responsible for enforcing federal laws related to workplace discrimination.

Subsequently, other federal laws were passed in order to

>> Prohibit age discrimination against candidates 40 and older (Age Discrimination in Employment Act)

>> Prohibit discrimination against individuals with disabilities and require employers to provide reasonable accommodations (Americans with Disabilities Act)

Though this Act doesn't explicitly mention sexual orientation or gender identity, courts have increasingly interpreted it to include protections for LGBTQ+ individuals.

Many states and localities also have their own equal opportunity laws that expand on federal protections related to hiring and interviewing. Here are a few examples:

>> **Ban-the-box laws:** Many states have passed laws that prohibit employers from inquiring about an applicant's criminal history on a job application or during the initial stages of the hiring process. (The term "ban the box" refers to the recent campaign against the practice of asking applicants to mark a check box on the job application if they have a criminal record.)

>> **Fair-chance hiring laws:** Some states have enacted fair-chance hiring laws that require employers to give candidates the opportunity to explain their criminal history before making a hiring decision.

>> **Salary history bans:** Multiple states now have laws that prohibit employers from asking candidates about their salary history. The goal is to stop perpetuating pay gaps for workers who are underpaid.

>> **Drug testing:** Now that a number of states have legalized marijuana, new laws protect applicants from being discriminated against based on the lawful use of marijuana outside of work.

Note that laws related to hiring and the interview process can vary significantly by state, and new legislation may continue to emerge.

Dealing with discriminatory questions

So, how do these antidiscrimination laws affect job interviews? The bottom line is that employers cannot discriminate against job applicants based on any qualities protected by law. That means they should not ask interview questions that touch on these topics.

To recap, the protected qualities include these:

>> Race

>> Color

>> Religion

>> Sex

>> National origin

>> Age

>> Health or disability

>> Marital status

>> Family obligations

Unfortunately, there's a long history of employment discrimination in the United States. Asking questions about these subjects opens the door to bias and discrimination.

Be on the alert for questions that are unrelated to your ability to do the job, especially any that touch on personal or protected matters. Sometimes, these questions are asked innocently, with no intention to discriminate. For example, an interviewer may ask about your family to make conversation.

In other cases, the questions are asked with inappropriate intent. If you answer, that information could be used against you by biased interviewers.

If you encounter an inappropriate or discriminatory interview question, here are some tips on how to handle it:

» **Stay calm.** Take a deep breath and avoid responding emotionally. If there's a chance that the question was an innocent mistake, your goal is to redirect the interview to more appropriate topics.

» **Distract with a non-answer.** If you can, tactfully avoid any inappropriate parts of the question and give a diplomatic non-answer to move the discussion along. For example, if an interviewer asks you "where you're from" because of your surname, ignore the implications and say something like, "I'm actually based here in the Philadelphia area, and I love it."

» **Redirect back to the job.** If it's difficult to answer the question without disclosing personal details, try to redirect the question back to topics relevant to your qualifications to do the job. For example, you might redirect with something like this: "I appreciate your interest, but I'd love to focus more on my work experience."

  It's possible that an interviewer might see this response as unfriendly or rude. However, if the question is truly inappropriate, it's better to stand your ground. You can make up for it with extra friendliness later, if the interview takes a turn for the better.

  On the other hand, if the question was a slip-up, it might draw their attention to the misstep and refocus them on more appropriate topics.

» **Be firm, if necessary.** If the interviewer continues to press for inappropriate information, you may need to address the issue directly. Take a firm but professional approach. For example, you can say something like, "I don't see that question as relevant to my qualifications for the position. Can we discuss my leadership experience instead?"

» **Report discrimination.** If you experience blatant discrimination during a job interview, consider reporting the incident to the interviewer's supervisor or an HR contact. You can also file a complaint with the EEOC. You can even post a review on a site like Glassdoor.com to alert other job seekers to discrimination at the company. These actions may close the door on future job opportunities at this organization, but they might also spark necessary change.

Accommodating candidates with disabilities

As I mention earlier in this chapter, employers are prohibited from discriminating against candidates with disabilities during the hiring process. This includes not making hiring decisions based on disability and providing reasonable accommodations.

If you need accommodations during the interview process, you have the right to request them. Employers are required to provide reasonable accommodations, as long they don't cause undue hardship on their business.

These are some examples of accessibility considerations:

>> **Interview venue accessibility:** In-person interview venues should accommodate individuals with disabilities. Accommodations may include accessible parking, ramps or elevators for wheelchair users, and accessible restrooms.

>> **Video Interviews:** It's important to offer accommodations for using the technology required for video interviews. Please see "The Video Interview" section in Chapter 3 for my advice on specific accommodations to consider.

>> **Appropriate interview questions:** Interviewers should not make assumptions about an applicant's disability or ask inappropriate questions. The focus should be on your qualifications, skills, and experiences relevant to the job.

It's generally okay to ask about ability to perform duties required for the job as long as they're also asking other applicants the same questions.

Overall, companies are getting more proactive about training their managers to understand and respect anti-discrimination laws. However, there is still work to be done. Knowing your rights as a job seeker will help you navigate challenging situations if they come up. This knowledge will also help you if you're a hiring manager or plan to move into a leadership role in the future.

Dissecting the Interview/Hiring Cycle

Continuing with the big-picture perspective on the world of interviewing, let's look at the overall hiring process from the hiring organization's perspective. This book is about interviewing, but interviewing is just one stage of your journey from application to new job.

It's helpful to know some backstory — in other words, how did you end up getting invited to interview, and what are the expectations? The more you know about the pre-interview stages, the more interview opportunities you'll be able to line up.

You also need to know what's likely to occur after the interview stage and how you can influence a happy ending to the story. I want to make you a pro at navigating from application to happily hired.

Let's look briefly at each major stage, including the company's goals and challenges and what you can expect.

Sourcing candidates

The first step is sourcing candidates. The company has a job opening and must attract a pool of qualified candidates for the position.

Companies use many different sourcing strategies, including internal referrals, job boards, social media platforms, professional networks, and recruitment agencies. The goal is to cast a wide net and attract a diverse group of qualified applicants.

TIP

For job seekers, it pays to be among the first to spot a high-potential job opening and submit your application. I recommend setting up automated alerts where you can (most job boards have them) and creating a daily schedule to check for new listings and apply promptly. This strategy will help you attract more interview invitations. If you apply too late, after they already have a flood of qualified resumes, you may miss out (or at least have to wait and hope none of the early birds is a good fit).

Resume screening

Once the applications start flowing in, it's time for the resume screening phase. Applications and resumes are reviewed to assess candidates' qualifications, experience, and skills.

Sometimes, this is done manually by a recruiter or sourcing person. However, many companies use an applicant tracking systems (ATS) to filter applications based on specific criteria (often using AI, as discussed earlier in this chapter). From the company's perspective, the aim is to identify candidates who meet the basic requirements and possess the necessary skills and experience for the job.

TIP

A well-written and customized resume gives you an edge. Screeners, whether AI or human, are scanning quickly for keywords and red flags.

Human reviewers spend an average of 6 seconds skimming a resume before deciding whether to toss it or give it a more thorough evaluation. Check out the latest edition of *Resumes For Dummies,* by Laura DeCarlo, for advice on how to make your resume irresistible.

Screening interviews

If your resume is deemed a fit, it's time for the screening interview, which can be conducted via phone or video or in person. Most often, this interview is conducted by a recruiter or HR representative.

The company's goal here is to quickly evaluate who's a fit to move forward and meet with the hiring team for more in-depth conversation. The screening interview is typically short and focused on validating key requirements and looking for red flags. See Chapter 3 for a detailed breakdown of what to expect from various interviewers (including screening recruiters) and interview formats.

After the discussion, your interviewer will decide whether to recommend that you move forward to the next round of interviews.

REMEMBER

The screening interview is your first nondigital interaction in the process. That means it's important to make a great impression and avoid raising red flags that can knock you out of contention. Many job seekers consider it an easier interview because it's more of a resume review and high-level discussion.

However, don't go in unprepared. Make sure you're ready for all the common questions and prepared to address any potential red flags on your resume. You never know when a screening interviewer might get tricky. In some cases, the hiring manager may conduct the screening interview and move directly into the tough questions.

Assessment

For some positions, assessments are important elements of the screening process. Sometimes, the assessment may even come before the screening interview, especially for roles that are highly dependent on certain technical skills.

REMEMBER

Assessments are most often used to evaluate a candidate's technical skills, but some companies also use assessments to examine critical thinking, problem-solving skills, and even personality traits. More advanced assessments are usually saved until later in the process, reserved for those who seem to be a good fit in other ways.

TIP

Assessments can bring back that school-test anxiety for some people, but try not to overthink it. In my opinion, the use of skill assessments is a positive sign that the company reps want to hire the most qualified person and are interested in objective, skills-based data to make a fair decision. Usually, you get enough of a heads-up to prepare if you're rusty in a particular skill area.

Critical thinking and strengths tests are harder to prepare for. However, if you're given the name of the assessment, you can usually search online for a bit of information about the format and what to expect.

I'm not crazy about the use of personality tests in the hiring process. I don't feel it's fair to base hiring decisions on personality, and most personality tests aren't evidence-based. If you're asked to participate in a personality assessment, your best bet is to answer the questions authentically. However, keep in mind that most people display slightly different personality traits in work situations (versus relaxing with friends, for example). Channel your work personality when responding to a hiring assessment.

Conducting interviews with the hiring team

After passing the screening and assessments, selected candidates are asked to meet with the hiring manager and other members of the hiring team. These interviews delve deeper into the candidate's skills, knowledge, and experience to determine their fit for the role.

Usually, a candidate faces at least two additional rounds of interviews after the screening. Sometimes you meet first with the hiring manager and gain their approval before returning to meet with others. If they're relatively confident in your fit, they may ask you to meet with multiple people in the second round, either in a series of one-on-one interviews or facing a panel.

Some companies drag out this process, asking top candidates to return for more than five different interviews on different days. They may keep you hanging between rounds, waiting for the call or email that says they want to continue the discussions. Usually, this isn't intentional torture, but rather bureaucratic delays (such as waiting for someone to return from vacation or for every member of the first group of candidates to complete the most recent round).

REMEMBER

The remaining chapters of this book talk about how to successfully navigate this critical interview phase. I strongly recommend that you read the chapters, do the prep work, practice, and go in there with confidence.

TIP

If you encounter delayed responses between rounds, it's okay to follow up with your point person (whether it's the recruiter or the hiring manager) to ask for an update. Some HR reps are notoriously bad about following up, so don't take it personally. If you're given a timeline for a response and don't hear back, send a short email respectfully asking for an update. If there's no response, try again in a few days or a week. Don't assume that a lack of response means you're out. However, don't pin your hopes on waiting for a call back. Keep looking and continue pursuing other options.

Making the hiring decision

After all the interviews and evaluations are complete, the field has been narrowed to a few finalists. Now it's time to make the final hiring decision and choose who will join the team.

You've been evaluated throughout the interview process. At each stage, interviewers weighed in on who should move forward and who should be cut. Strengths and weaknesses have been noted along the way. Once you make it to the final decision, it's down to which well-qualified candidate is *the one* (or, if nobody is quite the right fit, it may be time to restart the search).

Best practices of structured interviewing dictate that the company maintain a consistent scorecard for all candidates with key criteria and a rating scale. Then each interviewer should evaluate each candidate, scorecards should be reviewed, and the decision should be discussed by stakeholders before a decision is made. I train hiring managers in how to do this in my corporate training work. It's the best way to make a data-backed decision and minimize bias based on someone's gut feeling.

However, I can tell you that most companies don't structure their interviews this way. Many have scorecards that are ineffective or optional (if they have them at all). In these cases, the discussion may be more casual and opinion-based. Various stakeholders will share their input in meetings or via email or Slack, and the hiring manager will make the decision.

If outstanding issues are identified, the hiring manager may request more information from finalists.

Once the decision is made, the hiring manager will work with the HR team to put together offer details, including compensation, benefits, title, and desired start date. Then the lucky winner will get the offer call and have an opportunity to accept, decline, or counter.

If it turns out that the lucky winner isn't you, keep in mind that considerations beyond your knowledge or control — internal candidates, budget restrictions, company policies, for example — could have steered the decision.

If you do make it to the final round and don't get the offer, ask for feedback on why they decided on another candidate. To be honest, you probably won't get real feedback. Recruiters and hiring managers are often reluctant to say anything negative. If you've made it to the final round, it's unlikely there's a big problem with your qualifications or interview skills. More likely, it was a matter of a few small differences that put another candidate over the top. It doesn't hurt to ask, but you may hear something generic, such as, "We went with someone with a bit more experience in certain areas." It sounds like a bunch of malarkey, but it may be true from their perspective.

If you do receive genuine feedback, take it seriously even if you disagree with it. Remember that this is a perception of someone on the hiring team, not the unquestionable truth. It may be that you could be clearer or more convincing about certain qualifications or goals.

However, many rejections are not about anything you did wrong. Another candidate seemed like a better fit, maybe for reasons you don't know about.

REMEMBER

It's natural to be disappointed, especially if you feel you were misunderstood. Try to keep in mind that making it to the final round is an achievement in and of itself. You'll do it again and you'll land the next offer — hopefully, for an even better position. Learn what you can from the experience, but don't let rejection affect your confidence. It's part of the process for even the most accomplished and eloquent job seekers. Not every job is the right fit for you.

On the other hand, if you're chosen as the best candidate and offered the position, you'll move on to the next phase in the process.

Checking references and credentials and managing other red tape

At some point before finalizing the offer letter, the company will likely conduct a background check, which can include checking references, verifying employment, running a credit check, and possibly conducting a drug test.

Most often, companies don't take this step until they've narrowed their choices to one or two candidates. There's no point in spending time on a background check if you're not certain that you want to hire the person.

Most larger companies use a third-party service to conduct background checks. Pre-employment background checks may cover these areas:

>> Verifying the applicant's name, social security number, and legal right to work in the country

>> Confirming claimed education background, including degrees earned

>> Checking employment history, focusing on organizations worked for and dates employed

>> Validating other claimed credentials such as government-issued licenses, certifications, or security clearances

>> Running a criminal history search to identify convictions, probation status, or outstanding warrants

Some organizations will also run a credit check for roles that require financial management. They may review your motor vehicle records if the role requires driving.

When it comes to reference checks, I was surprised to discover that many companies just don't do them. Some do, but HR reps tell me they rarely gather valuable information from references these days. First, smart candidates provide references that say only positive things about them. More importantly, a large number of organizations prohibit their employees from providing detailed references for others — only basic confirmation that the person worked there and the dates employed. There can be legal ramifications from providing damaging information in a reference.

TIP

Take the time to build out your Recommendations section on LinkedIn. All those glowing endorsements will help you in the job search and will make companies more comfortable taking a chance on you when it's time for the hiring decision.

If your resume is accurate, your background is pristine, and your references love you, you can just relax and wait for the formal offer to arrive. However, if you're worried about negative info popping up in a background check, you should think about a mitigation strategy.

Honesty is the best policy, but you don't need to volunteer information that's unlikely to come up, especially if it doesn't affect your ability to excel in the job. If there's something serious in your background that you haven't disclosed (criminal conviction, fudged resume information), be prepared to address it if asked.

My coaching clients sometimes worry that a previous manager could cause problems by misrepresenting a difficult work situation out of spite. Choose only people you can trust as references. Hiring managers will understand that you can't always give your direct manager as a reference, especially if you're still employed while job searching.

Negotiating and accepting the offer

Once the offer is made, the candidate has the power to accept the offer as is, open up negotiations, or decline the offer. Most companies make offers in good faith, basing compensation and benefits on company policies and what they believe is fair. However, there is usually room for negotiation for the right candidate.

If the candidate counters the offer, it's negotiation time. In some cases, the company may immediately accept the counteroffer (leaving the candidate happy but also wondering whether they should have asked for more!). Often, the representative will have to go discuss the situation with colleagues and decide what they can do to sweeten the deal.

A few exchanges may take place before the company arrives at a final offer for the candidate to accept or decline. Once you accept the offer, you'll receive a signed offer letter, an official start date, and instructions for next steps (see the later section "Onboarding").

First, if you land the offer, celebrate your achievement. Express appreciation for the offer even if you're not sure you'll accept. More importantly, don't feel pressure to accept immediately if you're feeling unsure. You can say "Thank you" and ask for a little time to process the information and respond.

If you've done your research, you'll know whether that initial offer is generous or stingy. You've probably thought about the amount you need to be happy with the offer — not just compensation but also other factors, including title, benefits, flexibility, and schedule.

Decide what you want to ask for and prepare your proposal before you counter. Don't apologize, and don't offer an ultimatum. Keep it businesslike.

Onboarding

Once the offer is accepted, the onboarding process begins. Onboarding continues well into your first year of employment. It starts with completing necessary paperwork and setting up logins and passwords before your first day.

On day 1, you'll meet the team and learn all about the day-to-day duties and the company culture. You'll start training and get the hang of how things work.

Be proactive about your own onboarding experience. Some companies have a thoughtful, supportive process that takes the guesswork out of learning the ropes and getting settled in. If so, it's a helpful sign that they value their employees. But either way, you'll want to think about your own goals and the impression you want to make. Don't try to do everything on day 1, but do prioritize meeting people and establishing relationships.

You're not supposed to arrive already knowing everything (and if you try to act like you do, you'll only make the situation harder for yourself). The goal is to show up with genuine enthusiasm and curiosity. Show up excited to learn and ready to ask questions. Listen more than you talk.

Most importantly, prepare to say yes all day long. Do you want to grab coffee? Of course. Would you like a tour of the cafeteria? Definitely. Are you interested in sitting in on the sales meeting? Oh, yes. How about a drink after work? Sure.

It's the honeymoon period, after all. Later, you'll learn when to say no.

If you're an introvert or someone who struggles with imposter syndrome, remind yourself that you have new-colleague goodwill right now. Most people will be happy to get to know (and help out) the new person. It's not the high school cafeteria, after all (even if you have unpleasant flashbacks in these new-kid situations).

TIP

If you feel overwhelmed, focus on finding someone friendly and ask if you can tag along for a bit. Or ask your manager to introduce you to the resident experts.

A company with a well-planned onboarding process won't make you do all this yourself, but it's good to be prepared if you find yourself twiddling your thumbs and waiting for guidance.

Following the New Interview-Etiquette Rules

All rules of etiquette evolve with the times and the culture. The same is true for interview etiquette. Certain old expectations are now outdated. For example, nobody today expects a handwritten thank you note mailed on elegant stationery.

However, some guidelines have stood the test of time — and some new ones have emerged from the trends I cover in the first part of this chapter.

Rules to interview by

Let's start with the big-picture rules to always follow:

>> **Dress to impress:** Always dress well for the interview. Show that you made an effort and that you understand the rules of professionalism. These days, that doesn't always mean wearing an old-fashioned suit and tie or a conservative skirt with pantyhose (thank goodness). Do your research on the company's culture and dress for the job you want. See Chapter 15 for more detailed guidelines on what to wear for interviews and what to avoid.

>> **Be punctual:** Never show up late for a job interview. This rule has *not* changed. Interviewers tend to view a late arrival as a red flag — signifying a lack of professionalism, lack of interest, or lack of time management skills.

For in-person interviews, arrange to leave home early to make sure you aren't delayed by traffic or bad GPS directions. Aim to arrive at the interview location approximately 10 minutes early. Do your homework to determine whether you should leave extra time for parking, getting a security badge, or reaching the right floor or area within the building.

REMEMBER

For phone and video interviews, plan to be set up and in position early so that you can complete a final tech-check and adjust lighting and background if needed.

Interviewers may insist that candidates arrive on time, but they don't always follow this punctuality rule themselves. You'll find that this is the case with several of the other etiquette guidelines as well. Waiting is annoying, but don't take it personally.

If a disaster arises and you arrive late, apologize and offer a brief explanation if the cause was outside of your control. Make clear that you respect the interviewer's time and that you made every attempt to be punctual. Then move on quickly and do your best to wow the person with your qualifications and make them forget that you were ever late. Don't excessively explain or apologize or let the situation destroy your confidence. Yes, it's possible that your lateness will count against you, but you may be able to recover if you can avoid dwelling on the negative.

>> **Follow directions:** Always read and follow application and interview instructions carefully. If they tell you to submit a cover letter and writing sample, do it. If you're asked to confirm a time by email, respond promptly.

I realize that companies sometimes have ridiculously long and time-consuming application processes. However, if you're truly interested in the job, take the time to follow all the steps.

It's perfectly okay to judge them. A repetitive and difficult application process makes for a poor candidate experience. Companies should care about this experience and avoid wasting people's time. You can consider that when ultimately weighing the job offer.

TIP

Do you *need* to submit a cover letter? It's an ongoing and valid question. Many recruiters and hiring managers say they never read cover letters. However, some companies require them, and skipping this step can knock you out of contention. If the instructions say to include a cover letter, make the effort. If you create a standard cover letter template, you can quickly customize it for new opportunities.

>> **Proofread!:** Don't forget to carefully proofread all documents and communications related to your job search — even those quick emails. Typos and grammar mistakes make you look sloppy.

If writing isn't one of your strengths, ask a friend to proofread important documents for you. Consider using an app like Grammarly or Wordtune (both have free versions) for help with grammar, punctuation, tone, and wording.

>> **Don't ghost:** *Ghosting* an interviewer (cutting off contact with no explanation and especially when it includes not showing up to a scheduled interview) is bad form. If you're not interested in interviewing, don't schedule a time. If something comes up, be courteous and reschedule or cancel. It's basic business etiquette.

Ghosting has become more common with the rise of video interviews. I guess a video interview just feels like less of a commitment and easier to blow off. If you ghost an interviewer, you're unlikely to get a second chance.

Both interviewers and candidates are guilty of ghosting, but it's disrespectful and wastes everyone's time. Don't be part of the problem.

» **Do your homework:** Don't show up for an interview unprepared. At minimum, review the job description carefully and research the company. (See Chapter 4 for more on those topics.) Know your interviewers' names and titles.

It will be clear to your interviewer if you haven't bothered to prepare for the meeting. They'll wonder how much care you will put into your work.

Of course, I recommend additional preparation (see Chapters 5–14), but you know that already.

» **Show respect:** Hopefully, I don't have to tell you to be respectful to interviewers. That means following basic business etiquette rules — here are some examples:

Turn off your phone ringer (and noisy alerts) before the meeting to prevent interruptions. Stay focused on the interview to show your interest and consideration. Don't check for updates and don't pick up a call unless it's an emergency situation. During video and phone interviews, arrange for a quiet, private setting away from distractions that can interrupt the interview.

Follow the interviewer's lead when it comes to greetings. A handshake is still customary at the beginning of an interview (and often at the end). Shake firmly, but don't crush their hand. You don't get points for grip strength.

Get your interviewers' names right and pronounce them correctly. If you're unsure how to pronounce a name, ask and then remember to do it correctly from then on.

TIP

Some people may shy away from a handshake because they're germophobes (it's understandable, post-COVID) or simply not "touchy" people. Offer your hand, but don't be offended if someone doesn't respond with enthusiasm. It may make for an awkward moment, but it's their quirk, not a mistake on your part. Keep it friendly and move on.

Be friendly and try to make a personal connection with your interviewer; however, be careful not to get too personal and ask nosy questions about their family or life outside of work. This can make interviewers uncomfortable and bring up topics that aren't appropriate for the interview. (See my advice in the "Knowing Your Rights" section, earlier in this chapter, for how to deal with inappropriate and discriminatory interview questions.) If they bring up a hobby or interest outside of work, it's fine to respond. Just "read the room" and avoid irritating questions.

» **Keep your camera on:** For video interviews, make sure to keep your camera on, even if you don't enjoy being on video. They have arranged a video interview instead of a phone interview for a reason.

From your perspective, it's easier to make a memorable connection face-to-face, even via video. Occasionally, you may encounter an interviewer who keeps their camera turned off. This can be frustrating (why schedule a video interview if you're camera shy?), but it's still better to keep your camera on and try your best to approximate eye contact with their name in a box.

» **Keep it positive:** Never bad-mouth your current or former managers or even coworkers. Maybe your manager was terrible — certainly, plenty of terrible managers are out there. However, for the sake of the interview, you have to find a way to keep it positive (or at least neutral).

A job interview offers only a short window of time to make an impression. The interviewer has just met you and can't possibly know the full situation, so negativity may raise questions about your attitude or professionalism. Even worse, trash talking can take the interview off course to focus on the negative instead of the many positive qualities you want them to remember.

» **Don't lie:** Never, ever lie in a job interview. If you're caught in a lie, it's all over. If the interviewer catches it before the hiring decision, it will knock you out of contention. People have even been fired when lies were discovered *after* onboarding (sometimes, even years later).

That doesn't mean you have to tell the whole truth about every topic. Some situations are not the interviewer's business. Too much candor or self-deprecation can hurt you.

If there's a topic you're concerned about (for example, getting fired or making a mistake), take the time to prepare bullet points so that you can respond to questions with neutral language that allows you to tell the truth without hurting your chances. See Chapter 12 for more advice on answering tricky questions honestly but strategically.

» **Send a thank-you note:** Always send a thank-you note (an email is fine) after an interview. (Check out the "After the Interview" section, later in this chapter, for detailed advice on thank-you notes.)

» **Use social media responsibly:** Social media can be a valuable tool to support you in your job search. However, careless use of social media can also get you in trouble.

Many recruiters and hiring managers check out candidates' social media presence, especially when hiring for high-profile roles. If you've maintained a strong LinkedIn presence, that may give them enough of a sense of who you are — so they may not feel the need to look any further to other platforms, like Instagram, Facebook, or X/Twitter.

However, if you're active on social media under your full name and your activity is public, you never know what might show up in an online search. When you're in job-search mode, set all your social media accounts to Private. Review past posts and activities that have been shared and could come up in a search for your name. Be aware of who's following you on platforms where you post personal content. Avoid posting (or responding to) content that might be controversial.

>> **Respond promptly:** Again, this is basic business communication etiquette but good to keep in mind. When a recruiter or an interviewer contacts you, respond within a business day, if possible. That doesn't mean you have to reply immediately. If you need to think about how to address a question or when you can schedule that next round, take a little time but don't delay too long.

>> **Negotiate:** This is a reminder that it isn't presumptuous to negotiate an offer! Many people were raised to be polite and grateful and may hesitate to push for more money, for fear of seeming greedy or rude. Don't negotiate just to negotiate, but don't hesitate to ask for what you need in order to be happy.

Working with recruiters

Since this chapter talks about rules and etiquette, I want to briefly address how to work with recruiters during your job search. In Chapter 3, I cover what to expect in interviews with recruiters. But how do you connect with these recruiters and get considered for more opportunities? What are best practices for getting the most from working with recruiters?

If you're not actively engaging recruiters in your job search strategy, you should be. Recruiters often have early access to opportunities that haven't yet been made public. They also have inside connections and can help you move past the gatekeepers to meet with the decision makers.

However, as in any profession, you can find good recruiters *and* bad recruiters. A good recruiter has access to opportunities in your field, is transparent about their process, and communicates respectfully with candidates. Bad recruiters are clueless, rude, dishonest, or misleading.

REMEMBER

Most recruiters are managing many job searches at any one time. They get compensated based on their success in filling positions, so they focus on finding matches for their open roles and moving them through the process. They have limited time to nurture a relationship with a candidate who isn't a match for their current search; for this reason, you must be proactive about staying in touch. If you're passive in your approach, you may get spammed by plenty of bad recruiters but miss out on making the right connection at the right time.

Connecting with recruiters

You may naturally connect with recruiters when applying for opportunities posted on job boards. Once you work with a recruiter, make a note of the types of roles they represent (whether an internal recruiter for one company or a contract recruiter representing multiple clients). Even if the first role isn't ultimately a match, you can continue to check in and stay on the recruiter's radar for future opportunities.

To expand your network of recruiters, LinkedIn can be your best friend. Recruiters tend to be quite active on LinkedIn. It's easy to search for recruiters who are sourcing for your target companies or staying active in your field.

Most recruiters are open to connecting with potential candidates. Many of them post and comment regularly, aiming to build their network and influencer status. You can follow top recruiters, comment on their posts, and/or ask to join their network.

TIP

You can review recruiter profiles on LinkedIn to see their job history and gain a sense of what types of positions they represent. I also regularly see sensible advice and helpful resources posted by recruiters on LinkedIn.

Before you start reaching out to recruiters on LinkedIn, make sure your profile represents you well. At minimum, you should include these key components:

>> **A compelling headline:** Your profile headline is that line of text that appears directly below your name. Many people keep it simple by listing just their job title and company. Others like to include a brief description of their expertise. Job seekers should aim for a headline that will get the attention of potential employers. Examples include: "Award-winning marketing copywriter" and "Passionate K-12 educator."

>> **A descriptive About summary:** Your profile summary or About section is the text box that appears just below your photo. It is generally the first section someone scans to learn more about what you do. Use it to describe your key experience and achievements.

>> **A profile picture that presents you in a professional way:** A simple headshot is fine; no professional photo shoot required. A photo will make you more human to new connections.

>> **Your recent job experience:** Make sure to feature your recent positions, along with related accomplishments and skills, in the Experience section.

>> **Recommendations:** Reach out to close contacts to respectfully ask for a recommendation. These can help with credibility when a recruiter scans your profile. You can even ask your contacts to mention a specific skill or area of expertise to support your positioning.

You can also broaden your efforts beyond LinkedIn by searching online for information about the top recruiting firms in your industry. Search for keywords like *recruiters, search firms,* or *staffing agencies,* combined with your industry or profession (marketing or finance, for example). You can also try asking ChatGPT to generate a list of the top recruiting firms in your location and industry.

Once you have a list of top agencies, look them up on LinkedIn to find active job listings and connect with key people at the firm.

Finally, check in with people in your network and ask if they would recommend recruiters they have worked with.

WARNING

A colleague competing for the same jobs may not be as open about sharing their recruiter contacts.

Reaching out to recruiters

When you've identified recruiters you'd like to work with, reach out via LinkedIn or email to introduce yourself and let them know a bit about your background and what you're seeking.

If there's no current opening, they may suggest that you send or upload your resume to be considered for future opportunities. Then keep an eye out for posted jobs and reach out if you see one that's a fit. Even if you're in their system, they may need a nudge to be able to remember you and see the match with the new position.

REMEMBER

Once a recruiter reaches out about a specific role, you'll need to sell them on your qualifications before they'll advocate for you with their client. That means you must excel in the screening interview and take any advice the recruiter offers about customizing your resume.

Many recruiters will be happy to provide additional information about the company or job, so ask questions that will help you succeed in the interview. Ask why the role is open, determine the hiring manager's top priorities, and see where they are in the interviewing process.

Don't be surprised if recruiters sometimes drop out of contact or delay responding to questions — they're juggling multiple searches and multiple candidates for each search.

Follow up if you don't hear back or feel like you're being ghosted. In general, it's smart to keep the dialogue open with recruiters who are connected.

Whether you're interviewing and the process is dragging or you're looking for new prospects, don't be afraid to reach out and politely ask for an update. The worst thing someone can do to you is ignore you. You won't be blacklisted for respectfully following up.

Beware of dishonest and predatory recruiters. Some recruiters out there are running scams. Some are simply spamming you with inappropriate opportunities. They're "spraying and praying" that someone will respond. Others are running bait-and-switch strategies and will waste your time misrepresenting jobs that aren't worth your time. Still others will torment you by scheduling interviews and ghosting repeatedly.

Before you invest time in a particular recruiter, check their LinkedIn profile and online presence for red flags. Whatever you do, don't share sensitive information with anyone you haven't been able to vet.

Even good recruiters can be flaky sometimes. Try not to take it personally. If the opportunity is worth it, be patient and keep after them.

Working with recruiters should be just one part of your job search strategy. Keep networking and stay on top of new job postings on the job boards.

After the Interview

Even though the interview is over, your work isn't done. There are business etiquette rules that dictate what you should do after the interview to improve your odds of moving to the next round (and, ultimately, the offer).

Sending a thank-you note

The first follow-up step is the thank-you note. After the interview, you should send a personalized thank-you note within 24 hours.

Email is now the standard for this task, though some candidates still swear by mailing a handwritten note. Email is faster — and my experience is that few hiring managers truly prefer receiving a note by postal mail.

In recent years, I've noticed that fewer candidates are sending thank-you notes — they are viewed as unnecessary or old-fashioned. Some managers will admit they rarely read them, so it may seem like a wasted effort.

However, I can tell you that many managers *do* read them and appreciate the effort. To me, a thank-you note is a sign of true interest and follow-up skills. If I'm on the fence about someone and don't receive a thank-you note after the interview, I assume that they're not excited about the opportunity, so I put their resume in the No pile.

Whatever the format, the key is to express your appreciation for the opportunity to interview and reiterate your interest in the position. The thank-you email also gives you an opportunity to add or restate key information about your fit.

Keep the tone professional and focus on a few key messages. If you try to restate your entire resume, you'll lose your reader quickly.

If possible, send a thank-you note to each interviewer. Tailor your follow-up message to each individual, addressing them by name and referencing specific topics discussed. This shows that you paid attention and were actively engaged during each conversation.

TIP

If you lack contact information for all interviewers, ask your primary contact for the details, if possible. A legitimate Plan B is to send a note to your main interviewer asking them to pass along your gratitude to X, Y, and Z as well.

Writing an effective thank-you email

In general, keep thank-you emails concise and professional and don't try to do too much. To make it easy, here's an overview of the key components to include:

> **>> Subject line:** Don't leave out the subject line, or else you risk your email being overlooked or moving to the spam folder. Don't get too creative. You can't go wrong with just "Thank you."

- » **_Salutation:_** Starting with a professional salutation, such as "Dear Mr. or Ms. or Dr. <Last Name>," is always a solid choice for more formal interviewers. If they told you to call them Bob or Sarah, you can address them by first name. Make sure you know exactly how to spell the interviewer's name.

- » **Opening:** Start with a sincere expression of thanks, as in this example: "I appreciate the time you took to speak with me about Role XYZ."

  Then express a key positive takeaway about the position or organization. For example, share that you enjoyed hearing more about X or Y aspect of the role and why that has reinforced your interest.

- » **Body:** From there, you can add a paragraph or two to expand on your interest and fit and continue building rapport. You can use this opportunity to mention a topic that didn't come up in the interview or that you feel, in retrospect, you didn't articulate well.

  Another option is to expand on qualifications discussed in the interview or just reiterate your enthusiasm, mentioning any new positives that you learned and felt excited about.

- » **Conclusion:** If you haven't already done so, express your continuing interest in the opportunity and your desire to move forward in the process.

  Remind the interviewer that you're available if they have any further questions.

- » **Sign off:** Go with the classic "Sincerely, <your first and last names>." If you have another go-to option, that's fine too. Just keep it professional (avoid XOXO, in other words).

REMEMBER

Include your full contact information, and any relevant links, such as your LinkedIn profile or online portfolio.

A thank-you email example

Feel free to steal or adapt this example and use it as a template.

> Subject line: Thank you
>
> Dear Ms. Smith,
>
> I greatly appreciate the time you took to meet with me today to discuss the senior project manager position. I enjoyed learning more about the company and especially the details you shared about the upcoming product relaunch. It sounds like an exciting time to join the team.

Our conversation confirmed for me that the role is a great fit for my experience and interests. In addition to my track record in managing successful product launches on tight deadlines, I have extensive experience in keeping a cross-functional global team organized.

One of my strengths is process improvement, and I feel I could be a big help in achieving your goal of streamlining key processes and creating more consistency.

Please let me know if I can provide any additional information. I hope to have the opportunity to continue our discussion about the role.

Thanks again for your time.

Sincerely,

<your first name and last name>

<your email address, phone number, and any relevant links>

Dealing with the after-the-thank-you-email blues

You may receive a reply to your thank-you email. However, don't worry if you don't. Some companies have a protocol and prefer that HR serves as the contact with applicants. In other cases, your interviewer may wait until they have specific next steps to communicate.

If things go well, you'll continue to correspond with your interviewers to set up future meetings, discuss key aspects of the job, and eventually negotiate your offer and start date.

The biggest challenge is knowing when to follow up and when to wait patiently for their next move. If you were given a time frame to expect a reply and haven't heard back, it's fine to politely follow up and ask for an update.

REMEMBER

Take the time to proofread any emails before you click Send. Typos and errors only detract from the positive impression you're trying to cultivate.

Recruiters are notorious for failing to send updates or feedback, even when it's promised. It's one of the most frustrating parts of the job search process.

However, a lack of reply does not mean a lack of interest. Sometimes the process moves slowly, and recruiters get distracted while waiting for word from the hiring team. Yes, sometimes no response means they've moved on to other candidates. However, I've also heard many stories of recruiters reaching out about moving forward after weeks, or even months, of silence.

That doesn't mean you should put your job search on hold while waiting for word. And neither am I excusing this behavior. I believe that it's only common courtesy to take two seconds to let someone know that they're out of the running, especially if they've invested time and energy in multiple interview rounds.

If you're still excited about the position, you can check in periodically while also exploring other opportunities. Avoid excessive follow-up (more than once a week). Push too hard and you risk annoying them or seeming desperate.

WARNING

Don't pick up the phone and call unless you were specifically told to do so (or are returning their call). All the recruiters and hiring managers I know say that they detest receiving unsolicited calls from applicants. You're also more likely to get a response to an email or a LinkedIn message.

Maintain a professional tone in all your communications. Even if you aren't the final choice for one role, communication skills can help you expand your network and set yourself up for future opportunities or referrals.

» **Predicting questions to expect at each interview stage**

» **Preparing for different interview formats**

» **Getting comfortable with video interviews**

Chapter **3**

Getting to Know the Players and the Rules

Consider this chapter a field guide to the people you will meet — and how you will meet them — during the job interview process. Many different types of interviewers are out there — from recruiters to hiring managers to CEOs. You will also encounter various interview formats — including phone, video, in-person, panel/committee, and more.

To make a strong impression in your interviews, you need to understand each interviewer's perspective and what they care most about. There are some common considerations for all interviewers, but you will also find some variation based on the person's role in the hiring process and how they will interact with the individual hired.

You will also feel much more comfortable if you know what to expect on interview day in terms of format. There are best practices for each type of interview — and common mistakes to avoid, too. In this chapter, I cover the most common formats that come up across industries and professions.

This is an important chapter because fear of the unknown increases your anxiety and hurts your interview performance. Knowledge is power. I'm briefing you on what to expect so that you won't be caught off guard and can shine in every interview situation.

Assessing Your Interviewers

As with any communication challenge, knowing your audience is the key to success. If you understand whom you're talking to and what they care most about, you can tailor your messages to be persuasive.

For any given job opportunity, you will likely meet with multiple interviewers. (That's if you're lucky enough to advance past the first gatekeeper.) The interview experience varies based on who's evaluating you, so you have to be prepared.

Different interviewers will focus on different types of questions and will prioritize different criteria in deciding whether you're a good fit. The variations tend to be based on role (as well as on personality, though that's much harder to predict). For example, a recruiter's job is to validate your resume and decide whether you meet the minimum standards to move forward in the process. The hiring manager has a much better sense of the day-to-day work and technical skills required and will ask more in-depth questions.

Let's review the most common types of interviewers so that you'll know what to expect and how to prepare for each step in the process.

The screening recruiter

Typically, your first interview is with a recruiter or another HR contact. This is known as a *screening* interview because the goal is to screen out anyone who doesn't meet the basic qualifications.

To be selected for a screening interview, you must first pass the resume test. If your resume looks like a good fit, the next step is to have a brief conversation to validate that the resume is accurate and unearth a little more information. The focus is on identifying any red flags that would knock the candidate out of the running. These possible red flags might include resume falsehoods or exaggerations, weaknesses in key requirements, or lack of professionalism.

REMEMBER

Screening interviews are handled in a variety of ways. You may meet with someone via phone, via video meeting, or in person. These days, you may also be asked to answer and submit prerecorded questions. I'll delve into more information about these interview formats shortly. First, let's focus on the interviewers because the same people are likely to be evaluating you regardless of the format.

In most cases, your screening interview will be conducted by a recruiter. This might be an internal recruiter (employee of the organization) or an external recruiter (outside consultant). At smaller firms without dedicated recruiters, the screening interview may be with a human resources employee or even with the hiring manager.

It's helpful to know a bit about each of these roles. First, let's talk about external recruiters.

External recruiter

Companies hire external recruiters to do the legwork of sourcing and vetting candidates, allowing employees to focus on meeting with only the most qualified applicants.

The external recruiter typically makes money by sourcing candidates who get hired. They are vendors who are evaluated based on the quality of candidates they refer, so they don't want to send in someone who is a poor fit. They can't afford to annoy the client and risk losing future business.

However, the external recruiter also has a vested interest in your success if you advance past the screening interview and meet the client. If you do well, the external recruiter makes money. Some firms work with multiple external recruiters so that they face competition to send in the best candidate.

You should also know that the external recruiter is unlikely to be a true expert in their knowledge of the job and the organization. Occasionally, you'll meet an external recruiter who has worked with the firm for a long time and knows the process inside and out, but it's rare. External recruiters also typically work with many different clients and lots of candidates. As a result, some may not put in the time that an internal recruiter would.

The external recruiter will mostly ask basic questions to understand your background and qualifications. They will try to validate that your resume is legitimate and check on any gaps, short tenures, or other inconsistencies. They will also ask why you're looking for a new role now and what interests you about the open position. These questions are to determine whether you're serious about the opportunity and make sure no concerning reasons lie behind your job change.

They may also probe into a particular skill set that's a top priority for the job. To be efficient, screening interviews have to be focused. Not every issue can be covered, so the recruiter is usually given a short list of requirements to vet.

REMEMBER

Many of the questions may be yes or no. Do you have the required skill or not? Do you have the three years of experience or not? Be clear and don't assume they'll be able to read between the lines of your resume.

The screening interview is the shortest and the easiest (though maybe not exactly easy if you have a potential red flag that requires explanation). However, if you impress the external recruiter, they can become a valuable ally for you.

WARNING

Don't make the mistake of writing this screening interview off as easy and failing to prepare. Even if it's just 15 minutes on the phone, it's an essential step in the process. You have to win over this gatekeeper in order to move on to speak with the hiring managers.

REMEMBER

The external recruiter is evaluated (and compensated) based on the impression you make, so they succeed if you succeed.

If you make a connection with the external recruiter, don't be afraid to ask questions. This is someone who can become an advocate for you. They may even be willing to coach you on what to focus on, which can be a big advantage.

Take their advice seriously. If they suggest that you edit your resume or that you highlight certain skills in your interviews, they're doing it because they know more than you do about the hiring team's priorities.

Internal recruiter or HR rep

The other common type of screening interviewer is the internal recruiter or HR rep. This is the first company gatekeeper you'll face.

The goals of the screening interview are the same here as they are with an external recruiter: Validate the resume and look for red flags. The biggest difference is that the internal recruiter's motivations are more closely aligned with the hiring company's goals. Though the external recruiter wants to wow the client and get paid, the internal recruiter represents the company and has more invested in the long-term success of the hiring decision.

The HR interviewer also knows a lot more about the organization and the hiring process. They are likely to ask more challenging and nuanced questions. They will also judge against more specific criteria, not just look for general red flags, but consider candidates through the lens of the company culture and history.

This person probably has some solid experience in recruiting and interviewing and some insight into what the hiring manager wants and doesn't want. Their goal: Find out whether this candidate is a close enough fit that they should send them through to meet with the hiring managers. Their job is to pick potential winners and avoid wasting anyone's time.

Like an external recruiter, the internal recruiter or HR rep is judged on the quality of the candidates they refer, but it's different. They aren't paid based on a specific person getting hired. Their annual review and bonus will take into account the overall quality of the hire (often looking at long-term performance and turnover).

It can be harder to win over the internal recruiter or HR rep, mostly because they have more inside knowledge and thus more opinions on who should be screened out. However, if you impress them, you gain a useful advocate, even more so than the external recruiter. If they think you're a strong fit, they can answer more questions and offer more knowledgeable advice on what to expect in the next round. After all, they want the hiring manager to see that they're brilliant at screening candidates.

Regardless of who the interviewer is, the screening interview is critical. If you find that you're easily passing the screening phase, it's a sign that your resume is strong and your basic interview skills are solid. However, keep in mind that you'll need more advanced interview savvy to ace the next rounds with more complex and challenging questions.

On the other hand, if you're being invited for lots of screening interviews, but rarely moving forward, it's a sure sign that you need to improve your interview techniques.

The hiring manager

If you win over the hiring manager, you gain the support of the most influential player in the process.

The hiring manager will be your boss if you get hired, so it makes sense that the hiring manager is also the primary decision-maker. They may need the approval and support of others, but their vote carries the most weight.

That's because the hiring manager is the one who will succeed or fail based on who gets hired. Hiring is a key part of being a good manager. If the hiring manager makes a choice that doesn't work out, it will absolutely reflect on their performance evaluation (and affect future bonuses, raises, and promotions). They need to pick a winner to impress their bosses.

This decision will also impact the hiring manager's daily life for the foreseeable future. The right hire will make their life easier and help the whole team excel. The wrong hire will cause headaches and distractions at a minimum (not to mention cost them time and money to start the hiring process over again).

If you've been a hiring manager, you know the pressure of making a good decision — and the daily suffering of managing a bad employee.

The hiring manager needs someone who's going to do good work, meet deadlines, deliver what they say they're going to deliver, get along with the team, and generally make them look like a genius manager.

The hiring manager knows the job well and is more likely to ask questions about key competencies, technical skills, and experience with specific day-to-day responsibilities.

TIP

The hiring manager will also care the most about your personality and work style, because they will be working closely with you on a day-to-day basis. They will likely spend more time building rapport and getting to know you as a person.

Beyond the basic qualifications for the job, they need to evaluate your work ethic, your commitment, and your reliability. Will you stick around and perform if they take the time to hire and train you?

Be prepared for questions about your goals and culture fit along with behavioral questions about your past experience and deeper dives into key topics.

REMEMBER

Often, you will meet with the hiring manager more than once. First, you must win their approval and the opportunity to move forward in the process. Later, the hiring manager may play a role in introducing you to other interviewers and/or circling back for some follow-up questions after you've met with others on the team.

The senior manager

If the hiring manager likes you, you will probably move on to meet with their boss and/or other senior managers. This is a positive sign because a senior leader will take the time to meet with you only if you've made a strong impression with others already.

The senior manager's vote will carry a lot of weight. At a minimum, they will need to approve the hiring manager's decision. If the senior manager has concerns about you, the hiring manager will have to think twice, even if they love you.

REMEMBER

Just like the rest of us, the hiring manager has to show respect for their boss. Even if the senior manager is taking a hands-off role, ignoring their concerns isn't a good look (especially if the hire doesn't work out).

In most cases, the senior manager will ask more high-level fit questions and fewer detailed technical questions. They aren't as close to the details of the position as the hiring manager. However, if the interview is for a visible role or one that interacts frequently with senior management, the senior-level interviewer may be more invested in the process.

The senior manager likely has extensive experience interviewing and hiring employees. They may also have a deeper understanding of the organization's culture and future needs. As a result, they may see red flags that others don't — and ask questions accordingly. They may also be focused on culture factors such as leadership style, integrity, or work ethic.

In general, you want to prepare for this interviewer the same way you prepared for your interview with the hiring manager. This is an influential person in the hiring process, and you want to present yourself in the best possible way.

The team member

Often, key team members are asked to participate in the interview process.

You may be asked to meet with potential peers, managers from teams you would be working closely with — maybe even someone who held the position in the past and has been promoted.

If someone has been asked to be part of the interview process — and take the time away from their work to meet with you — it's a pretty good call that you're going to be working closely with them if you're hired.

That means these are people you need to impress, to show that you would be a fantastic and beloved coworker.

REMEMBER

Generally, team member interviewers are most interested in how well you would support their interests. If the person is an internal client, they will consider your ability to deliver what they need. If the person is a peer, they will wonder about how you collaborate and whether you can pull your weight on shared projects.

They're thinking, "Can I get along with this person? Can I count on them to deliver what I need to succeed in my job?"

That's really what it comes down to with every single one of these interviewers: "Will this person help me do my job better? Will this person make my work life easier?"

They're likely to ask the usual common interview questions as a way to get to know you and evaluate your experience. They may focus on a particular work experience or competency area that's important to them as a colleague. For example, you might be asked behavioral questions about teamwork from a potential collaborator. You might be asked to elaborate on a technical skill that's critical to pulling your weight on the job.

When it's time for your questions, it can be helpful to ask for more information about how you would be working together if hired. This can give you more insight into the job in general and give you an opportunity to address related strengths.

The direct report

If you're interviewing for a management position, you may be asked to interview with employees who would be reporting to you if hired. This can be a tricky interaction at times.

For this interviewer, it's not just a hiring decision; it's choosing who will be their future boss — the person responsible for their career prospects.

In addition to the typical interview questions, the direct report is wondering: "Can I see myself working for this person? Would they be a good and fair boss? Is there any obvious personality conflict here? What is their management style? How would they approach leading the team?"

Occasionally, you face an added awkwardness here. For example, you could end up interviewing with someone who had hoped to be promoted into the position you're interviewing for. They may resent being passed over for the role and take it out on you. They may have loyalty to another internal candidate or preconceived notions about the kind of manager they want.

You can't change these situations, certainly not in one interview. All you can do is focus on building rapport, show respect for the current team, and hope that you can win over the direct report, despite any hidden agendas at play.

Look for opportunities to show that you care about being a good manager, and talk about positive relationships with your current and/or past direct reports.

When it's time to ask questions, you can ask about what type of management style works best with the team. Again, the answer will provide useful information about the job and the culture, but it may also give you a chance to address how your management style is a good fit.

The bar raiser

Some companies now include a new type of interviewer in the process — a special agent known as the *bar raiser*, who is usually an employee from a different team or department, specially trained in interviewing and brought in to add more rigor to the process. The bar raiser's job is to be an advocate for the company's hiring criteria and talent standards.

Since this person has no personal connection to the job, they can be more objective. Usually, bar raisers also have a deep understanding of the company's values and culture and how to evaluate whether a candidate is a fit.

Bar raisers have been common for years at many large tech companies, including Amazon and Google. Other companies have since jumped on the trend and adopted the bar raiser approach.

Bar raisers are rarely identified as bar raisers. From the candidate's perspective, this person is just another interviewer. However, here are some clues to look for:

>> **Department and role:** Look for interviewers from departments that have no obviously strong connection to the role, especially if no explanation is provided.

>> **Probing questions:** Bar raisers often ask more structured and challenging questions. They come prepared because they take seriously their role as a bar raiser. They interview people a lot and have an arsenal of well-designed behavioral questions to choose from.

>> **Focus on culture:** Bar raisers will likely ask thoughtful questions related to culture fit. Though most untrained interviewers judge fit based on overall impression, the bar raiser has been educated in how the organization defines culture and values alignment.

Since you won't know in advance whether you're meeting a bar raiser, it's good to go into every interview prepared for the possibility. This is also smart because you may encounter other interviewers with training and interview skills at the bar-raiser level.

REMEMBER

If you research the company's interview process on its website and sites like Glassdoor.com, you may be able to predict whether a bar raiser is likely to show up. If so, pay special attention to any information provided about hiring criteria and values.

For example, Amazon has 16 leadership principles that are widely publicized. Bar raisers often ask behavioral questions related to these leadership principles. For example, the leadership principle of customer obsession might prompt a question like this: "Tell me about a time you went above and beyond for a customer."

TIP

Bar raisers tend to like behavioral questions in general, so pay attention to Chapter 11 and prepare your greatest hits stories. Make sure you feature a strong R (result) that demonstrates how you "raised the bar." These examples will serve you well with other interviewers too.

Some bar raisers may challenge you to think on your feet. If you field a curveball question, take a moment to think about the reasoning behind it and do your best to answer. The bar raiser is probably more interested in your ability to adapt and think critically than in hearing a specific "right" answer.

If you spot a bar raiser, that means the company is serious about their hiring process and has high standards. Don't let that intimidate you. If you've made it to the bar raiser round, they obviously see valuable qualities in you. Now you just have to seal the deal.

Mastering the Various Interview Formats

Though knowing your audience is vital, you must also master the method of communication. In job interviews, that means getting comfortable with the various interview formats.

If you're a public speaker, you prepare differently for presenting to a giant auditorium of strangers versus a small conference room of close colleagues versus a live YouTube stream to casual viewers with short attention spans. You take a different approach to a 2-hour keynote speech versus a TV talk show appearance versus an investor pitch.

It's similar with job interviews. Luckily, you have to consider only a few common interview formats. Yes, the questions can vary greatly (as I explain in the remainder of this book), but interviewers don't typically try to get too creative when it comes to format.

I cover all the common interview formats, what to expect, and how to prepare effectively. You're probably familiar with some of these, but I want to share advanced tips to help you make the most of each format and avoid common mistakes.

In terms of your interview answers, you should prepare the same way for a phone interview as you do for an in-person interview or a video interview. In other words, anticipate the common questions, outline your bullet points, and practice. (See Parts 3 and 4 of this book.)

You'll find that interviewers ask similar questions regardless of the format. I point out wherever there are some differences to be aware of. However, the formats differ mostly in how you connect and communicate.

Some formats will feel more challenging and uncomfortable, depending on your preferred communication style. Others will feel more comfortable in the moment but limit your ability to make a strong impression. For example, some of my clients prefer phone interviews because they don't have to worry about how they look, but it's easier to establish rapport in person. By understanding the formats and their challenges, you can customize your approach for various scenarios.

Traditional one-on-one

The one-on-one in-person interview is the classic format. Before COVID-19 entered the picture, the majority of job interviews consisted of two people chatting in the same room. For obvious reasons, COVID-19 isolation led to more reliance on phone and video interviews. However, in-person interviews are gaining popularity again, because many managers prefer to meet candidates in person if possible before making a hiring decision.

This type of interview usually lasts from 20 to 45 minutes. After the introductions and small talk end, the majority of the interview is the interviewer asking questions and you answering them.

As you now know, the same questions come up time and time again. You should be ready for a curveball or two, but most interviews are pretty predictable. They want to find out whether you can do the job and whether they can see themselves working with you.

After you finish answering their questions, you'll generally get a chance to ask them questions of your own. The interview then ends with some sort of wrap-up and discussion of next steps. If all went well, you might be offered a tour of the office or be asked to spontaneously meet with someone else on the team before you leave.

With many companies, you may be scheduled in advance to face a series of back-to-back, one-on-one interviews on the same day. The goal is to be efficient and obtain as much information as possible in one day, avoiding the scheduling headache of bringing candidates back multiple times. This is in theory, of course, because I know some of my clients have been asked to interview more than seven times (between in-person visits and phone or Zoom interviews) before getting an offer.

The in-person one-on-one interview sounds pretty straightforward, and it is, in many ways, but that doesn't mean it's easy. Some of my coaching clients have truly struggled with the in-person format. They were passing their phone interviews with flying colors and then being rejected after the first in-person meeting.

Most of us don't have to present ourselves for judgment on a regular basis (thank goodness). It tends to feel more vulnerable in person. On the phone or on Zoom, you're in a comfortable environment and can control your surroundings. You can have your notes nearby in case you need them.

An in-person interview presents a bunch of additional challenges — including an unfamiliar environment, a stranger who might turn out to be intimidating or rude, and more focus on your physical presentation.

In person, your nonverbal communications play a much bigger role. When you're anxious or self-conscious, you're more likely to forget your thoughtful talking points and fall back on nervous habits like fidgeting, rambling, or using filler words.

Some people do just fine when the interviewer is friendly and puts them at ease but get thrown off when faced with someone who is confrontational or poker-faced.

REMEMBER

When preparing for an in-person interview, practice is crucial. Practice makes you more comfortable with both your talking points and the delivery of those talking points. That means your trained instincts are likely to kick in even in the face of nerves or an unreadable interviewer.

Live on video

Video interviews have become a standard part of the hiring process. Companies are increasingly using Zoom, Microsoft Teams, Google Meet, and other video conferencing platforms to interview candidates.

During the COVID-19 pandemic, video interviews became the standard. Most people became comfortable using video conferencing in their day-to-day lives, not just for interviews but also for work meetings and PTA meetings and family gatherings.

Many companies (and candidates) found that video interviews were much more convenient, so now they're here to stay. Video interviews offer all the flexibility of a phone interview with the bonus of the visual element that makes the connection feel more human.

In some cases, video interviews have replaced the screening interview that was traditionally conducted via phone, with in-person interviews to follow for those who make the cut.

Other organizations prefer to use video interviews during all phases of the hiring process. They're useful for easily including interviewers who are based in other cities or countries. They're also perfect for hiring for remote roles or for interviewing nonlocal candidates, even those who plan to relocate to work onsite if hired.

For a video interview, you'll want to prepare in much the same way that you would prepare for an in-person interview in terms of your bullet points and practicing your presentation. The video interview is easier in some ways — you don't have to worry about parking or logistics or what pants to wear (*Note:* Please wear pants. You never know when you'll have to stand up to close the door or fix the webcam, and I have heard horror stories from recruiters about sights they can't unsee.)

TIP

You can also keep your notes nearby in case you need them — you probably won't, but it can be reassuring to know they're there in case you go blank.

However, acing a video interview requires some skills and knowledge (and equipment) that you don't need in a phone or in-person interview. If the video format is relatively new for you, you'll need to get comfortable with being on camera and working with the technical components.

Technology

Two technical components are necessary for video interviews. First, you need the right hardware — the equipment necessary to connect with interviewers and record or stream video and audio. Then you'll need access to the software application(s) required to join the interview.

For hardware, you just need an Internet-connected device (computer, tablet, or smartphone in a pinch), a webcam, and a microphone and speakers for audio. Most laptops and tablets now come with built-in webcams and speakers/microphones, though you may want to consider a headset for higher-quality audio.

REMEMBER

A strong, reliable Internet connection is vital. Video interviews require significant bandwidth and a weak or unstable Wi-Fi connection can lead to technical problems, and you don't need that distraction during an interview.

If you're using a desktop or your laptop's webcam isn't reliable, you need an external webcam. It has the added benefit of giving you more control over image quality and positioning. You can find many good webcam brands out there, but Logitech is usually a good bet.

If possible, position the webcam just above your monitor. This allows for a flattering angle and also helps you approximate natural eye contact. (I tell you more on video eye contact in a moment.)

With a built-in webcam, you can achieve a similar effect by placing your laptop on something (a laptop stand, a box, a few books) so that the webcam is positioned slightly above your eye-line, in line with the top of your head.

Even though I personally prefer a headset during a video interview, you don't necessarily need one. Webcams and laptops have built-in microphones now, but the sound quality tends to be tinny and they pick up ambient sounds (neighbors, nearby construction, air conditioning) that can be distracting.

Now let's talk about software. Most video interviews are conducted using one of a few popular video conferencing tools — Zoom (still number one in my field reports from clients), Google Meet, and Microsoft Teams. Occasionally, you see other platforms, but they tend to be similar to the Big 3 in terms of candidate user experience.

If you have a Zoom/Meet/Teams account already, be sure to clean up your profile and privacy settings if you're going to use it with potential employers. Your college account with the ID stoner-yolo1993 will *not* inspire confidence.

Usually, you don't even need to download software or set up an account to participate in the video interview. The interviewer simply sends you an invitation with a link (and maybe a password and dial-in number).

However, be sure to read the interview invitation carefully. Some interviewers may ask you to download software, set up an account, or provide a number for them to call.

Sometimes you see special instructions if you have a series of video interviews or interactions on the same day. You may be asked to prepare documents to share in the video conference room or to complete an assessment before the meeting.

If you receive the invitation and see that the interviewer will be using a platform that's unfamiliar to you, take a few minutes to read up on the functionality or user experience and try a test call with a friend to avoid surprises on interview day.

Once you have your video interview setup ready, be sure to do a trial run to make sure no technology adjustments are needed. You can wait to do this until you also have the lighting and background ready (see the following section) so that it's a true dress rehearsal.

If possible, avoid using your phone for video interviews, especially in environments you can't control. With a phone, it's harder to set up a hands-free, flattering angle (a phone stand can help). You don't want to be worrying about holding the phone in the right position when you should be focusing on your speaking points. More importantly, phones also tend to be more temperamental — they drop or switch Wi-Fi networks or hit you with incoming calls or alerts at exactly the wrong moment.

Environment

A video interview gives you control over your environment, so take advantage of that power. If you prepare for optimal lighting, background, and other environmental factors, you can feel confident that you'll look and sound impressive and prevent distracting surprises.

BACKGROUND

First, set up a spot for your video interview with a neutral, professional background. The interviewer doesn't want to see your messy bed or your spouse or roommate wandering into the background.

Avoid any background imagery that might embarrass you or distract the interviewer. It's hard to go wrong with a neutral background — a plain wall, a bookshelf, a screen, a painting. You can use a custom background if the video software allows it. If you choose to do so, don't get too creative — a colorful or quirky scene can be fun but might prove distracting over the course of an interview.

If you choose to use a custom background, be aware that it can fail you — I have seen weird warping and flickering at times. To be on the safe side, test out the background before the interview — and make sure there's nothing mortifying behind you, just in case you have an issue.

Try not to sit in front of windows, especially uncovered windows. If you do, you may experience glare, shadows, or reflections. Keep in mind the time of day of your scheduled interview — that window background may look great at 10 a.m. but too bright at 2 p.m.

LIGHTING

After you set the background, you should pay attention to the important topic of lighting — the right lighting can make you look like a movie star, but the wrong lighting can be extremely unflattering.

You don't need an expensive lighting setup unless you're interviewing for a job as an influencer or on-camera talent. However, a little bit of time and ingenuity can make a big difference.

The ideal setup for video is to position lights on either side of you at about the same height of the webcam (or a little higher). This helps you achieve nice, even lighting across your face, which minimizes shadows, blurs wrinkles and imperfections, and makes you look fabulous.

You can create this effect on a budget by positioning two lamps or desk lights, one on either side of your desk, with the light source ideally at the height of the webcam or slightly higher.

You may need to test and adjust until you find the perfect positioning. The lighting can vary based on factors like the ambient light in the room, the time of day, and the height or wattage of the lamps, so move around your lights and your laptop, if necessary.

ELIMINATING DISTRACTIONS

I've mentioned this topic already, but it's important to do whatever you can to prevent distractions during the interview. Distractions can throw you off your A game. They can also draw the interviewer's attention away from your thoughtful answers and even lead to misperceptions about your professionalism.

First, do your best to arrange a private, quiet location for your interview. Turn off the ringer on your phone and any noisy or annoying alerts.

If you're in a shared space, let people know not to disturb you during the interview period. Yes, we're all human and we all have lives, but a surprise guest appearance by your housemate or toddler could diminish your credibility. Personally, I'm a fan of cute pet appearances, but some interviewers may disagree.

Sometimes a distraction is unavoidable (sudden construction, tap-dancing neighbor upstairs). If you're using a high-quality headset, a noise that sounds loud to you may not even be audible to the interviewer. If the distraction is obvious, just address it briefly, apologize, and move on. If necessary, excuse yourself for a moment and mute your mic or turn off your webcam to address the issue.

WARNING

Do not connect to your video interview from any public place (especially not a Starbucks). You're just setting yourself up for noise, distractions, and Wi-Fi instability. The message to your interviewer: You didn't care enough to find a quiet spot to talk.

PRESENTATION

The biggest challenge for many of my clients is making natural eye contact in a video interview. In Chapter 15, I cover why it's important to maintain confident eye contact during a job interview (and I give you tips on how to get better at it). This is more difficult to do via video than in person.

When you're speaking to someone via video conference, your eyes naturally tend to focus on the face of your conversation partner. Depending on where that face is positioned on your screen and the location of your webcam, this can cause you to appear as though you're looking down or away.

You can avoid this problem by resizing and moving the window with the person's video image. Move it as close to your webcam as possible. This way, when you're looking into their eyes, you're also looking toward the camera. This will give the closest approximation to real human eye contact.

At this point, most people are used to being on video calls regularly, so they don't think much about eye contact. It's mostly noticeable when there's a problem. If you're repeatedly looking down or up or to the side, it can translate as disconnected or avoidant. Sometimes the interviewer notices it not as an eye contact problem but rather as lacking a connection.

If you try to force yourself to look continuously into the camera instead of at the interviewer's face, it can feel awkward or forced on your end and limit your ability to read reactions and visual cues. However, it tends to look fine to interviewers if that's your preference.

TIP

There's a difference between good eye contact and the serial killer stare. Because webcam eye contact can feel awkward at first, some people respond by overcompensating. Just try to relax and act natural. It's fine to look away to think occasionally, and blinking is allowed.

Though it's fine to glance at your notes or your resume occasionally, be careful not to go overboard. This is the equivalent of sitting in an in-person interview and staring down at the table instead of looking at the person you're speaking with.

Another potential challenge is the temptation to stare at yourself. If the video software displays your image on the screen (most do), be careful not to get distracted by looking at your own image. This will look odd to the interviewer and make you self-conscious when you should be thinking about your answers.

TIP

Remember to smile. I know it's a cliché, but it's a cliché for a reason. Your first impression in a video interview is made during the first few seconds, before words are even spoken. A smile, good posture, and confident eye contact communicate interest and enthusiasm. Don't force a continuous smile (that's downright creepy), but make a point of starting with a smile (and don't hold back when it feels natural). Practice helps you become comfortable enough to relax and smile more.

On a related note about presentation, you should dress for your video interview just as you would dress for an in-person interview (see Chapter 15). However, you should consider a few additional issues for a video interview.

First, certain colors and patterns don't work well on video. I've never heard of someone being rejected because of wearing an unflattering color — however, if you want to look your absolute best on camera, avoid too much solid white or busy patterns.

You might also want to consider paying a little extra attention to makeup, if you wear it. In a video interview, most of the focus is on your face, and the lighting can make you shiny. A little makeup on your nose and forehead can fix that.

If you wear glasses, glare-proof is best so that there's no reflection. You want the interviewer to see your eyes and not a distracting glare. If you have contacts, it might be a good idea to use them.

TIP

Many of us have been guilty of dressing professionally on top but keeping our pajama bottoms on during a video call. Once again, I advise wearing real pants in case you have to stand up to adjust the camera or grab your water bottle.

Dress rehearsal

One advantage of video interviews is the ability to do a realistic dress rehearsal and make adjustments before the big day. You can test your technology, see how your background and lighting look, check your outfit, and practice your video eye contact.

WARNING

Before starting your dress rehearsal or actual video interview, close out of any other programs that connect with your webcam and/or audio. I've seen clients experience problems connecting their webcam to Zoom, for example, because their camera was streaming to another app.

Ideally, you've already spent time practicing your interview answers and presentation style. If you haven't practiced on video yet, do it now. This is valuable preparation for interviews in general, not just video interviews.

When the time comes to prepare for a specific video meeting, you'll also want to do a dress rehearsal using your actual location and setup. This helps you identify any issues that need attention, including these:

- » Internet connection
- » Webcam settings
- » Webcam position or angle
- » Audio settings
- » Software functionality
- » Software settings
- » Lighting
- » Background
- » How you look on camera (hair, makeup, clothing)
- » Eye contact

This way, you can troubleshoot problems before interview day. A dress rehearsal also gives you a realistic sense of how you come across on video.

Accommodations

Employers are required to offer reasonable accommodations to candidates with disabilities, including options for video interviews. If you're invited to a video interview and no information about accommodations is provided, don't hesitate to ask.

Here are some possible accommodations to consider requesting:

- » Additional technical assistance using the required video conferencing platform and any assistive technologies
- » Real-time captioning and/or transcription for those with hearing impairments
- » Flexible scheduling to interview at an optimal time (taking into account the need for a certain environment or technology)
- » Assistive technologies, including screen readers or voice recognition software

I recommend researching the accessibility of the required platform. This can help you identify whether accommodations will be needed. You can also see the accessibility tools available (such as display settings, captioning, and keyboard shortcuts) and practice with them to see whether they're sufficient. The following links are good places to start:

- » **Zoom accessibility:** https://explore.zoom.us/en/accessibility
- » **Microsoft Teams accessibility:** www.microsoft.com/en-us/microsoft-teams/accessibility-closed-captions-transcriptions

» **Google Meet accessibility:** https://support.google.com/meet/
answer/7313544

Prerecorded video

In addition to the classic live video meeting, you have a new video interview format to prepare for these days: the prerecorded video interview. This format is also sometimes described as a *one-way* video interview or an *asynchronous* video interview.

With these, you're sent a link to a page with prerecorded questions you need to answer. Sometimes these are video or audio recordings of someone asking the questions, and sometimes you just see the text question and a prompt to record your answer.

You're given a defined amount of time to complete the interview (submit all your answers). Usually, you also have a time limit to answer after you view a given question and a defined number of takes allowed per question. (*Takes* are opportunities to redo your answer before submitting.) Companies can customize the settings, so you won't know the exact requirements until you see the questions.

Most organizations use special platforms to create these prerecorded interviews and then view and evaluate the answers. Some popular ones are HireVue, AsyncInterview, Wepow, and Sonru, among others.

These video questions are most often used as a screening step, especially for positions with a high volume of applicants to screen. The questions are usually basic ones designed to eliminate those who aren't a strong enough fit to meet with in person.

This format has become increasingly popular with hiring organizations. They see it as a time saver, especially when having to narrow down large pools of applicants.

Unfortunately, many candidates find the format to be impersonal and disrespectful. As one of my clients put it, "Why would I want to work for a company that can't even be bothered to talk to me one-on-one?"

I understand where he's coming from, but most recruiting teams are overscheduled and looking for ways to make the screening process more fair and efficient. Prerecorded interviews allow them to consider more candidates in the first round. The in-person interviews happen later in the process.

Other job seekers dislike the prerecorded interview because it's unfamiliar to them and feels awkward. They're put off by the idea of talking to a computer screen and being recorded and evaluated.

What to expect

If you're asked to participate in a prerecorded interview, don't let it freak you out. I'm going to walk you through what to expect and how to prepare.

The exact user experience will vary somewhat by company and platform, but the process usually goes something like this:

1. **Visit the platform.** You'll click a link and go to a page with general interview information and instructions. Here's where you usually see how many questions you must answer and details about settings such as time limits.

   Take the time to read the instructions carefully. If there are time constraints, wait to start the interview until you feel fully prepared and know you have time to focus for the length of time required.

   Make sure your setup is ready (follow the same advice in the previous section to set up your technology, background, lighting, and wardrobe) before starting the interview.

2. **Start the interview.** When you're ready, click to start the interview. You'll be asked to fill in some information about yourself and then launch the first interview question.

   You might launch a video or audio recording of the question, or you might see just the text. You'll see whether there are time constraints at the question level (versus the overall interview level). Sometimes, you have only a certain amount of time to "count down" after you play/read the question. In some cases, the recording automatically cuts you off after a certain amount of time. Sometimes you have only one chance to record, whereas other interviews allow for multiple takes.

   Once you know the question and the parameters, take a moment to collect your thoughts. Even if there's a countdown to start, you'll be better if you pause just a bit before jumping into the answer.

   If time permits, check your notes and try practicing the answer out loud before you record (recommended if you haven't had a chance to practice it recently).

   If the question stumps you and you have time, jot down some bullet points and organize your thoughts.

   One advantage with this format is that nobody is looking at or judging you until you press the Submit button. Take a deep breath and strategize.

3. **Record your answer.** When you're ready, go ahead and record. Follow the guidelines for eye contact and nonverbal communication that I cover in the "Live on video" section, earlier in this chapter.

   One interesting difference is that you may not have anyone to look at. This makes eye contact understandably difficult. If a paused video face appears on your screen, do your best to position the image near your webcam and make eye contact. If not, your best bet is to look at the webcam. If it feels weird, give yourself a minute to warm up; try imagining someone's face under that green webcam light.

   After recording, you may have the option to discard your first answer and try again. If you feel good about the answer, go ahead and submit. If you stumbled or left something out, give it another go.

   Sometimes it helps to do a "rough draft" and the second take feels smoother. Just don't get too caught up in endless re-dos in pursuit of a "perfect" answer. Remember that they will be focusing on the substance of what you say. Don't stress out and re-record for a hair out of place or a few ums.

4. **Submit your answer.**

   Once you're happy (enough) with your answer, it's time to submit and move on.

   Remember that you don't have to be perfect. By reading this book and following the advice, you're better prepared than 95 percent of the other candidates.

5. **Complete the interview.** Now you're warmed up and you can navigate your responses to any remaining questions. If you get stuck or aren't feeling the right energy, you may have the option to step away and come back. However, once you get into a flow, it usually makes sense to complete all the questions while you're in interview mode.

That's it. All that's left is to wait for them to invite you in for one-on-one meeting for the next round.

Common questions

Because prerecorded interviews are used mostly for screening, the questions are usually screening questions designed to develop a general overview of your background and fit.

In my experience, these are the most common questions used in prerecorded interviews:

>> **Tell me about yourself (or some variation).** See Chapter 6. The interviewer is looking for an overview of your experience, your general professionalism, and your communication skills.

>> **Why are you interested in this opportunity? (Or some variation).** See Chapter 7. They want to determine whether you're serious about the position and whether you have done some research about the organization.

>> **Basic behavioral questions.** See Chapter 11. Sometimes, you see basic behavioral questions about teamwork or problem-solving or other key competencies. I often see these in prerecorded interviews for internships or entry-level positions — situations where applicants have no proven experience working in a professional setting.

Phone interview

Even with video interviews gaining popularity, phone interviews continue to be quite common, especially as a first interview with the recruiter or HR person.

Many of my interview coaching clients prefer phone interviews because they feel this format is less intimidating than a face-to-face meeting, or even a video conference.

In a lot of ways, they are. First, you don't have to worry about how you look. You don't have to consider wardrobe or body language or eye contact.

You can also have your notes nearby to reference. That can really help with nerves.

However, a phone interview has some special challenges.

It's much harder to make a strong impression in a phone interview, for a couple of reasons.

First, it's harder to connect and build rapport without nonverbal cues. It's difficult to feel like you're getting to know someone when you can't look into their eyes or smile or lean forward to show your interest. You can't see when they perk up to listen more closely, when they zone out, or when they nod and smile.

This is particularly limiting for people who are "good in the room," as they say. You can't convey charisma or magnetism as clearly with only your voice.

REMEMBER

In general, people are much more likely to remember you if they've met you in person. This is why salespeople always want to snag the in-person meeting.

In the phone interview, all you have is your voice and your words, so you have to make sure that your voice and your words are on point. To compensate for the lack of engaging eye contact and body language, make an extra effort to bring out positive energy in what you say and how you say it.

Because it's harder to read the interviewer during a phone interview, you're more likely to talk way too much in phone interviews. My clients ramble on, subconsciously waiting for a sign that the interviewer is satisfied.

You can avoid this problem by getting comfortable with moments of silence. You may hear the silence as, "Oh my goodness, they hate my answer. I had better keep talking and salvage this." More likely, the silence simply means that they're making a quick note or checking their phone.

TIP

Don't rush to keep talking just to fill the silence. If the interviewer wants more or has a follow-up question, they'll let you know. You'll sound more confident if you're concise and stay on point.

In terms of questions, phone interviews tend to cover topics similar to those covered in video or in-person interviews. They're more dependent on the interviewer and the stage in the process than on the format.

If it's a phone screen interview, the questions will be basic resume review questions, though some may include tougher fit questions or technical questions as well.

Whatever you do, don't blow off preparation for a phone interview, assuming it will be easier than an in-person meeting. Go in prepared for any type of question that might come up.

Panel interview

Sometimes, you'll be asked to interview with more than one person at the same time, either in person or via videoconference (occasionally, by phone). This is known as a *panel* interview.

Panel interviews can be anything from a casual chat with two interviewers to a formal interview by committee of eight or nine people. In some professions, the panel interview is the norm. For example, a panel interview is standard for most academic hires, for certain government roles, and at many large nonprofit organizations. These panel interviews can be highly structured and formal, with five or more interviewers taking turns to ask questions.

However, many companies take an informal approach, with two to four interviewers sitting in with the candidate for a more free-flowing discussion. For companies, the panel interview saves time, allowing for multiple decision-makers to get to know the candidate in a single meeting — there's no need to schedule a series of separate meetings with repetitive questions if you can arrange a panel.

This arrangement can be useful for the candidate as well. Most of us have had the experience of having to take time off to schedule interview after interview before landing an offer. And it really hurts when you invest time and energy in attending six different interviews and then get "ghosted."

However, for many job seekers, a panel interview sounds terrifying. They picture a row of judgmental faces and questions being fired from every corner of the room.

Don't worry! Most panels are pretty friendly. In fact, sometimes they can feel more comfortable than a one-on-one. Adding another interviewer or two can make it feel more like a group conversation than a grilling.

Also, more interviewers means more potential allies. In a one-on-one, if you don't vibe with the one and only interviewer, that's it. In a panel, your odds are good of winning over at least one of your interviewers.

Luckily for you, I have some tips to reduce your anxiety and help you embrace the positive aspects of the panel interview. First, the worst part is the fear of the unknown. Try to find out in advance as much as you can about the specific format and the panel members.

For the more structured panel interviews, you're likely to get some advance information regarding the number and/or type of questions, perhaps even biographies of panel members. Some organizations (universities, government agencies, or nonprofits like the United Nations) even provide advice on how to prepare for their hiring process.

At a minimum, you should receive an invitation with the names of your interviewers. Now you know how many to expect and can look up their LinkedIn bios for a better understanding of their perspectives. Learning their titles and backgrounds can help you anticipate their priorities and the questions they might ask. (See the section "Assessing Your Interviewers," at the beginning of this chapter, for more about types of interviewers and what to expect from each one.)

Your interviewers may represent senior leaders, future internal clients, likely collaborators, close team members, direct reports, and/or HR representatives. The more you know about what you're walking into, the more confident you will feel.

Next, the most important thing to remember in the panel interview is that you need to connect with everyone. This is the big difference, compared to the one-on-one interview.

When three people are sitting across from you, you have to make sure that you include everyone in your answers — and that you build rapport with each individual.

Sometimes this comes naturally, with each interviewer asking their own questions and interacting with you individually. In some panels, each interviewer is assigned a specific question or topic to cover. For example, someone may be the technical-question person and someone else may be the leadership expert.

In other situations, you may need to make an effort. For example, you may have a leader asking most of the questions, with the others chiming in as the spirit moves them. You may have a quiet panelist who is easy to overlook.

Make an effort to alternate your eye contact and your focus. You want to make sure that every person on the panel walks out of that interview thinking you're a great fit.

TIP

In video interviews, you may encounter panelists who keep their cameras turned off. This makes it more challenging to develop rapport. It's hard to know if they're even listening. However, your best bet in this scenario is to give your best video eye contact to the faces of those you can see. (See my video interview tips in the "Live on video" section, earlier in this chapter, for more on this topic.) This should translate well for anyone who's camera shy but paying attention.

Occasionally, you may run into interviewers who are hard to read or are even unfriendly. Don't let this person throw you off your interview game! I have learned that it's extremely difficult to know exactly what some interviewers are thinking. Some interviewers are poker-faced and dismissive even with candidates they love. Others will treat you like their best friend but then never call you back.

The only thing you can control is your own behavior — what you say and how you present yourself. At least in a panel interview, you're not reliant on only one person's perception. Try to connect with everyone, but know that one prickly panelist won't necessarily sink your chances.

WARNING

In a video interview, more participants means more risk of technical issues. Inevitably, someone's connection will drop, someone's audio won't work, or someone will be called away mid-interview. Don't let these glitches throw you off. Follow the lead of your interviewers and remain calm. Be prepared to wait patiently if someone needs to troubleshoot or repeat an answer for a late-joining panelist. Relax knowing it was their mistake and not yours.

In panel interviews, the questions tend to fall into the same common categories I cover in Part 3 of this book. You'll find that behavioral questions are quite common in panel interviews — especially the structured panel ones with pre-set questions. Be prepared with your greatest hits stories (see Chapter 11) so that you can wow the panel with relevant examples.

If you're able to research your panelists, prepare a question for each person. For example, if you know that one panelist represents another department, ask them about how the role collaborates with their team. You may not get a chance to ask all these questions (especially with a large panel), but this is a good way to engage any interviewers who still seem unconvinced.

After the panel interview, try to send a thank you note (email is fine) to each panelist. If you don't have everyone's contact information, you can send a note to your main contact, mention how much you enjoyed meeting all the panelists, and ask them to pass along your thanks.

Group interview

A *group interview* takes place when a company gathers a group of applicants and interviews all of them simultaneously. Sometimes, this is a full-day experience. It can include some group activities combined with separate one-on-one interviews.

Group interviews aren't as common as the other formats I've covered, but they do come up. They are most common when an organization is hiring for multiple openings. For example, a company may be hiring a new class of analysts or sales reps or customer service associates. Group interviews are also used when recruiting for management training programs for students and new graduates.

Because group interviews require more planning and organization, companies usually provide an agenda and some instructions in advance. For large, well-known companies and training programs, you can often find details online, posted by those who have completed the process in the past.

Why would a company choose a group interview format? A group format allows the hiring managers to observe candidates interacting with each other and gain a better sense of how they approach tasks.

As you prepare for the group interview, remember that you're going to be observed throughout. If there are group activities, that means teamwork and interpersonal skills are important to the interviewers. Don't sit back and relax. Participate even if it feels a bit forced and awkward.

They're watching and considering the answers to these questions:

>> What role do you play in a group?

>> Do you step up with ideas?

>> Do you respect other people's perspectives?

>> Are you comfortable jumping into a new group and a new environment?

REMEMBER

In the group activities, focus on being yourself, but be yourself at your best.

Case interview

If you're planning a career in consulting, you will first have to master the case interview. In fact, most business schools and undergraduate business programs provide training in the art of the case interview. In recent years, other industries have also started experimenting with using case interviews, or at least case questions, as part of their hiring.

Case interviews 101

First, a definition: In a case interview, the candidate is provided with a detailed situation, problem, or challenge and asked to analyze it and come up with a solution to present to the interviewer. Usually, the candidate is permitted to ask clarifying questions, though the interviewer may decline to answer them.

A case interview question can be based on a common business situation faced by the company or its clients in real life, or one manufactured to deduce your abilities. Questions can range from the basic ("How do you know the light goes off when you close the refrigerator door?") to the sweat-inducing ("How do you estimate the volume percentage of disposable diapers in the total U.S. household garbage?").

Case questions test your knowledge of certain business and industry scenarios, but also force you to demonstrate your critical thinking, analysis, and communication skills. They work well for consulting because companies hire consultants to strategize solutions to business problems. Case interviews are also sometimes used in investment banking and other industries that require strategic business thinking.

Answering case interview questions

In most cases, your interviewer is more interested in your overall approach to the problem than the final outcome. Your future employer is trying to see if you can analyze complex problems critically and break them down in a logical manner.

If you arrive at the "right" answer or close to it, you get a gold star. However, it's not always possible to get the right answer — either because there are multiple correct responses or critical information isn't provided.

You *can* ace the case interview without getting the answer correct if you show that your thinking and problem-solving processes are sound.

Here are some high-level guidelines for answering case interview questions effectively:

>> **Listen carefully.** Pay attention to the question, including specific word choice, and make sure you understand what the interviewer is asking for. If possible, take notes so that you can refer back to provided data points.

>> **Ask clarifying questions.** Make sure that you understand the purpose of the case. You should also ask for additional information and/or direction if needed. By asking smart questions, you show off your critical thinking skills and can gain valuable information to guide you.

>> **Outline your approach.** After you've considered the case and asked any clarifying questions, explain to the interviewer how you plan to structure your response. This shows purpose and framework.

>> **Think out loud (but take your time).** Tell the interviewer the factors you're considering and strategies you plan to use. However, don't feel the need to express every thought that you have. Pause to consider before sharing a particular thought process with the interviewer.

>> **Stay focused.** It's tempting to get distracted by detail and possibilities. Keep the original question in mind and don't allow yourself to wander too far from the main objective.

>> **Pay attention to feedback.** Many interviewers provide feedback — verbally or via body language or facial expression. Be observant and you may see clues that you're on track or way off base. If you get stuck, ask for input or validation of your understanding.

>> **Wrap up and summarize.** When you've worked through the problem, take time to end crisply and confidently with a summary of your approach and key findings.

Case interview preparation

Preparation is the key when it comes to acing the case interview. The best way to get good is to practice (but you knew that, didn't you?). Your competitors for the job will be practicing, and you should, too.

You never know exactly what case questions you will get. However, you can hone your skills by reading and solving as many as possible. Some common case types come up frequently, and some accepted frameworks are used to solve them. (Examples here are segmentation of a market, analysis of a competitor's initiative, and product pricing.)

Most of the top management consulting firms offer case interview advice and practice questions on their websites (see the following links) — these can be valuable preparation resources when preparing for any case interview:

>> **Deloitte case interview prep:** https://caseinterviewprep.deloitte.com

>> **McKinsey case interview resources:** www.mckinsey.com/careers/interviewing/getting-ready-for-your-interviews

>> **Bain Interviewing:** www.bain.com/careers/hiring-process/interviewing

>> **Boston Consulting case interview preparation:** https://careers.bcg.com/case-interview-preparation

Informational interview

An *informational* interview is basically a networking meeting mixed with a job interview. In an informational interview, you're meeting with someone to learn more about opportunities at their firm (and maybe a referral or recommendation if all goes well). You're not there to discuss a specific position (there may not even be any openings at the moment).

This can be a helpful first step to landing your dream job at a target organization. An informational interview is a way to expand your network, gain some inside information about a company and/or career track, and position yourself for future opportunity. You'll also gain some valuable interview experience.

Informational interviews are generally arranged through networking. Maybe a friend or family member knows someone at one of your target firms and offers to make an introduction. Maybe you take the initiative to reach out to people in your own network (through LinkedIn, your alumni networks, or your volunteer and extracurricular activities).

For your interviewer, the informational interview may be mostly a favor to you or your friend or family member. However, many professionals actually enjoy being helpful and offering career advice.

At the same time, your interviewer would probably love to refer a great hire, especially if their company offers referral bonuses. Even if there's no open position now, they can pass your resume along to the right internal contacts for future opportunities. It makes sense to meet you first to make sure you'd be a good fit and they can feel comfortable recommending you.

If you make a great impression in the informational interview, you'll be at the top of the list when a position opens up. You'll also establish trust with your interviewer so that you can reach out if you see a new job posting and ask for help getting past the gatekeepers.

Though this is not an official job interview, you can expect some of the same questions to come up. Generally, informational interviews are more informal, but your ultimate goal is still to communicate your qualifications and establish credibility. Often, the interviewer will ask questions like these:

>> Tell me about yourself.

>> Why are you interested in working here?

>> What type of role are you looking for?

>> What experience do you have in the field?

>> What are your strengths?

Prepare and practice your talking points for answering these questions. If you present yourself well, your informational interview could very well morph into a real job interview, so be prepared to present yourself in the best possible light.

REMEMBER

Since you won't have a specific job description, it's harder to tailor your responses. Spend a little time researching the company so that you have an idea of what departments/roles would be a good fit. You'll make it easier for the interviewer to refer you if you tell them exactly where you fit and why.

If you're interested in multiple position types, it's okay to say that. You can say you're flexible — just make it clear that you have researched the company and have some goals in mind. (Avoid the temptation to say, "I'm interested in whatever you have available!")

I also recommend preparing thoughtful questions to ask. In an informational interview, there will likely be more time for your questions. As in a traditional job interview, choose questions that show your interest in working for the company. Good questions can also help you establish rapport with the interviewer and make them more comfortable with the idea of recommending you.

Here are a few recommended questions beyond the ones in Chapter 13.

>> What made you choose to work here?

>> What do you like most about the company?

>> What can you tell me about the hiring process here?

>> What is your advice for someone looking to build a career at this organization?

>> What is your career advice for someone in this industry or on this path?

Listen carefully to any career advice offered. This may be your opportunity to gather some honest feedback about your qualifications and how you may be able to improve your odds of landing a job (through a more polished resume or additional experience or training). After all, you rarely get truly honest feedback after a real job interview.

TIP

Don't ask repeatedly about available positions. Your interviewer knows you're interested. If you're too aggressive about asking for a favor, you may make them uncomfortable and less likely to keep you in mind for future opportunities.

If the conversation goes well, your interviewer may volunteer to recommend you to HR or introduce you to colleagues who are hiring. However, if they don't mention it, conclude the interview by asking about the best way to stay in contact about future positions.

Then, don't forget to follow up with the interviewer to thank them for their time — by email within 24 hours and/or promptly by handwritten note, if that's your thing. You can ask to be kept in mind if a position becomes available that aligns with your skills and experience.

However, don't rely on your interviewer to reach out. Even if they loved you, people get busy or may not be in the loop on hiring plans. Check the company's site periodically for new openings. When you find a position that looks like a good fit, reach out to your informational interviewer and politely ask for advice on the best way to apply. If you made a positive impression, your new contact may be willing to forward your information directly to the hiring decision-makers, improving your chances of getting a call.

Internal interview

In general, you should prepare for an internal interview in the same way you prepare for any other important job interview.

Don't assume it will be a slam-dunk just because they know you. Internal opportunities are usually pretty competitive — with both internal and external candidates in the running.

On the plus side, you already know how your company conducts interviews. You may also have an edge if the hiring managers know you and your work. On the other hand, you might have to counter preconceived notions.

Again, I recommend preparing in the same ways that you would for any other interview. However, here are some additional issues to think about when preparing for an internal job interview.

Your interviewers

Do you know any of the people who will be interviewing you for this position? Do you know someone who knows any of the people who will be interviewing you? Good internal relationships can give you a real edge.

You can go into the interview with more information about what to expect and some established goodwill. However, don't be too relaxed about it.

Even if the hiring manager loves you, you still have to persuade others that you're the best person for the job. Most hiring decisions involve multiple people. Even your strongest advocate will face pushback if you don't impress the other decision makers.

REMEMBER

Make sure you shine in all your interviews. I have seen internal candidates lose out even when they thought they had it in the bag.

In some cases, knowing the interviewers may be a disadvantage to overcome. Maybe you know that one of your interviewers isn't your biggest fan — or maybe you're aware that someone on the team is advocating for another candidate.

These are issues that can be overcome by interviewing well. If you're aware of potential objections, you can try to proactively address them.

Your reputation

Sometimes, interviewers know you only by reputation. It's helpful to have a sense of how you're generally perceived within the company. This can help you to emphasize the right strengths and counter any misperceptions.

If you're at a large organization and don't feel the interviewers know much about you, it might make sense to leverage your network for some recommendations. You likely have at least one internal fan who knows someone on the hiring team. I'm sure your fans would be happy to put in a good word for you, as long as it's appropriate (not compromising confidentiality or showing unfair favoritism, in other words).

Your current role

How clear is it that you're qualified for this internal role? In some cases, you may be making your obvious next move — with your current role preparing you well for the one you want next.

In other cases, it may be more of a stretch. Internal interviewers are more likely to take a chance on a candidate with great potential, even with some gaps in their experience. You know the company and have shown yourself to be a reliable employee in general, so there's less risk than with an external candidate.

If it's a stretch move, be prepared to make the absolute most of this opportunity to interview. You got your foot in the door through your reputation, but the interview is where you win or lose the prize.

TIP

Be prepared to sell your transferable skills and related experience and to counter any concerns. For example, if you have no experience with a key software program for the new job, start teaching yourself before the interview and prepare to talk about your ability to learn new technology quickly.

If you're moving from an individual contributor role to managing a team, think about how to demonstrate your desire and ability to step up. Prepare your leadership examples. If you've never officially managed a team, be prepared to talk about managing projects, unofficially taking the lead, mentoring others, or facilitating other experiences with leadership.

2

Using the Big Interview Approach to Interview Preparation

Chapter 4

Understanding Your Mission

nterview success is all about preparation. Once you learn my approach to interview prep, you'll know exactly what to do every time you have a new interview opportunity — now and for the rest of your career.

These strategies will work for you even as you rise in seniority, even as you change careers, even as technology and the job market continue to evolve.

I'm going to lay out this approach as a linear process over this chapter and the next one — starting from the moment you snag that interview invitation. In this chapter, you get a chance to find out all about the first stage — the research and strategic thinking required to create a plan for success. In Chapter 5, I dig into how to use that knowledge to predict interview questions, outline answers, and practice for the big day.

Let me emphasize how important it is to approach each new opportunity strategically. For each role, the hiring team will have different priorities and different concerns. You can't use a generic approach or else you'll come across as a generic candidate.

The more you know about the organization and its needs for the role, the more you can accentuate your strengths and neutralize any weaknesses. In other words, you can take both an offensive approach (hit them with your best selling points!) and a defensive one (head off any possible concerns — spoken or unspoken).

Always start with a critical reading of the job description. The job description tells you a lot about what to expect in the interview.

It's shocking to me to see how many job seekers fail to take advantage of the clues that have been laid out for them. Many candidates don't take the time to closely examine the job description. They give it a quick skim and that's it.

However, a close analysis will help you understand what the employer is looking for and even predict the questions you'll hear. Even if you're adept at interviewing, customizing your approach is the key to standing out from the pack.

For the purposes of this book, I define *job description* as the written overview of the qualifications, duties, and responsibilities of a particular position.

Some job descriptions are more detailed and useful than others. In fact, most job descriptions fall into one of two categories:

>> Stuffed with so much information that it's overwhelming

>> Too short or generic to offer much insight

Occasionally, you'll see a description that's just right, with just enough clear, specific information to be useful.

In all cases, take what you can from the information that's offered and use the research techniques I share with you in this book to expand on the description in any way you can.

If you're preparing for an interview and have no job description to work with, you're at a disadvantage — but all is not lost. Here are some strategies to try:

>> **Work your network to see what you can learn about the position, the hiring manager, and the organization.** Read the later section "Researching the Opportunity" for my tips on LinkedIn research to leverage your online network for this task.

>> **Search for similar job descriptions at the same organization (current or recent).** Especially at big companies, they have likely hired for this job in the past or for a related position (in a different department or region, perhaps). Though these are not guaranteed to be exact matches, they will give you some context.

>> **Look for descriptions of similar roles at similar companies (in terms of industry and size).** By looking at a few, you can identify some common themes to focus on. Often, the core competencies and required skills are similar.

Many times, the challenge lies in having *too much* information. If you have three pages of job duties and requirements, it can be hard to know where to focus. Don't worry — I'm here to help.

Knowing the requirements

The first step is to review the job description closely, making note of the qualifications that stand out.

When I say, "stand out," I mean it in multiple ways:

>> **The most important requirements for the role:** These tend to be featured at the beginning of any section and mentioned multiple times. (Even if the wording is slightly different, you're looking for recurring themes.)

>> **Areas where you know you're a strong match:** Know what to highlight to make the strongest impression.

>> **Potential gaps or weaknesses:** Be prepared to counter concerns about your weaknesses.

There should be some overlap — hopefully, you're a strong match in some of the most important requirements!

REMEMBER

You may have already completed some of this analysis when you applied for the job and customized your resume accordingly: If you did, now is the time to revisit your notes; if you didn't, it's a good idea for the future to help you land more interviews, but you can start now for this opportunity.

Next, let's examine the components of the typical job description.

Requirements

These are the dealbreakers that dictate which resumes advance past the gatekeepers. Requirements include education, minimum years of experience, certifications, language fluency, and core technical skills.

You may be asked questions about any of these areas that aren't clear from your resume, probably in the first screening interview to determine whether you should move ahead in the process.

Responsibilities/duties

The list of job duties gives you more information about what you would be doing from day to day. You should review these and think about how your experience aligns.

They are likely looking for someone who has experience with similar projects and tasks. The job responsibilities also give you some insight into important skills and competencies, based on what's needed to perform key duties.

Qualifications

Here I'm grouping all the other items you commonly see in job descriptions: competencies, skills, and areas of knowledge or expertise. Most of these are hard to evaluate by resume alone, so they are likely to inspire interview questions.

REMEMBER

You may see a listing of core competencies, such as teamwork, leadership, or problem-solving. The terms *competency* and *skill* are often used in similar ways, but they are different. By definition, a *skill* is a single hands-on ability (like programming in a particular language, writing advertising copy, or processing invoices). A *competency* tends to be broader, requiring multiple skills as well as specialized knowledge and capabilities.

TIP

Core competencies often inspire behavioral questions. (You can find much more on those in Chapter 11.)

Identifying the priorities

When preparing to coach a client for an upcoming interview, I read the job description and highlight all the words and phrases that seem important. This exercise helps me see the top priorities for the role and how my client's experience compares. From there, I'm able to anticipate the most likely interview questions and work with the client on answers that will truly impress.

Let's use a sample job description and client profile to illustrate this process, starting with identifying the priorities for the position.

REMEMBER

This one is based on a real-life job description but has been streamlined. Normally, you'd have to skim over lots of "nice to have" bullet points in order to distill the real deal-breakers, but I won't waste your time with that.

Take a look at the job description featured in Table 4-1 and note which information stands out for you as critical.

TABLE 4-1

Sample Description: Manager, Advertising Sales Team

Requirements
* Bachelor's degree: MBA preferred
* Minimum four years of experience in B2B sales
* Two years of experience in managing high-performing sales teams
* Successful sales track record

Responsibilities
* Meet or exceed assigned sales goals
* Serve as account lead for key advertiser accounts and ensure client satisfaction
* Train, manage, and motivate a large sales team
* Assess customer needs and gather feedback to improve on advertising solutions

Competencies
* Leadership
* Results focus
* Communication skills
* Analytical skills
* Coaching

I see three dominant themes here:

>> Sales ability

>> Leadership/management of a large sales team

>> Client service skills

As you might expect for a sales job, company reps are looking for sales skills. That category is a bit broad, though — sales ability can be defined in many ways.

By reading the Responsibilities section, you can see that the focus is on business-to-business (B2B) advertising sales. Experience in this area isn't listed as a requirement, but you should be prepared to show how your background is relevant.

Previous sales of similar products or to a similar customer segment will help you stand out. Researching the company (I tell you more on this later in this chapter) will give you more insight into the products and customers.

The job description also has a strong emphasis on proven sales results. For sales roles, that's sometimes more important than product knowledge. The company would rather hire a sales whiz with the ability to become an expert on the products.

I highlighted the phrases "successful sales track record," "high-performing," "meet or exceed sales goals," and "results focus." You can bet that you will be asked about your sales strategies and accomplishments.

Leadership is also a huge component of this job. They want experience in managing sales teams, and a key responsibility is not just supervising daily activities but also motivating a large sales team to meet ambitious sales goals. Finally, leadership is a core competency, along with related competencies of communication and coaching.

As a candidate, you know you want to highlight leadership experience, especially how you motivate and coach team members to produce results.

Finally, account management is also a responsibility, so I highlighted "client satisfaction," "key advertiser accounts," and "customer needs." The Competencies list shows that you'll need to excel at relationship-building and communication.

REMEMBER

The idea here is to read carefully for themes, paying particular attention to anything featured prominently or multiple times.

In Chapter 5, I show you how to use these themes to predict interview questions.

Spotting red flags

I write a lot about how to avoid raising red flags with interviewers. However, *you* should pay attention to red flags, too. You don't want to waste your valuable time or — worse — get conned into accepting a nightmare job in disguise.

In some cases, the job description and company research can raise enough concerns for you to skip the interview altogether. Unfortunately, you can encounter a *lot* of job scams out there. Do your research and be cautious.

WARNING

If a job description sounds too good to be true ("Make millions at home!") or requires you to pay or provide personal details, it's probably a scam. Here are a few specific scam red flags to watch out for:

>> The URL in the email address is fake, but made to look legitimate. For example, instead of microsoft.com, they are using recruiting-microsoft.com and hoping you won't notice.

>> They ask for sensitive personal information (birth date, social security number, ID) early in the process.

>> They ask for credit card or payment information (Venmo, PayPal, and so on) to confirm the interview or for a deposit, verification fee, or other sketchy reason.

>> They reply immediately after you submit the application. Scammers reply quickly, but real employers are busy and will need time to review applications and reach out.

Even with legitimate job openings, there are danger signs to look out for. Here I'm not talking about potential scams, but clues that the job may not be a good fit for you. It's important to investigate any potential issues before deciding to accept a job offer. After all, you'll be investing a lot of time and energy in your next position and you want to make the right choice.

REMEMBER

These red flags don't always mean danger, but they are signs to ask questions and pay close attention to the answers.

Here are a few potential red flags and advice on how to follow up:

>> **Lack of compensation transparency:** If you can't get a straight answer about compensation, that raises doubts about the company's transparency and willingness to pay what's fair. In some states, companies are required to include a compensation range in every job posting. Even then, some companies try to skirt around the issue by posting a ridiculous salary range, like "$18K to $500K." It could be just an oversight, but it's fair to ask the recruiter for this information if they don't share it. It's not always concerning if the compensation isn't in the job description, but you should at least know the range before you invest a lot of time in interviews.

>> **Vague or confusing job duties:** It could be that they haven't fully decided what they're looking for. This means the job requirements could easily change between interviews or even after you've accepted the job. It could also be that they're just not good at writing job descriptions. Ask lots of questions about the day-to-day expectations to determine if the reality of the job is a good fit for you.

>> **Bad candidate experience:** Is the recruiter rude? Is the application process endless and confusing? A bad candidate experience can be a sign of a company that doesn't value their employees. Don't jump to conclusions, but pay attention to the people you meet and ask questions about company culture.

>> **Requiring free work:** Be wary of requests to work for free. If you're being asked to complete time-consuming projects, especially early in the interview process, it could demonstrate lack of respect for your time. Of course, many legitimate companies also require take-home projects when hiring for certain roles. It's part of the evaluation process. Only you can decide whether it's worth the time investment, based on your interest in the job and the amount of work involved.

Sometimes you just develop a bad feeling about a company or a manager. You don't want to be too quick to make a judgment, but pay attention to your instincts and investigate further.

It's hard to judge someone accurately from a short interview interaction (as job seekers know all too well). Ask yourself where the feeling is coming from and what questions you could ask to clarify your concerns.

TIP

In the later section "Researching the Opportunity," I share some tips on how to get the information you need to determine if a red flag is real.

Evaluating Your Fit

Once you have a sense of the position priorities, it's time to evaluate your fit from the hiring manager's perspective. Every candidate has both strengths and weaknesses. The key is to make the most of what you offer.

Everyone who makes it to the interview is mostly qualified on paper. The interview is all about determining who the *best* candidate is.

REMEMBER

To stand out from the crowd, you need to know your strengths so that you can be sure to sell them in the interviews. You also need to know whether your resume has gaps or issues that the interviewer may be concerned about. If you can neutralize doubts about potential weaknesses, you have a much better shot.

Focusing on your strengths

Let's start with getting clear on your strongest selling points for the position.

To illustrate this step, I'm going to talk about a fictional candidate for the sample job description I discuss in the "Identifying the priorities" section, earlier in this chapter:

> Meet James T. He would love to land this job as manager of the advertising sales team for a media company.

It's a dream job for him. But what does he bring to the table?

Well, James has five years of experience in B2B sales, including three years in advertising sales.

So far, so good. He has more than the required amount of experience.

He also has a proven sales track record and lots of big sales wins he can talk about. He was even promoted last year to manager of the sales team at his organization.

James also has relationship-building and communication skills. How can he prove it? He has a strong performance review. He has won awards internally. His clients love him and sing his praises to senior management.

James clearly has multiple strengths that will position him well for the job.

For each opportunity you pursue, you will have top selling points. Those may be very similar from position to position, but there will also be some variation.

The job description helps you see which strengths and experience to emphasize to make the best possible impression in the limited amount of time you will have. (Chapter 8 shows you how to articulate those selling points in a compelling way.)

This understanding empowers you to go into each interview with a strategy: to make sure you communicate your strengths. You can prepare the right examples and be on the lookout for any opening to bring up one of your key selling points.

Knowing your weaknesses

Let's go back to James T. He seems pretty qualified, but nobody's perfect.

I always recommend trying to focus on the positive, but there are a lot of qualified people out there.

The interview process is about narrowing down the number of candidates to find the perfect person for the job. Part of the process of elimination is looking for red flags or potential areas of weakness.

So, what could be potentially perceived as negative about you? What are areas in which another candidate could be stronger?

REMEMBER

Go through the process of honestly identifying your weaknesses or what could be perceived as weaknesses by others. You may not agree that you need an MBA for this position, for example, or at least four years of experience, but you have to think from the perspective of the interviewer. That way, you'll be prepared to proactively address and, ideally, reframe potential weaknesses if they come up.

Based on your analysis of the job description, jot down any potential issues and some notes about how you think you could counter concerns.

Let James T. illustrate:

On the plus side, he does have more than four years of sales experience, but only three years in advertising sales.

More concerning, this advertising sales experience was two years ago. His most recent job is in B2B software sales, not advertising.

The work is related, but not the same. You can bet that a smart interviewer will ask James about why he left advertising sales for his current job, whether he's kept up with advertising trends and technology, and whether he has enough current knowledge for the job.

He might be going up against somebody who has more years in advertising sales and is now working in the field.

What else? James is managing a sales team, but he was promoted to manager only about a year ago. It's also a small team, and the job description stresses managing a large sales team.

He needs to think about how to position the management experience he does have — as well as his knowledge and potential — in a way that shows he will be able to step up and manage a larger team.

Finally, James doesn't have an MBA. Now, you may recall that the job description said that having one was a plus, so it isn't required.

However, you can bet that some candidates will have MBAs. James must be prepared to position himself, his experience, and his other training and education to show why he's as qualified as anyone with an MBA.

Weaknesses are tough to talk about. However, with preparation, you can play a strong defense and make a compelling case for how your strengths far outweigh those weaknesses.

Researching the Opportunity

Your pre-interview plan should also include some research on the organization and your interviewers.

This research will help you with answering important interview questions and give you data you need in order to evaluate that offer when it comes. (You'll be such an impressive interviewer that the offers are inevitable.)

REMEMBER

In every interview, you can expect some version of the question "Why do you want to work here?" (It also happens to be the title of Chapter 7.) Research will help you speak thoughtfully about the company and how it fits with your interests.

TIP

Company research can also help you land more interviews. You can use these techniques to uncover more job leads beyond the job boards that everyone else is checking. Look for additional tips on this area in the remainder of this chapter.

Researching the opportunity thoroughly also means researching the industry, the interviewers, and the work environment.

Learning about the organization

First, you'll want to find out as much as you can about the organization.

Your research will give you insight into business priorities and challenges, the company culture, current hiring needs, the qualities valued in employees, and much more.

So, how will you acquire the information you need in order to dazzle the interviewer(s) with your knowledge?

Step 1: The company website

You can begin your information-gathering by visiting the organization's website.

Visit the company's About Us section, where you can learn about its mission, history, values, key leaders, and more. Elsewhere on the site, you can read about products, services, and offerings — if you're not already an expert.

Check out the Press or Media section, too. The press releases and media mentions that are posted tend to represent major initiatives the company wants to share with the world.

I also recommend reading the Careers section thoroughly. This is where an organization shares what they want job applicants to know about them as an employer. Some even share interview tips and details about the hiring process.

Most also feature current job listings. It can be interesting to see how actively they are hiring, especially in the department or area you're applying to join.

If you're in job-search mode, I recommend visiting the Careers section of the companies you're targeting. Look for interesting job descriptions to apply for, of course. Even if you see no relevant openings right now, you can often find names of, and contact information for, recruiters and HR contacts. Many will be open to connecting with candidates on LinkedIn, which can help you stand out when a fitting job opens up.

Some organizations put a lot of time and effort into their Careers section. They might include information about benefits and important policies, such as diversity and inclusion and remote work. You might find interviews with current employees about their experience, videos showing the office environment, or descriptions of the typical career paths in various roles and departments. This is a sign of an organization that values the candidate experience and transparency — important issues to consider when choosing your next employer.

REMEMBER

Some smaller organizations lack the resources to create an award-winning Careers section. Even the best sites can't tell you everything about the organization. It's always smart to expand your research to other sources.

Step 2: Social media

Social media can provide a wealth of information about your target organizations.

LinkedIn is a terrific resource for job-seekers in many ways. Most organizations now use LinkedIn for recruiting, and many also post frequently for marketing and PR purposes.

Many have LinkedIn Careers pages specifically for communicating with candidates. You may also be able to follow the company and any internal experts to see updates and keep up on big announcements.

You will find profiles for most key people within the organization. Look for profiles of those in jobs similar to the ones you're interested in. This can help you learn more about what the company looks for in related roles and perhaps even give you a networking opportunity.

TIP

Create a compelling LinkedIn profile to support your job search. Many recruiters will check out your LinkedIn profile after you apply. Your profile is also more likely to come up in recruiter searches if you include the right keywords.

Your LinkedIn network can also be a helpful resource. If you're lucky enough to have a contact who works for your target company (or has in the past), you might be able to get the inside scoop on the position.

Finally, LinkedIn has groups for every industry. You can join and see whether members are talking about the organization and what they're saying.

In addition to checking LinkedIn, you might also want to explore the company's presence on other social media platforms, like Twitter, Facebook, Instagram, or TikTok. A search can tell you a lot about how the company positions itself to consumers and the public.

Step 3: Check the news

Search for headlines to see if the organization has been in the news recently or if there are hot industry stories you should know about. Check mainstream news as well as industry publications for the full picture.

You may find interesting information in these areas:

>> Financial news about the company (find out if they just reported record earnings or if the stock is in free fall)

>> Economic outlooks for the industry

>> Labor market news and outlooks

>> Competitor information and activities

REMEMBER

The more you know, the better poised you are to speak intelligently and answer any questions that come up. This information will also help you later when deciding whether to accept the offer.

You may also want to search for news on recent activities related to your job. If you're in marketing, search Google or another search engine for information about the company's latest marketing campaigns. If you're a product designer, look for product news and check out the products firsthand, if you can. (Go to the store, download the app, and browse product reviews.)

Getting to know your interviewers

Once you know the names of your future interviewers, you can also research their backgrounds to see whether you share any common ground.

The first place to look is LinkedIn because your focus should be on learning about their professional history — not stalking their family pictures or personal Insta posts. The LinkedIn profile should give you information on education, job history, professional organization affiliations, volunteer work, and other work-related activities. You might even spot a common connection or interest area.

If you're lucky enough to share a connection with one of your interviewers, consider reaching out to ask for information if you're close enough to your shared contact. Best case scenario: Your shared connection is a close friend of your interviewer and glowingly recommends you for the job.

TIP

Some professionals are quite active on LinkedIn, and you can get a good sense of their interests and personality from their posts, likes, and follows.

Of course, you should also check the company website for bios of your interviewers or any other pertinent information — maybe a Q&A or a white paper or a video of a recent conference presentation.

For senior-level or high-profile interviewers, it may be worth searching on Google to see whether they are quoted in any industry publications or have spoken at events or panels.

Once you've gathered information about your future interviewers, how should you use it? Some of it may help you in the interview. If you know that the hiring manager is passionate about a certain industry trend, you could make a point to highlight your common interest.

WARNING

Avoid coming across as a stalker. These days, interviewers expect that candidates will research them on LinkedIn. However, if you start getting into personal information that they haven't shared with you themselves, it can feel intrusive.

Your research on your interviewers can also help you when it comes to decision time. Your direct manager can make or break the job. If their style doesn't fit with yours, it's good to know in advance.

Investigating the work environment

These days, you can research what the work environment is really like before accepting the job. Glassdoor (www.glassdoor.com), for example, is a job board and online community that allows users to post reviews of companies they've worked for and interviewed with. You can read what other employees, past and present, have to say about a business and their experience working for the company.

REMEMBER

The anonymous nature of Glassdoor allows people to give honest, unvarnished opinions about the business. This can give you a heads-up about culture fit before the interview.

If most of the reviews paint the organization as collaborative and inclusive, you can talk about why those qualities matter to you when asked about your interest in working there.

Then again, if multiple reviews mention lack of work/life balance, you may want to ask a question about workload expectations before accepting the offer. Of course, you should do this in a diplomatic way. Some reviews may be biased, and often experience varies a lot in different departments.

Researching salary ranges

You should always be prepared with your desired salary range before the interview.

If you're lucky, the organization will be transparent about compensation in the job description. It's always a good sign when an organization is transparent when it comes to pay ranges. Too much mystery could be a sign they're looking to get a bargain by paying you as little as possible.

TIP

For advice on how to talk money in job interviews to get yourself the best offer, see Chapter 12.

Even if the company provides a range, it may be a broad one. You'll want to think about what would be an attractive offer for you. Is there a minimum amount you'd need to even consider it as a fair offer? Is there a number that would delight you?

To figure this out, you'll need to assess the current market rate for the position. Sites like Salary.com (www.salary.com), Payscale.com (https://webflow.pay scale.com), Glassdoor.com (www.glassdoor.com/index.htm), and Salary Expert.com (www.salaryexpert.com) provide information on average compensation for specific job types, taking into account aspects like geography and years of experience. In some cases, you can even find salary ranges for specific companies.

This data will help you set some parameters around what you're worth in the free market. It's good to go into the interview prepared, in case the subject comes up. Later, you can use your research to support your salary negotiation and get the best possible offer.

Chapter **5**

Preparing to Impress

You've reviewed the job description, analyzed your fit, and researched the company. You now have the information you need to do the real work of the interview preparation process.

The next phase starts with anticipating the key interview questions based on your research and job description analysis. Then you outline your answers to the most critical questions, preparing how you will highlight your fit and make an unforgettable impression.

There is also a final step that most job seekers neglect: practice. Skip the practice step at your own risk. It really does make a difference, but you have to do it the right way.

This may sound like a lot of work, but trust me when I say it's worth the time. I have seen the magic with so many coaching clients and participants in our Big Interview training courses. Also, once you learn the process and go through it the first time, you'll find it's pretty efficient.

REMEMBER

Master the steps and you acquire a life skill that you'll use again and again at every career turning point.

Anticipating Questions

To prepare efficiently, you must focus on the right questions. You can't possibly prepare for every one of the hundreds of possible interview questions you'll find during your late-night Google searches.

I'm not claiming that you can perfectly predict every question, word for word. Interviewers are human and complex and some of them are downright clueless.

However, if you've done your homework, you can develop a pretty good idea of the core questions that will be asked in any given interview.

That homework includes understanding the most common types of questions asked. This knowledge gives you a huge head start on your process because certain questions come up in most interviews, across industries and job types and experience levels.

These questions are entirely predictable, for a couple of reasons: First, they all ask about key topics that are important to evaluating a candidate's fit for any job. Second, most interviewers don't have the time or interest to get creative with their questions. They ask the same questions they've been asked over the years, the same questions they got from HR or that article they skimmed before conducting their first interview.

This predictability gives you a big advantage.

REMEMBER

Review the chapters in Part 3 of this book for detailed advice on how to answer all these predictable and important questions. You should always be prepared to answer them.

Based on the job description and your research, you can customize your approach for different opportunities. However, if your target positions are similar, you can create a standard go-to answer for most of them and then tweak them where needed as new opportunities come up.

Beyond the most common questions, you want to look to the job description and fit analysis (see Chapter 4 for guidance in analyzing your fit for any job opportunity) to predict other questions likely to come up, such as specific aspects of the job, culture fit, and potential weaknesses in your background.

Predict behavioral questions

Behavioral questions are those that start with the words "Tell me about a time" or "Give me an example" or with similar phrases. Chapter 11 is all about behavioral questions and how to prepare for them, so you'll be an expert soon.

For now, it's important to know that many of the job-specific questions you'll hear will be behavioral questions. Interviewers like to ask behavioral questions about hard and soft skills, core competencies, and accomplishments.

Hundreds of behavioral questions are out there, but analyzing the job description helps you determine which types of behavioral questions to prepare for. They're almost always predictable, based on the job description and your background.

Let's take a look at an example from Chapter 4 to illustrate. There I talk about candidate James T., who is applying for the position of sales team manager.

Table 5-1 summarizes the job description:

TABLE 5-1 · **Sample Description: Manager, Advertising Sales Team**

Requirements
Bachelor's degree: MBA preferred
Minimum of 4 years of experience in B2B sales
Two years of experience in managing high-performing sales teams
Successful track record in sales
Responsibilities
Meet or exceed assigned sales goals
Serve as account lead for key advertiser accounts and ensure client satisfaction
Train, manage, and motivate a large sales team
Assess customer needs and gather feedback to improve on advertising solutions
Competencies
Leadership
Results focus
Communication skills
Analytical skills
Coaching

James T. is an excellent fit for the role in many ways, including his sales track record, though his management experience is a little light and he hasn't managed a large team. Finally, he has advertising sales experience but is now in a software sales position, and he does not have an MBA.

Based on this information, what are some of the behavioral questions that he's likely to hear in his interview?

Here are some that I would prepare him for if he were my client:

>> **"Walk me through your sales results."** We know that proven sales success is an important requirement. In most sales interviews, you can expect questions about your track record. In this case, this is a behavioral question that James T. should welcome because we know he has impressive numbers to talk about. He should prepare his best examples and look for openings to talk about them.

>> **"Give me an example of one of your greatest management challenges."** The company needs a strong manager in this role, so James can expect multiple questions about his management experience. He should prepare examples of his successes, but also challenges he has overcome. For James, it's especially important to prepare for these questions, because his management experience can be seen as weak at first glance (relatively few years in a management role and experience managing a smaller team). If he shares a story that shows strong management skills and the ability to overcome challenges, he can counter any concerns.

>> **Tell me about a time you dealt with a difficult client.** Client management is essential for this position. Interviewers will want to evaluate James' skills in building client relationships and handling demanding clients. Communication, problem solving, and other competencies come into play here. James should prepare his best examples of saving the day for an important client.

Other topics are likely to come up, but you get the idea.

REMEMBER

See Chapter 11 for much more on common behavioral questions and how to craft impressive story examples.

Identify other critical questions

In addition to behavioral questions, other questions are likely to pop up based on your specific background. These may include some of the tricky questions about resume red flags that I discuss in Chapter 12 (including gaps and job-hopping).

Many of these questions will be related to potential gaps or weaknesses. It's important to consider your background with a critical eye so that you're not caught unprepared.

Often, interviewers just want to clarify details in your background to better understand your fit.

For example, you know that James T. has never managed a large sales team. If I were the hiring manager, I would want to dig into his management experience to determine whether he has the potential to step up and lead a bigger team. Here are some questions I would ask:

>> What's the largest team you've managed?

>> What experience do you have in hiring and firing?

>> How do you approach performance management?

Another question specific to James involves a recent career move. He was successful in advertising sales for several years but then moved to his current role in software sales. Again, putting myself in the hiring manager's shoes, I would want to be certain that James is now committed to moving back to advertising sales and has kept his knowledge fresh. Questions might include:

>> Why did you leave advertising sales for your current role?

>> Why are you interested in an ad sales job now?

>> What are your long-term career goals? (It's a common question but an important one in a situation like this one.)

These are just a few of the pointed questions likely to come up for James. A similar analysis helps you prevent feeling blindsided in your own interviews.

Be prepared to discuss anything on your resume if asked. The focus will be on recent projects and transitions, but you never know what an interviewer will focus on. For example, if you're claiming fluency in Spanish, you'd better practice if you're rusty!

Drafting Your Speaking Points

Once you've anticipated the most important and challenging questions that might come up, I strongly recommend outlining your speaking points.

The process of writing helps you organize your thoughts and think through what you want to say. Your answers will be much more compelling if you think about them in advance, when you're not distracted by nerves.

REMEMBER

By writing notes for key answers, you create a useful cheat sheet for practicing. The acts of writing, editing, and reviewing your bullet points also help with recall later, when you're working without notes.

Don't script it

Don't try to script your answers word-for-word. Answers that are scripted and memorized tend to sound scripted and memorized.

It's also difficult to memorize multiple long answers. This can lead to anxiety and overwhelm.

The best preparation leaves room for some spontaneity and personality. I recommend outlining bullet points highlighting your key ideas. This way, you create a flow of ideas and ensure that you're covering the most important points, but your answer will sound slightly different each time.

REMEMBER

You don't want to sound like a robot — or like ChatGPT (the AI chatbot) scripted your answer. This can lead to interviewers questioning your authenticity.

Save time with frameworks

Luckily for you, I have created some frameworks to save you a bit of time in outlining your bullet points. In the chapters on common questions — Chapters 6 through 10, if you're checking — you'll find detailed instructions for using frameworks to organize your thinking, including these:

>> **Tell me about yourself:** My 3-part model can help you organize your career story.

>> **Why do you want to work here?** This one also calls for covering two important components.

>> **Strengths:** My proof-point approach makes the most of your strengths.

>> **Weaknesses:** The simple 2-part answer structure makes talking about weaknesses easier.

>> **Behavioral questions:** My model for behavioral questions uses the STAR format to help you tell impressive stories.

Here's an example of how a bullet point outline might look for James T.'s answer to "Tell me about yourself."

JAMES T.: TELL ME ABOUT YOURSELF

Part 1

» 5 years of experience in B2B sales for large brands

» Expertise in advertising sales

» Promoted to manager based on performance and leadership skills

Part 2

» Current role: Manage team of six sales reps

» Responsible for $5 million key client accounts and meeting my own sales quotas

» Exceeded last year's sales goal by 35%

» Led team to a record year, hired two new reps

» Previously started sales career at ABC Co.

» Earned Chairman's Club award both years at ABC Co.

Part 3

» Excited about this role — love the company

» Goal is to grow career in ad sales

You can see how the bullets provide an outline of key ideas, but not exact wording. This ensures that no important points are forgotten while avoiding an over-rehearsed delivery.

Occasionally, some of my clients have found it useful to script certain phrases or transitions. For example, when discussing a recent layoff, you might want to describe it in a certain way to keep it neutral and avoid negativity. In other cases, knowing the first few words of an answer can help with recall.

Practicing the Right Way

I can't emphasize this advice enough: Practice your answers out loud before the interview. Quietly reading your answers to yourself isn't enough.

Many people shy away from practicing because they think it feels unnatural. I know I've had to beg and persuade many clients to do it, though they've always thanked me later.

If you detest the idea of practicing, it's especially important for you to do it. It feels uncomfortable at first. But wouldn't you rather feel uncomfortable practicing with your webcam? Don't save the cringing and fumbling for the interview, when the stakes are *much* higher.

Recognizing the power of practice

You've heard the expression "practice makes perfect" a million times. Every athlete and performer knows that practice is the key to improvement.

Passive learning expands your knowledge, but it takes active practice to build a skill. You can know all about what makes a great interview answer and still mess it up if you don't practice.

Practice develops your interview skills in many ways. First, when you've just outlined your speaking points, practice shows you how the answer flows and whether anything needs to be added, reordered, or tightened up.

Then, once you feel good about your speaking points, practice makes you more comfortable with your responses, reducing your anxiety and your chances of forgetting an answer at the worst possible moment.

Practice even improves your delivery, smoothing out filler words "um" and "uh," nervous gestures, and other issues.

I have seen countless clients transform their presentation skills through practice. I record them on video, and we originally created the practice tool on our Big Interview platform so they could practice on their own. I can see the dramatic difference between their first practice answer and their final dress rehearsal.

If you have trouble thinking on your feet, practice lets you work out the kinks in advance. If you tend to ramble when you're nervous, practice keeps you more focused when it matters most.

Perfecting your practice

You can practice on your own or recruit a friend to help. I first created the practice interview tool on my Big Interview training platform because I found that my clients weren't practicing between sessions, despite their best intentions. They felt self-conscious about asking a friend to role-play with them and didn't think practicing in the mirror would have the same effect.

The Big Interview practice tool has an interface similar to a video interview, with you on your webcam interacting with a recording of an actor playing your interviewer. You can practice in your PJs, make mistakes, or curse the interviewer and nobody ever has to know about it. You can review tips and sample answers if you get stuck.

When you're ready, you can record your answer, play it back, and evaluate yourself. You can also share the recording with a trusted friend or advisor if you want external feedback. You can even receive automated AI feedback on factors including pace of speech, eye contact, filler words, and vocabulary.

A mock interview with a live human can also be quite valuable. If you have a friend with expertise in hiring, ask for the favor of a mock interview. Fill them in on the job details and give them a list of questions, if you like.

This approach is most useful when your practice partner has some knowledge of the interview process and the ability to provide objective, constructive feedback. Think critically about any feedback you receive. Your best friend knows and likes you already, so they might think you sound awesome even when you're rambling. On the other hand, your sister might be hypercritical because she knows you too well and lacks a background in job interviews.

For expert feedback, you can work with a career coach, if you have the budget. Look for someone with lots of interview experience — ideally, in your industry. Ask questions about how the coaching works to ensure that you get what you need from the feedback.

If you're a student or a recent graduate, your school may offer free coaching and mock interview services via the career center (along with resume help and other types of assistance). More than 600 schools and universities also offer Big Interview as a free practice resource for their students (and many offer access to alumni as well).

Finally, if you have no access to any of these resources, practicing on your own is still much better than no practice at all. Practice in your mirror, practice by creating a voice memo on your phone, practice talking to a photo of your favorite celebrity, or practice with your dog. You won't get feedback, but the act of practicing alone will increase your confidence and improve your interview skills.

Learning to shift into Interview mode

Practicing feels uncomfortable at first. I'm surprised at how many clients fidget the first time I start recording or cringe at the idea of watching or listening to themselves. Confident answers can feel like bragging or performing when you're not used to talking about yourself that way.

To interview well, you must move past this awkwardness. A job interview is not a normal conversation. It *is* a conversation, but it's also a persuasive presentation.

To succeed, you must be able to adjust your communication style for the audience. The interview version of you doesn't talk like you're hanging out with your best friends over lunch. The interview version of you is even different from the regular job version of you, where everybody already knows you and your work.

REMEMBER

To succeed in job interviews, always be your authentic self — that is, a slightly more confident, focused, and self-promotional version of yourself.

Maybe you've played video games that allow you to shift into Superhero mode or Beast mode. I teach my coaching clients to shift into Interview mode. They're all sort of the same concept — though I admit Interview mode is not quite as much fun.

Interview mode is similar to how you communicate when you give an important presentation, especially a persuasive one. You don't stand up in front of an auditorium full of people and just wing it and "be yourself." The world's greatest presenters prepare and practice extensively to sound polished and authentic up on the stage.

Moving past self-consciousness

At first, it doesn't feel natural to shift into the Interview mode persona. You're not accustomed to talking about yourself in this way, so it's awkward. In regular life, you don't often talk about your strengths or summarize your accomplishments, so when you try it, it doesn't feel like "you" at first.

At the same time, you judge yourself more harshly than anyone else does. Self-consciousness can make you overthink whether you sound like you're bragging.

Practice helps you move past embarrassment and overly critical self-judgment. In presentation skills training, they take the same approach. Early in my career, I took a presentation training class, and it was an eye-opener. I felt ridiculous standing in front of the room, but practice and feedback from the instructor forced me out of my comfort zone.

I learned that what felt over the top to me looked great on video. Meanwhile, when I was acting like my normal, laid-back self, I came across a bit meek and bumbling. (Hey, I was in my early 20s and struggling with some imposter syndrome.)

This was a valuable learning experience that I have tried to pass along to my coaching clients: Confidence persuades. And if you're feeling unsure of yourself, you can actually build confidence with practice.

Gathering feedback

You can multiply the value of practice by asking for feedback, but it has to be the right kind of feedback.

It is difficult in the moment to know how you're doing in an interview. Later, your memory may be a blur because you were intensely focused on answering the questions and completing the interview without making a blunder.

Whether evaluating yourself or seeking feedback from a practice partner, it's important to gather specific and actionable feedback. It's not helpful to receive generic feedback specifying that you sounded "fine" or "arrogant" or "boring."

When you recruit someone as a feedback partner, be clear about the kind of feedback you're looking for. Encourage them to be candid (without being rude) and to take notes on any wording or gestures that stand out either positively or negatively.

If you have specific topics or questions you're concerned about, tell the person to pay special attention. If you're self-conscious about eye contact or saying "um" or making distracting hand gestures, remember to ask them, after the practice interview, what they noticed.

You can even create a scorecard. In my feedback to coaching clients, I rate each answer based on the following criteria and provide suggestions for how to improve:

- >> Answers the questions well overall
- >> Conveys relevant qualifications
- >> Communicates enthusiasm
- >> Keeps answers concise
- >> Avoids filler words ("um," "uh," and "y' know," for example)
- >> Speaks clearly
- >> Maintains steady eye contact
- >> Displays appropriate body language
- >> Wears appropriate attire
- >> Minimizes the use of nervous gestures

When you've prepared for the anticipated questions and are ready to start practicing, see Chapter 14 for additional tips and resources to make the most of your practice time.

Don't become overwhelmed by striving for perfection. It's okay to say "um" occasionally, for example. The goal is to identify any major issues that can be distracting or make a negative impression.

Read Chapter 15 for advice on nonverbal communications and eliminating nervous habits. Hint: Practice is key.

Staying fit

Keep practicing until you're game-ready. Then get out there and get some real-world experience. If you've followed my preparation tips, you'll be more polished and prepared than 90 percent of your competitors.

You won't waste a single real interview opportunity on trial-and-error. However, each interview gives you additional input on what you're doing well and what you can refine.

If you score a new interview invitation and it's been a while, practice a bit to refresh your memory. I recommend answering a practice question or two as a warm-up right before each interview, just to get back into that Interview mode mindset.

I see the value of warming up every day with coaching clients. I'll often have a session with a returning client, and maybe it's been a few weeks since our last session or maybe it's been a few years since they were looking for their previous job. Almost always, they struggle with that first question — they're rusty and meandering, even though I know they possess the skills.

Then, magically, after a few questions, they get their groove back and sound confident again. I like to circle back for a redo of the "Tell me about yourself" statement after they've warmed up, and it's always much stronger.

Once you've landed your job offer, celebrated your achievement, and started your new job, you can forget about interviewing for a while. You've earned that privilege!

Eventually, though, it will be time for a new career move. Next time, you'll know exactly what to do to get back into interview shape.

Chapter **6**

"Tell Me About Yourself"

"Tell me about yourself. . . ."

It's a question that is guaranteed to come up in most (if not all) of your job interviews.

You'll hear this favorite opening question whether you're a brand-new grad or executive material. You'll hear it across industries and job types, too.

Since it's often the first question of the interview, it's your big chance to make a first impression. However, most job seekers are not prepared to make the most of it.

When working with my coaching clients, I always recommend investing whatever time it takes to prepare a compelling answer to this question. That's because a strong answer helps you

» Start the interview strong and make a solid first impression

» Position yourself the way you want to be seen

» Build rapport with your interviewer

» Reduce jitters with the knowledge that you're 100 percent ready for at least that first question

In this chapter, you too can discover how to master your response to the statement "Tell me about yourself." I give you insight into the interviewer's thinking, help you outline your bullet points and fine-tune your approach, and inspire you with some sample answers.

Understanding Why They Ask

First, let's get this out of the way: I *know* that you dread hearing those words, "Tell me about yourself."

It's just *so* open-ended. Are you supposed to tell your life story here? Is the interviewer looking for a full recitation of your resume? Or are you supposed to be dazzling them with wit and personality?

Many job searchers detest hearing "Tell me about yourself" because they're not sure what's expected of them.

I've heard venting about it from coaching clients, LinkedIn followers, and training workshop attendees. I created a YouTube video with my advice on "Tell me about yourself" and it has been viewed more than 6 million times. Obviously, job seekers are looking for answers.

The good news is that this question is an opportunity in disguise once you know how to prepare. It's an opening for you to set the tone of the job interview, emphasize your most impressive qualifications, and make a fantastic first impression.

From the interviewer's perspective, "Tell me about yourself" is an easy and open-ended way to start the conversation with any candidate.

Their ultimate goal for this interview is to find out enough about you to decide whether you're a good fit for the job opening they're trying to fill. In most cases, they want to like you. Their life will be easier if they can find the right candidate quickly.

However, it's also their job to spot red flags. A bad hire reflects poorly on their judgment and looks bad on their next performance review.

With "Tell me about yourself," they're hoping to get you talking and, ultimately, collect the data they need to make a hiring decision.

It's almost always the first significant discussion of the interview, right after making small talk about the weather. Your answer establishes the interviewer's first impression of you and sets the tone for the rest of the interview, letting you lead with your strongest selling points — if you follow my advice.

TIP

Be aware that you may hear some common variations on "Tell me about yourself." You can use the advice in this chapter to respond to any of the following as well:

>> "Walk me through your resume."

>> "Give me an overview of your background."

>> "Tell me more about your professional experience."

All these are similar in that they are open-ended and give you lots of autonomy to tell your story in your own way.

Creating Your Elevator Pitch

Think of your answer to "Tell me about yourself" as your interview elevator pitch. In case you're not familiar with the term, an *elevator pitch* is a short summary used to quickly and simply define a product, service, or business and its value proposition. It answers the question, "Why should I buy/invest?"

Your elevator pitch should be concise enough to be delivered during a short elevator ride (to the 5th floor, not to the 105th floor). At the same time, you need enough details to intrigue your listener and make them want to hear more.

TIP

Create an elevator pitch for yourself as a job candidate. It's a helpful way to respond to "Tell me about yourself," and it comes in handy for networking as well.

A stellar pitch covers these aspects:

>> **Your career story so far:** A condensed overview of your career path helps put your experience into context and deliver more info about your background.

>> **Your primary selling points for this job:** These can include experience, accomplishments, special training, technical skills, competencies, and other key strengths.

» **Your career goals:** These goals help specify why this role is a fit with your objectives.

» **A bit of personality:** Give a sense of who you are and what you're like to work with.

Does this task sound daunting yet? It's a lot to cover.

To make crafting an elevator pitch even more challenging, remember that you also need to keep it focused and short — ideally, less than a minute and no more than 2 minutes.

In my experience, that's the sweet spot in terms of answer length. Attention spans are short. Talk much longer than 2 minutes and you're likely to lose your listener.

Of course, you can't fit *all* your outstanding qualities and resume high points into 2 minutes, so you have to spend some time thinking about how to present yourself in a way that starts the interview on the right note.

Is it any wonder that it's difficult to come up with an appropriate elevator pitch on the fly in an interview?

Preparation is the key to success with the pitch. In the next section, I help you craft a noteworthy reply to the statement "Tell me about yourself" so that you can relax and feel confident in your interview.

Benefitting from the Big Interview 3-Part Model

In my early days of career coaching, I came up with a handy 3-part model that has since helped millions of job seekers ace the "Tell me about yourself" request. I call it the Big Interview approach because it became a key part of the curriculum on Big Interview, the online training platform I founded, which is how it has been tested and approved by millions of job hunters so far. It's a framework to help you shape your speaking points in a way that flows smoothly in an interview.

The following sections outline the three components.

Part 1: Who I am

Your first sentence should be an introduction to who you are professionally — an overview statement that establishes credibility, shows off some strengths, and maybe gives a little sense of your personality, too.

For example: "I've worked in customer success for software companies for the past five years, starting as a customer service troubleshooter and working my way up to leadership roles — most recently, running the customer success team at SoftwareCo, where I've had a productive experience building and training the team to support the company's rapid growth . . ."

In this example, the job candidate immediately establishes credibility in the field and relates some impressive experience (five years in customer success, promotion to leadership roles, building a team at a fast-growing company). In fact, in this example, Part 1 seamlessly transitions into Part 2.

Part 2: Why I'm qualified

Here's where you highlight the strengths and expertise you want the interviewer to notice. Don't assume that they have closely read your resume and know your qualifications. Many skim and miss — or quickly forget — your key details.

One way to approach Part 2 is to walk through your last few job roles, describing key accomplishments and experience gained for each one. If you do this, it's usually best to start with your most recent (and relevant) position and then discuss earlier roles.

You may also want to talk about special training, key projects, awards, publications, or other highlights.

You won't have time to cover everything in your resume, so the key is to choose three to five key bullet points to focus on.

REMEMBER

You will have time later to walk through your resume in more detail and fill in any gaps. Don't try to squeeze in too much information or else your interviewer will start to tune out.

TIP

A good interview is a dialogue, not a monologue. Keep your elevator pitch concise but intriguing and leave the opportunity for the interviewer to ask questions and continue the conversation.

Part 3: Why I'm here

Wrap up your answer by stating that you want the position and why.

You don't have to go into a ton of detail. You will likely be asked a question like this one later: "Why are you interested in this company or opportunity?"

However, establishing your genuine interest here can help you connect with the interviewer early and set the right tone.

REMEMBER

My clients have also found it useful to have a crisp, confident way to end this answer — and Part 3 can definitely provide that. It's easy to get lost in rambling while trying to cover Part 2. If you find yourself wandering into too much detail, Part 3 can help you get back on track and end purposefully.

Your ending statement can be short and simple — for example:

"Although I love my current role, I feel I'm now ready for a more challenging assignment, and this position really excites me."

If time permits, you can also share a detail or two about why the position is so interesting.

Putting it all together

Once you have listed bullet points for each of the three steps, it's time to put them all together into a polished, powerful elevator pitch. You have an outline now, so the next step is to bring it to life out loud in a natural way.

The key is to practice a bit and find your rhythm. Start by practicing out loud with your notes handy. This helps you identify where you need to make adjustments. You'll find out if your answer feels too long or if it has awkward transitions or phrasings that you stumble over.

Edit your bullet points, if necessary, and then practice again until you've internalized the general outline. You're not memorizing a script, just creating a structure to keep you focused.

This way, it comes out a little bit different each time, which sounds more natural and allows your personality to shine through as you become more comfortable.

Practice also helps you refine your delivery, eliminating filler words and nervous body language.

Avoiding Common Mistakes

Before you start crafting your own pitch with the 3-part model, let's talk a bit about how *not* to respond to the statement "Tell me about yourself."

Know what not to do

I frequently see the same mistakes made over and over again by smart, capable people. If you recognize yourself in any of the examples in the following sections, don't feel bad — you're about to become one of the few with the knowledge to avoid these mistakes in the future.

The resume rehash

WARNING

A common response to "Tell me about yourself" is to launch into a recitation of the resume in detail from the beginning. Don't do it!

The Resume Rehash inevitably turns into an overly long monologue that starts with your oldest — and probably least relevant and impressive — experience. By the time you get to the good stuff, your interviewer has zoned out and is thinking about lunch.

Don't get me wrong: It's important to prepare a summary of the high points of each of your past positions. You may be asked about your accomplishments and day-to-day responsibilities in any of your previous roles.

However, these details should, ideally, emerge in an engaging conversation, not in a long monologue at the beginning of the interview. You'll only confuse your interviewer with information overload.

Even if the interviewer specifically asks you to "walk me through your resume," don't take the suggestion too literally. You can still lead with your elevator pitch and focus on the high points of the most recent or relevant positions, letting the interviewer ask for more detail as needed.

Mr./Ms. Modesty

Many of my interview coaching clients let modesty get in the way of a strong start. They answer with a humble or vague introduction that fails to clearly communicate their strongest qualifications.

Some of these clients are just humble people who aren't comfortable with "selling" themselves. Others have never had to worry about making a strong pitch — they haven't had to interview in a while, or they've always relied on an accomplishment-filled resume to tell their story.

Today, the competition for any good job is fierce. You can't rely on the interviewer to see past your humble exterior and figure out how wonderful you are.

You don't have to be arrogant or pushy. If you take the time to prepare, you can find a way to present yourself to full advantage while staying true to your personality. See Chapter 14 for advice on how to be more self promotional even when you're modest by nature.

The first-date approach

An interview isn't a first date. (I truly hope your first dates are a lot more fun than the typical job interview!) Resist the urge to answer the way you would reply to "Tell me about yourself" on a date or with a new friend. It's fine to share a hobby or two in normal conversation, but don't put more focus on your personal interests than on your professional qualifications.

Yes, it's helpful to make a human connection in a job interview. However, you don't want the interviewer's main impression to be, "Cool person, but I'm not sure about fit for the job."

The clueless ramble

I have heard too many smart candidates flub the "Tell me about yourself" statement because of overthinking. Their answers sound something like this: "You want me to tell you about my job experience or about my schooling or what kind of information are you looking for?"

I know that these candidates are aiming to please and that "Tell me about yourself" can be interpreted in many different ways. However, asking for too much clarification only makes you look hesitant and confused.

Dive right in with your 3-part pitch. If they're looking for something else, they'll ask you for it.

Keep it concise

My general rule of thumb (yes, I've mentioned it before, and I'll do it again) is to keep your answers in the range of one to two minutes.

This is the sweet spot in terms of length. I base this opinion on many years of experience in working with interviewers (hiring managers, recruiters, career counselors, and others).

Attention spans are short, and job interviews are meant to be dialogues. Even if your content is good, you will lose most listeners' interest after about two minutes of talking. If your answer is unfocused, wandering, or off topic, you'll lose them even faster.

TIP

If your answer is shorter than one minute, you're probably missing an opportunity. Even with a yes-or-no question, you often have an opportunity to elaborate by sharing a relevant example or your thinking on the subject.

With "Tell me about yourself," it can be especially tempting to talk too much. After all, it's quite an open-ended topic. You may have years of experience, dozens of projects, and multiple career or job transitions that you could discuss.

That's why winging it with this question often leads to a long, rambling response.

By outlining your key points with the 3-part model, you ensure that you're focusing on the right details and presenting your story in a concise, impressive way.

Focus on what's relevant

To keep your pitch concise, you need to understand which details will grab the interviewer's attention — and which details you should cut or save for later.

The 3-part model I discuss earlier in this chapter works well because it allows you to "front-load" your answer with the most relevant information to make your interviewer sit up and pay attention.

In Part 1, you establish credibility with an overview of your career focus. For example, let's compare the Big Interview approach with the most common resume rehash:

Big Interview 3-part model: "I'm an operations analyst with more than six years of experience in the financial services industry."

This response immediately conveys the breadth of the candidate's experience and their industry expertise.

Resume Rehash: "Well, I graduated from college in 2016, and my first job was as an entry-level operations assistant at Mega Corp, where my job entailed . . ."

It may seem logical to start at the beginning of the story, but your first job isn't the main interest of someone who is evaluating you for a position requiring multiple years of experience.

For similar reasons, I recommend leading with your most recent experience in Part 2. Your most recent role will almost always be the most relevant and interesting to your interviewers.

REMEMBER

You don't have to cover every job on your resume in detail if you've been working for a while. Remember that your "Tell me about yourself" response is meant to be a highlight reel. If the interviewer is interested, they can ask you later for more information about those early or otherwise-less-relevant positions.

Neither do you have to address every job transition in this response. For example, if you have a gap or short tenure, you might be tempted to explain it. However, this can muddy the narrative and distract from your positive points.

Sometimes, it makes sense to address a recent transition in your "Tell me about yourself" response. If you have a clear and understandable reason, briefly explaining it can help you proactively counter unspoken concerns.

In Chapter 12, I cover how to discuss common resume red flags in interviews and include some strategies for using "Tell me about yourself" to confidently explain unusual career moves.

Sell yourself

You may detest the very idea of having to "sell yourself." This is one of the most common issues I see with my coaching clients.

In Chapter 1, I talk about how a job interview is one of the few situations in which you're expected to talk about yourself and brag a little. I also cover how to become more comfortable with shifting into Interview mode, a slightly more polished and self-promotional version of the real you.

One of your best opportunities to sell yourself is in your response to "Tell me about yourself." When someone makes this request of you, they want to hear the story of your career in all its glory.

Don't hold back. Own your strengths and accomplishments. Don't make the interviewer dig to figure out why you would be a fantastic hire.

Yes, it feels strange at first if you're not used to talking about yourself in this way. Practice is helpful in finding the right language and projecting confidence.

For modest types, one trick is to focus on factual statements.

You may not be comfortable with this type of bragging: "I'm the best salesperson in the world." Instead, you could state, "I led my division in sales for the past three years and had the opportunity to bring in more than $18 million worth of new business during that time."

I also recommend forcing yourself out of your comfort zone while practicing out loud. Often, my clients shy away from making certain statements that they believe are arrogant. I encourage them to try an over-the-top confident version just for fun and record it. Usually, they begrudgingly agree with me that they sound self-assured, not obnoxious.

Experiment with a bolder way of saying it and see how it feels. Ask a trusted advisor for honest feedback if you have trouble seeing yourself objectively.

Be human

REMEMBER

Don't be a robot. Prepare what you want to say, but don't memorize a script word-for-word.

You are more than a walking resume. Yes, you want to grab the interviewer's attention with your credentials, but you also want to make a human connection.

Give them a sense of your personality and what motivates you. For some, it might make sense to share a detail or two about your personal interests to round out your "Tell me about yourself" statement.

For example, talk about any personal connection to the organization's products or mission. Share a hobby or cause you're passionate about. Mention in passing where you grew up, where you went to school, or why you moved to or love your current city.

Keep the focus on your professional story but remember that they're also evaluating whether they'd enjoy working with you.

Practice

You might notice that I never miss an opportunity to remind you to practice.

This reminder is particularly important with your response to "Tell me about yourself." When you employ the 3-part model, you have a lot to cover. Practice helps you find your flow and commit your outline to memory.

Also, practicing this response ensures that you start your interview strong and create positive momentum. It's usually the first interview question you're asked, and you want to be your best from the beginning. First impressions matter.

Sample Answers

Now let's take a look at some sample answers for inspiration.

These examples are based on real-life interview responses that worked for my interview coaching clients. Identifying details have been changed.

Everyone is different, and your "Tell me about yourself" response will be unique to you. However, these examples may spark ideas that you can adapt for your own pitch.

I've chosen examples for three common types of job seekers so that you can see how the 3-part model can be customized based on your situation and experience level.

New graduate

Who I am: Well, I grew up here in Chicago and I just graduated from Springfield University, where I majored in business.

My courses helped me discover a real passion for marketing. In particular, I love digital marketing because it taps into both my analytical and creative sides.

Why I'm qualified: In addition to my courses, I spent a lot of time starting and running our campus branch of ReadWrite, a tutoring nonprofit. That experience taught me a lot about leadership and project management. I also took on responsibility for our social media presence to attract volunteers and donors.

We were able to line up major sponsors to fund our backpack drive and after-school events. We also expanded from just two of us to more than 80 active volunteers in just one year.

Last year, I also had the opportunity to intern in marketing for a new fashion brand, and that was an amazing experience. I got to work closely with the founder and the head of marketing, who taught me so much about the fashion industry, branding, and all aspects of marketing. I was in charge of social media marketing and was able to achieve some dramatic results in growing our following and driving traffic to our site. It was a lot of hard work, but I learned *so* much.

In my free time, I'm into running. I'm actually training for my first 10K race.

Why I'm here: I'm excited to be talking to you about this opportunity because I love the brand and your products. And I feel like the role is a great fit for my strengths.

Why I like it

This is a nice, concise overview that highlights interest in the industry and career path, along with relevant experience from school, an extracurricular activity, and an internship.

Most students and new graduates don't have a lot of work experience, so they must show how their coursework, extracurriculars, and internships have prepared them for a job in their field. This answer shows our hero has a strong work ethic, enthusiasm, and some hands-on experience collaborating on marketing projects.

Some personality is shining through via the enthusiastic language and the mention of hobbies.

The response wraps up with a sincere statement of interest in the company and the job.

Career changer

Who I am: I'm an experienced technical project manager looking to transition into an entry-level data science role. I have a lot of transferable skills and am passionate about investing in a data science career.

Why I'm qualified: In my role as a project manager, I have spent more than a year working closely with our internal data and analytics teams. This experience has helped spark my interest in data science as a career.

As a project manager, I have successfully led several complex projects, including a major data-quality initiative that wrapped up last month.

I have developed strong analytical, problem-solving, and communication skills that will serve me well in a data science role.

To prepare for this career change, I have also taken a number of courses in data science and programming, including courses in Python, SQL, and machine learning.

In my current data analytics certification course, I recently completed a real-world data analysis and visualization project for a healthcare start-up, which helped me confirm that this is what I want to do in the long term.

Why I'm here: I am excited about this opportunity in particular because it's such an innovative company and the role has some project management components in addition to data analysis.

Why I like it

With this answer, our applicant sounds confident about the plan to change careers and the value of their transferable skills and experience.

This job seeker talks about their real-world exposure to data science and relevant experience and training. It's clear that they're committed to making this change and have put some work into preparing for it.

I also like the clear description of strengths and the obvious enthusiasm about the company and the position.

Senior-level

Who I am: I have more than 8 years of experience in leading business operations for growing software companies.

Why I'm qualified: In my current role at Unicorn, Inc., I lead a team of 16 and oversee finance, HR, and customer success. When company reps brought me onboard, the company was growing fast and needed to put more structure in place to scale more profitably. This is something I was able to do successfully in my previous role at DataMaster.

I built out the teams to support our aggressive growth targets and the hiring and expansion plans we needed to support them.

It has been a rewarding experience, and I'm very proud of the team we've built and the results we've seen. Thanks to our hiring success and process improvements, we have been able to exceed our revenue goals for the past three quarters.

I was able to build on my experience at DataMaster to achieve these results at a larger scale. At DataMaster, I started out as finance director and was later promoted to COO and spent three years in that role during the company's growth and eventual acquisition.

Before that, I started out working in financial operations for XYZ Corp. and was able to pursue my MBA part-time, which gave me a much deeper understanding of business strategy.

I think my greatest strengths are in leadership and process improvement. I have a proven track record of building high-performing teams and guiding them to success.

Why I'm here: I am excited about this opportunity to be part of leading your next stage of growth. Though I was not actively looking for a new role, I have started to think about what's next, and this role really intrigues me, based on the huge potential in the market and the innovative team you've put together.

Why I like it

For senior-level roles, it's even more important to immediately establish credibility. Our hero starts by stating their overall length of experience in similar roles and then moves right to the highlights of their most recent and relevant position. They talk about scope of responsibilities, achievements, and key strengths.

They go on to fill in a bit about previous jobs, with more detail about what's recent and closing with just a little about earlier roles.

Finally, they provide a clear statement of interest in the opportunity and why they think it's a fit.

3

Acing Common Questions

IN THIS PART . . .

Grab them with your answer to "Tell me about yourself"

Show enthusiasm when answering "Why do you want to work here?"

Sell your strengths

Avoid raising red flags about weaknesses

Demonstrate fit with your response to "Where do you see yourself in five years?"

Project confidence when answering "Why are you looking for a new role now?"

Wow them with great examples when responding to behavioral questions

Be prepared for tricky topics

Ask smart questions

» Seizing the opportunity to show your enthusiasm

» Covering the two critical components of a strong answer

» Planning a great answer for every interview

Chapter 7

"Why Do You Want to Work Here?"

"**S**o, why do you want to work here?"

This is a question that's certain to come up in every job interview. It may not sound particularly challenging. You applied; you showed up for the interview. You're obviously interested in the opportunity.

But that's not enough for most interviewers. A weak answer to this question can raise red flags and knock you out of consideration.

On the other hand, a thoughtful answer can help you stand out from other qualified candidates and win you an offer.

Understanding Why They Ask

In addition to basic qualifications, the hiring manager is looking for the best fit in terms of motivation and work preferences when it comes to filling a position.

They're not looking to hire someone who showed up because, "Hey, the job was open, and the salary looks decent. I'm available."

They want to feel confident that you're excited about this position and this company in particular.

This question isn't just about the hiring manager's ego (though, yes, that may play a role). Every company wants engaged employees, workers who feel a true connection to their work and their teams. High employee engagement is closely linked to business performance — including increased profitability, higher productivity, lower turnover, and greater customer loyalty.

If you genuinely see the role as the perfect next step in your career, you're much more likely to excel and get results. If you're lukewarm about the opportunity, you're a risky hire, for multiple reasons. You present a higher risk of performance problems and attitude issues. You're also more likely to leave as soon as something more appealing comes along.

REMEMBER

A bad hiring decision is very expensive for the company. In addition to lost productivity and wasted time and money spent on training, they now have to start all over with recruiting.

There are two ways this particular question uncovers your potential to thrive as an engaged employee. First, the hiring manager gets to hear whether your reasons for wanting the job sound authentic, enthusiastic, and realistic. Your answer will help that person understand more about your career priorities and work preferences and will also clue them in to which aspects of the company and the job are most appealing to you and why.

Second, any thoughtful and well-researched answer shows both interest and professionalism. If you haven't even bothered to research the company and think a bit about the job fit, that's a red flag. If your answer doesn't ring true, that's also a red flag.

REMEMBER

The advice in this chapter applies to any question about your interest in the job opportunity. Here are some common variations to listen for:

>> Why are you interested in this position?

>> What made you respond to this job listing?

>> What do you like about the company or organization?

A related approach takes a different angle by asking, "What are you looking for in your next role?" You can interpret this question as, "Why is *this* role what you want to do next?" Your answer may start with some general information about your career goals but should also cover the same points recommended in answering "Why do you want to work here?"

Conveying Your Enthusiasm

A thoughtful answer to the question "Why do you want to work here?" (or WDYWTWH, for short) is all about showing genuine enthusiasm for the opportunity. Hiring managers tell me this is often the deciding factor. Most of the candidates who interview are well-qualified — at least on paper. When it comes down to two candidates who are both fantastic, the offer usually goes to the one who wants it more.

Many job seekers don't do a good job of expressing their interest. Some feel like they're supposed to play it cool. Others just assume their interest is obvious and don't articulate it. Still others focus on preparing for all of those questions that seem trickier and then fall back on platitudes when it comes to discussing how they feel about the role.

A generic or half-hearted answer gives the impression that you're interested in the job mostly because it's available. Compare job interviewing to dating (hopefully, dating is at least a little bit more fun for you). No date wants to hear, "You were the only one who would go out with me." It's the same with job interviews. If you want the company to woo you, you have to make them feel at least a little bit special.

To show your love, you must provide some detail about why you would enjoy the work and how the job fits into your goals. This is particularly important if the job represents even a slight career shift or a step up to more responsibility.

Handling Special Challenges

An enthusiastic answer may come naturally in some cases, but it's not always so easy.

When you're not sure

You may find yourself interviewing for roles that don't particularly excite you. To be clear, I don't recommend wasting your time pursuing jobs that obviously don't match your needs. I'm talking about those opportunities that have real potential but need to be investigated further.

Maybe the job description is unclear and you need to learn more about the duties and expectations to know whether it's a fit. Maybe you're unfamiliar with the organization and you want to gain a better sense of the team, culture, and reputation. Maybe there are missing details that could be deal-breakers — for example, schedule flexibility, remote work options, or benefits.

You see enough positives to want to learn more, but you don't yet know whether this job is "the one."

The challenge here is that you don't want to lie, but neither do you want to hurt your chances with a half-hearted answer to "Why do you want to work here?"

Your best bet is to answer as if you know the job will turn out to be everything you're hoping for. Imagine that your best-case scenario for the position is true. Why would you be excited about that optimistic vision of the role?

I'm not advising you to blindly believe in that vision. You will need to ask questions, do your research, and keep an eye out for red flags.

However, this look-on-the-bright-side approach will help you advance through the process until you gather the information you need to make a decision. You can always say no to a job offer.

REMEMBER

If you fail to show sufficient interest in the early interviews, you won't progress far enough to find out whether the position is a great fit or a potential disaster.

Exploring multiple options

Many of my clients struggle with how to answer the WDYWTWH question when they're looking at a few different career directions.

I see this a lot with recent graduates, but also with many others who are at a career turning point. For example, some may be torn between staying on their current track or making a career change. Others might be debating a lateral move versus taking on a larger role.

Interviewing is part of the exploration process. However, if you're too candid about being unsure, you can sabotage your odds of receiving an offer, even if you're well-qualified.

In this situation, I tell clients to channel the part of them that sees the role as the perfect next career step. This thought exercise can also be quite helpful in evaluating your options and eventually making a decision about which career path to take.

Covering the Two Key Factors in Any Terrific WDYWTWH Answer

Any top-notch answer to the "Why do you want to work here?" question (or any of the variations I mention) covers two key components:

First, why are you interested in working for this organization? And second, why is this particular position appealing?

Let's start with the *here* part of the "Why do you want to work here?" question.

Why this organization?

When you take a job, you're joining a team. You're tying your professional fate to the company or institution (nonprofit, government, or academic). You're devoting at least half of your daily waking hours to this organization.

Do your homework so that you can talk about the organization in a knowledgeable way. Identify specific details that inspire you to want to work there.

So, what do you talk about? Here are some issues to consider:

>> The company's general reputation

>> The organization's mission

>> The reputation of the organization's key leaders

- » The quality of the company's products or services

- » The quality of the company's other initiatives (marketing campaigns, community involvement, training programs)

- » The company's culture and values

- » The company's growth and success

- » The kinds of awards and recognition the organization has received

It's not enough to give a general answer, such as "It's a well-known company with a great reputation." Be specific and focus on the aspects that are most meaningful to you. If it's relevant, talk about *why* a particular detail resonates with you.

REMEMBER

If you're coming up blank here, you need to do some research.

You can start with the corporate website. It's likely to feature a wealth of information about the company's mission, values, and recent activities. You'll find details about products and services and maybe even bios of the leadership team and key personnel.

The Careers section highlights the facts the company's leaders most want applicants to know about the organization. You may find information about department structure, common internal career paths, and day-in-the-life interviews with current employees.

The Press section is also valuable because you'll find both press releases and references to recent positive media coverage and awards. Press releases give you insight into major company initiatives and points of pride.

You'll also want to search for recent media coverage. You may find some useful information in industry publications — or maybe even a quote from your future boss that you can mention in the interview!

TIP

Be sure to check out the organization's social media presence. LinkedIn is a good place to start. Most companies actively recruit on LinkedIn and maintain a LinkedIn company page with news, updates, and current job postings. You can also find profiles of past and current employees.

Many organizations are also active on other social media platforms — including Facebook, Instagram, Twitter, and TikTok.

Also investigate Glassdoor and similar platforms to read about what it's *really* like to work at the company. Former and current employees post their candid reviews, including pros and cons of the work environment.

REMEMBER

Most Glassdoor reviews are posted by people who either really love the company or really hate it, so you don't take every word as gospel.

For more inside information about the organization, look to your network. LinkedIn makes it easy to determine whether you have a past or current employee in your extended network. Maybe the person won't be 100 percent candid if they still work there, but they should still be able to give you some helpful information.

Best case scenario: You may even find someone willing to serve as an advocate for you internally. A recommendation like that is hugely valuable.

Sample answers: Why this organization?

Let's look at a few examples of good reasons to want to work for a particular organization. Don't limit yourself to just one reason. Do your homework and cite as many positives as you can.

EXAMPLE 1: PRESTIGIOUS FIRM

"Well, the J.P. Morgan reputation is certainly a factor, I'd be proud to work for a company with such a long history of leadership in the industry."

"Also, a good friend of the family has been working in corporate finance at J.P. Morgan for the past two years, and he told me that the culture supports learning and development on the job and truly rewards hard work."

WHY I LIKE IT

The first part is a bit general, but let's face it: Everybody knows J.P. Morgan. The prestige of the brand is obviously a draw.

And the company does indeed have a long history in the industry. So that part sounds fine because the answer then delves into some specifics.

To make the response more personal, the candidate has sought out a friend of the family who works at the firm and asked about the culture. That shows initiative.

EXAMPLE 2: LEADERSHIP

"I saw an article in *Business Week* magazine about your new CEO, John Jacobs, and the firm's renewed focus on technology innovation. I consider myself an innovator, and I would love to work for an organization that's leading the future of the industry."

It's smart to seek out recent press on any company that interviews you. In this case, the candidate found an article about the firm's new CEO. Quoting it makes the person sound smart, prepared, and interested.

The candidate also singles out the bit from the article about innovation and articulates that this aspect is a shared value. It doesn't hurt that they compliment the firm as a leader in the industry. A little flattery can be effective — just be careful not to lay it on too thick.

Why this role?

Many candidates go all in on the employer's charms when they answer the question "Why do you want to work here?" They don't think to talk about the appeal of the role or the day-to-day work unless asked directly.

But regardless of the question phrasing, you'll make a better impression if you also address the appeal of the opportunity you're interviewing for. It's just as important, if not more so, to show enthusiasm for the specifics of the position. After all, every manager wants to hire someone who will love the work that's required and be committed to doing an excellent job.

A thoughtful answer also allows you to sneak in information about your expertise. Though the interviewer wants to know why you're attracted to the job, they'll be even more interested in hearing about how you can contribute to the company with your knowledge and experience.

If you struggle with how to articulate why the job is a great fit for you, revisit the job description with a focus on finding shared values. (See Chapter 4 for more on analyzing job descriptions.)

Sample answers: Why this role?

Let's look next at a few examples of complete answers that combine "Why this organization?" and "Why this role?"

Example 1: Reputation for innovation

"Well, I have great respect for your company's reputation, and I would welcome the opportunity to work with some of the best developers in the industry."

"At the same time, I understand from my research that the company culture is focused on collaboration and rewarding innovation. I think my proactive style would fit in really well here — especially in this particular role."

"The position seems like a perfect match for my skills and interests. I'm looking for a role that will allow me to work on projects that are challenging and provide an outstanding user experience."

WHY I LIKE IT

This sample answer addresses both the organization and the role. The candidate compliments the products, the employees, and the work environment. (Companies do love to say they're innovative, don't they?)

The candidate then talks about how their personal style would be a good fit for the culture and goes on to describe what they find appealing about the role.

Example 2: Superiority of product

"Your app was one of the tools we used at my previous company, and I've always been a fan of both its functionality and intuitive design. When I saw the job opening at your company, I thought it was the perfect opportunity for me."

"Based on the job description, I have the skill set you're looking for, and I believe I could contribute a lot in the role, given my understanding of user needs and my design sensibilities."

"Finally, the reviews on Glassdoor make it clear that you value your employees and encourage internal development, and that's the kind of company I'd love to work for."

WHY I LIKE IT

This candidate is an enthusiastic fan of the company's products and has done their homework on Glassdoor to learn about the work environment.

This person goes on to articulate how their skills are a good fit for the job description and expresses their unabashed enthusiasm for working at the company.

Chapter **8**

"What Are Your Strengths and Weaknesses?"

E very human being has both strengths and weaknesses — and it turns out that interviewers want to hear about all of them.

During the interview process, you'll often be asked to describe your strengths and weaknesses, and this is difficult for many to do well. On the strengths side, many job seekers struggle to sell themselves, so to speak. When it comes to weaknesses, it's easy to blurt out the wrong thing and raise a red flag.

When so many of your competitors are clueless about how best to answer these questions, you can stand out from the crowd by following my advice and learning how to ace them.

Understanding Why They Ask

The hiring process is all about finding the best candidate for the job. That means the person with the right strengths to excel — and with none of the weaknesses that can get in the way.

Questions about strengths and weaknesses are asked in job interviews for all levels of positions in all industries. That's because it's almost impossible to judge strengths and weaknesses based on a resume alone. You can use assessments to test certain skills, but these represent only part of what's required for most jobs. Complex soft skills and competencies are much more difficult to assess. Interviews certainly aren't perfect tools for this task, but they're currently the best we have (and the ones most relied on by hiring managers).

REMEMBER

It's the interviewer's job to find someone who will perform in the position *and* get along with the team. Interviewers ask you for your perspective on your strengths and weaknesses and then follow up to determine whether your answers are believable.

When it comes to strengths, the interviewer is seeking to find out whether

>> Your strengths align with the position's needs.

>> You have the skills and experience to be a star in the role.

>> You are someone who will make an excellent addition to the team.

>> You are the best person for the job — there's no need to hold out for someone better.

And then there are those dreaded questions about weaknesses. These are also quite common, though they're less likely to generate reliable data about a candidate's limitations. Job seekers are understandably reluctant to confess their greatest flaws in the middle of a job interview.

However, the weakness question has become a cliché for a reason: Interviewers continue to ask it even though they know they're unlikely to hear answers that are 100 percent honest.

They're trying to forge past your nice, presentable interview facade and gain a sense of what you're *really* like to work with — the good, the bad, and the ugly. The question may be annoying, but if you answer it the right way, you can actually counter concerns and inspire the interviewer to become more comfortable with you.

Let's talk next about how you can prepare to ace these questions, starting with advice on selling your strengths.

Selling Your Strengths

I cannot overemphasize the importance of learning to talk about your strengths. This is one of the most common challenges I see with my coaching clients. Even the most accomplished, confident professionals struggle with this idea of selling themselves in job interviews.

But why? This is a positive question. The interviewer wants to know what's so great about you.

The problem is that most people aren't accustomed to talking about themselves in this way, so it feels weird. We don't walk around in day-to-day life talking about how great we are. It would be obnoxious to brag about our strengths at a team meeting or cocktail party.

Just remember that a job interview is different from every other type of interaction. The whole point is for the person to learn about your strengths and determine whether they fit the position's needs. Of course, you don't want to sound arrogant or over-the-top, but you must be a bit self-promotional.

REMEMBER

You have an oh-so-brief opportunity to make the interviewer love you and want to hire you. You don't have time to be awkward or shy or to hope that they read between the lines of your resume.

Many candidates fail to take advantage of the opportunity given them. Interviewers hear a lot of lame answers, such as "I'm a people person and a team player." That's why a strengths question is an opportunity for you to stand out from the crowd — if you can speak about your strengths in an authentic and compelling way.

TIP

Even when this question isn't asked, you should be prepared to articulate your strengths and look for opportunities to talk about them. You want the interviewer to walk out of the meeting with a clear understanding of what you can do for the organization and why they should hire you instead of someone else.

Recognizing similar questions

When I talk about asking *strengths* questions, I'm referring to any question that prompts you to talk about your strengths. There are quite a few variations on this theme, and some of them don't even mention the word *strength*. Here are some of the most common alternative wordings:

>> What are your greatest strengths?

>> What makes you a good fit for the position?

>> Why should we hire you?

>> What would you bring to the role?

>> What makes you stand out from other candidates?

>> What makes you a good engineer/copywriter/assistant/whatever?

>> How would your last manager describe your strengths?

The proof-point approach

I strongly recommend taking the time to prepare your strengths bullet points and practice talking about them in advance. That way, you'll be ready when you walk into that interview for your dream job.

I'm going to walk you through a proven approach that has worked for hundreds of my coaching clients over the years. The goal is first to identify the most relevant and impressive strengths for you and then develop a "proof point" (as described in Step 2 of this section) for each one to show how you bring those strengths to life at work.

Step 1: Identify your strengths

Sit down and make a list of your top strengths: Aim for at least five — and be creative. Banish your modest internal editor to another room. Start by jotting down everything that comes to mind. You can refine the list later.

Your strengths might include

>> **Experience:** This can mean experience with using a certain software program or type of task, expertise in a particular industry, or a track record of working with similar products or clients, for example.

>> **Talents:** Picture abilities such as programming in a desired language, writing proposals, selling widgets, litigating cases, organizing events, or translating from Mandarin, for example. (The possibilities here are truly endless.)

>> **Soft skills:** Here, competencies such as problem solving, influencing, team building, negotiating, and leadership would be worth mentioning.

> » **Education/training:** Here, relevant background on topics critical to the job — including college degrees, certifications, training seminars, mentoring, and internships — could be highlighted.

If you have trouble coming up with enough work-related strengths, jot down positive personality qualities or personal strengths. You may find ways to relate these to job performance.

Step 2: Prepare proof points

It's not enough to just list a bunch of strengths in an interview. You must also be able to talk about each strength in a convincing and memorable way.

To prepare to do this, write a brief proof point for each strength. A *proof point* can be a single example that shows a strength in action, or it can be a more general — but still detailed — overview of how you've displayed that strength over time.

For example, here's a generalized proof point for strength as a manager:

> "I have more than six years of people management experience and have been recognized as one of the most effective managers in our division. I've been consistently promoted to manage larger teams, I now have 18 people in 4 locations reporting to me, and I've had 0 percent turnover in the past year."

It's an overview versus a single example, but it has plenty of detail to set this candidate apart.

Here's another proof point that focuses more on a specific example to illustrate a candidate's work ethic:

> "One of my strengths is my strong work ethic. When I commit to a deadline, I do whatever it takes to deliver.
>
> "For example, last week we had a report due and got some numbers back late from our team in Singapore.
>
> "I pulled an all-nighter to finish the spreadsheet because I knew that the client had to receive the report on time."

Anyone can claim to be a hard worker, but this candidate talks specifically about how they embody their strength by being reliable, deadline-driven, and committed to meeting those deadlines.

"I'm a hard worker" is a common answer, but this candidate makes it their own.

Step 3: Focus

Now it's time to narrow your list to the top three you want to highlight in your upcoming interview(s). Because you brainstormed at least five in the previous step, you have options. However, you won't have time to cover more than three in detail in 1–2 minutes.

You may decide on a go-to Top 3 to use for every interview, or you may choose to customize your strengths list for different positions.

You'll also have "spare" strengths from your initial list and can look for opportunities to bring them up.

Step 4: Practice

Once you've done the work of outlining your top strengths and proof points, you should practice describing them out loud until you feel confident and your delivery is polished.

REMEMBER

Practicing helps you feel more comfortable bragging about yourself — something that can feel truly awkward until you develop a feel for it.

EMBRACING SELF-PROMOTION

If you get stuck trying to develop a list of your strengths, try these techniques to move past your modesty:

- **Get a second opinion.** Ask a trusted friend or colleague what they think are your greatest strengths.

- **Dig for clues.** Go back to previous performance reviews and analyze the positive feedback. Dig up old emails praising your work. (If you haven't been saving these, start a folder now.) If you're a student or new grad, think about the feedback you've received from professors and supervisors from past internships and jobs.

- **Review your resume.** Look for common themes in your achievements. Sometimes, we're so close to the subject that we lose perspective. Try to read your resume with fresh "eyes" — as though it were the resume of an admired friend. What stands out?

- **Get scientific.** Try a strengths assessment. I often use the CliftonStrengths assessment with my clients to help them gain a greater understanding of their strengths. The cost is $19.99 to take the assessment and see your top 5 strengths report (https://store.gallup.com/p/en-us/10108/top-5-cliftonstrengths). The results can help with answering interview questions and also with your professional and personal development. There is also a free strengths assessment called the HIGH5 (`https://high5test.com/`). They provide your top 5 strengths for free but do charge $29.99 for a detailed report on how to use the information. I have not used HIGH5 with clients, but I have tried it out for myself and found it provided some interesting insights.

Choosing your best strengths

When it comes to narrowing your strengths list to the best ones to highlight, follow these guidelines:

>> **Be accurate.** Choose strengths that you actually possess. Don't pick a strength just because it's specified in the job description or it worked for your buddy. You want to be yourself in an interview — just the best and most professional version of yourself. You will be much more convincing and likable if you talk about authentic strengths.

>> **Be relevant.** Take the time to analyze the job description and identify the most important strengths for each opportunity. You likely have many strengths, but which will be most relevant to this interviewer?

>> **Be specific.** Choose specific strengths. Instead of "people skills" (too broad and boring), go with "relationship building" or "persuasive communication." Don't be generic. Could 90 percent of your friends claim your strength? Pick another one.

>> **Don't be too humble.** Avoid weak praise and lame strengths. Pick something impressive. Don't go with "pleasant to work with" as your main selling point. Just about everybody can and should be pleasant to work with. To land the job, you have to show you would bring more to the position.

>> **Be prepared to demonstrate.** Prepare proof points (refer to the earlier section "Step 2: Prepare proof points") that describe how you personally have developed and demonstrated each strength you mention.

Avoiding common mistakes

Unfortunately, many candidates struggle to present their strengths in a compelling way. Here are some common mistakes that can be avoided with proper preparation:

>> **Lack of self-awareness:** Most job seekers don't spend enough time analyzing their strengths and thinking about which ones are most relevant for each position. Knowing your strengths will serve you well in job interviewing and in

the rest of your life as well. If you don't feel you have a clear sense of your job-related strengths, read on for some advice on how to identify them.

>> **Modesty:** Many candidates are too humble or just too uncomfortable articulating what makes them great. This is particularly true for introverts and for people who never really had to sell themselves before because new jobs always fell into their laps. You must put aside any hesitation to say nice things about yourself. You can do it in a way that feels comfortable and authentic if you prepare in advance.

>> **Choosing lame strengths:** People often choose strengths that don't help them stand out — strengths that aren't important for the job at hand or strengths that just about anybody could claim. This mistake makes a candidate bland and forgettable at best. At worst, it can raise red flags with the interviewer — who wants to hire someone whose greatest strength is the ability to show up on time?

Sample answers: What are your strengths?

I've given you the lay of the land when it comes to answering the "What are your strengths?" question. Now it's time to look at some examples that do a first-rate job of answering that very question.

Example 1: Strengths for a technology team leader

"I think one of my greatest strengths is as a problem solver. I have the ability to see a situation from different perspectives, and I can get my work done even in the face of difficult obstacles.

"I also feel that my communication skills are top-notch. I feel just as comfortable presenting to senior executives as I do mediating a conflict between junior team members. I worked as a programmer in the past, so I have the perspective of a developer, and I think they respect me for that."

Why I like it

This is an effective answer that lists two relevant strengths and illustrates them with proof points. In this case, the candidate talks about how their problem-solving skills work (seeing things from different perspectives) and gives examples of their communication skills (presenting to senior leaders and mediating team disputes). I also like the discussion of their programming past and how this makes them a better manager.

Example 2: Writing skills

"I am proud of my writing skills and am confident that they make me a better analyst. I am able to communicate complicated topics to various types of audiences.

"I also have the ability to take a lot of data and information and find the story and themes that clients need to know about.

"I honed my research and writing abilities during my days of writing for the college paper, where I learned how to write well on deadline from demanding editors. I even won an award for my series on the financial crisis."

Why I like it

This answer from a recent college graduate succinctly explains why the candidate is a good writer and how that skill applies to the position. The example adds credibility by showing that others also believed that the candidate's writing skills were top-notch (editors and award judges).

TIP

"WHAT IF THEY DON'T ASK ME ABOUT MY STRENGTHS?"

If the interviewer doesn't think to ask you about your strengths (not every interviewer has been trained to ask the right questions), you'll have to look for opportunities to bring up the topic.

You should walk into every interview with a clear goal: to communicate your greatest and most relevant strengths to the interviewer. If you aren't asked directly, look for openings. For example, when asked a behavioral question ("Tell me about a time . . ."), share an example that illustrates one of your top strengths and emphasize it.

If all else fails, wait until the end of the interview when you're asked whether you have anything else to add (after you have asked some smart questions of the interviewer). Then take the opportunity to bring up the key strengths you haven't had a chance to mention.

Addressing Weaknesses

Let's get real about weakness questions: Nobody likes them. They aren't particularly effective. And most people's answers are terrible. I say that as an interview coach who has now worked with thousands of job seekers. At least 90 percent of my clients need help with answering weakness questions in a way that won't raise red flags.

It's awkward and intrusive to ask someone about their weaknesses. Certainly, it would be considered a nosy and rude question in most settings, but it's somehow considered perfectly appropriate in job interviews.

Most candidates detest this question, and many consider it pointless. After all, they aren't about to confess candidly to their biggest flaws in the middle of a job interview. And, most of us don't have much practice speaking in a neutral way about our flaws and insecurities.

Unfortunately, the weakness question is still asked a lot across industries, companies, and levels of seniority. Interviewers love this question because it makes them feel like they're being thorough and hard-hitting.

You may get lucky and have a more enlightened interviewer, but I recommend that every candidate be prepared with a good answer to the weakness question, just in case.

Figuring out how to answer weakness questions

I have seen many excellent candidates get tripped up by the weakness question. It can be extremely difficult to talk about your flaws in a stressful situation like a job interview. The fact is, negative topics require added diplomacy. Meanwhile, you're nervous and thinking about a thousand other topics. Is my hair sticking up? Is my breath okay? Why did my interviewer just frown like that? What am I going to say if they ask why I left my last job?

However, there is a way to answer that is honest and authentic and still increases your odds of getting a job offer.

A good weakness answer has these two important components:

>> **Your weakness:** Here, you should briefly describe a real-life weakness that wouldn't be a major handicap on the job. (Read on to see how to choose a "good" weakness.)

>> **How you're already working on it:** The second part is the critical component. Discuss your proactive efforts to improve. This shows that you're self-aware, you have a drive to be your best, and the weakness won't slow you down.

Now let's talk about how to tackle each of these two parts. First off, here's how to choose a "good" weakness:

>> **Be authentic.** Don't select a weakness just because it sounds good. You will make a better impression with sincerity. That doesn't mean you have to share a weakness that makes you look bad. If you're like most of us, you have several weaknesses and at least one of them will be interview friendly.

>> **Pick a weakness that's acceptable for the job at hand.** Be aware of the job requirements, and don't cite a weakness related to any of the required skills or desired qualities. If you're an accountant, don't talk about despising math or lacking attention to detail. If you're in sales, don't confess to being too reserved or lacking persistence.

>> **Select a weakness that's relatively minor and fixable.** By *fixable,* I mean that it's something you can improve through work and motivation — for example:

> Fixable: *"I get nervous when speaking in front of large groups."*

> You can get better through practice and learning new skills — and this is a common development area.

> Harder to fix: *"I am very shy and often have trouble speaking up in meetings."*

> Though there's nothing wrong with being shy, an interviewer might assume that the candidate would have trouble collaborating in a team environment. This is a preference or personality quality that would be more difficult to change.

>> **Describe your weakness in a concise, neutral way.** Don't feel like you have to go into great detail. Be brief and, most importantly, avoid sounding defensive or overly negative.

Now let's look at how to best describe how you have already taken steps to improve in your area of weakness. (Keep in mind that a decent candidate is always looking for ways to learn and grow, but a fabulous candidate then takes the initiative to improve!) Use your answer to demonstrate your motivation to be the best at what you do. This is how to truly emphasize the positive when talking about your weakness.

Avoiding red flags

And now, a few words about what not to do.

Here are the mistakes that candidates typically make (you may be able to relate):

>> **Dodging the question:** Even if you don't answer honestly, your answer tells the person something about you. If you dodge the question or try to fake your way through, the interviewer will wonder whether you

- *Have scary secret weaknesses that you won't discuss*

- *Think you're perfect because you have no self-awareness*

- *Think you're perfect because your standards are very low*

- *Are a con artist*

>> **Trying to pass off a positive as a negative:** You'll find many books and articles that advise you to avoid negativity by sharing a supposed weakness that is actually a desirable quality in an employee. Here are a few examples:

- *I am too much of a perfectionist.*

- *I work too hard sometimes.*

- *I care too much about my work.*

Clever idea. At this point, though, it's an old trick and the interviewer will see right through it. They have seen many candidates try the same song-and-dance. In fact, this approach will likely make them think you're hiding something.

>> **Refusing to answer the question:** Some candidates will assert that they can't think of a single weakness. This is probably because they don't prepare for the question properly and freeze up, afraid to say the wrong thing. This answer also makes you look like you're hiding something.

>> **Revealing a weakness that raises red flags:** Another mistake is to be too candid and confess to a weakness that would hinder your ability to excel in the role. I once had a coaching client answer this way: "I have trouble getting up in the morning and getting to work on time." His true weakness was that he was way too honest.

Looking at Sample Questions and (Excellent) Sample Answers

Here are some of the various weakness questions that are regularly asked in job interviews:

>> **"What is your greatest weakness?"** Yes, the interviewer is going for it here — not just a weakness, but your *greatest* weakness.

>> **"Name three of your weaknesses."** Here you're being asked for more than one. The interviewer realizes that you have that one totally inoffensive weakness prepared and wants to push you for more. (See also the follow-up questions in the list that follows this one.)

>> **"What are your strengths and weaknesses?"** Some interviewers ask you to sum up both strengths and weaknesses in one answer. That's a lot, but there's always the possibility that you can lead with strengths and divert them from the weakness part.

>> **"If I called your current or former manager, what would they say you need to work on?"** This phrasing is tricky. By planting the idea of calling the manager, the interviewer is trying to subconsciously encourage more honesty. (Some candidates immediately start thinking, "What if they actually call them?")

>> **"Tell me about a development goal you have set for yourself."** This question is a roundabout weakness question. If you set a development goal, it was probably to address a weakness.

>> **"If you could change one thing about yourself, what would it be?"** Here's another phrasing — again asking for your greatest weakness, or at least the one that you feel is most limiting.

>> **"What do you most want to improve in the next year?"** This phrasing takes a more positive approach, but it's still a question about weaknesses.

You should also be prepared for follow-up or probing questions, especially if your answer to the original weakness question was vague or unconvincing. Here's what they might sound like:

>> **"How has that weakness negatively affected you?"** You'll often hear this follow-up question if you've failed to describe a *true* weakness rather than that totally insignificant flaw you came up with. (See the bullet entry about "Trying to pass off a positive as a negative," which I describe in the earlier section "Avoiding red flags.")

- ❯❯ **"Okay, how about a true weakness?"** This is a more pointed follow-up when the interviewer is more than skeptical about your answer.

- ❯❯ **"Can you share another weakness or area for development?"** A tough interviewer may ask for more than one weakness, especially if the first one sounds false or over-rehearsed. Some interviewers realize that candidates often prepare only one weakness description and want to see what they come up with on the spot.

The following sections highlight examples of strong weakness answers.

Example 1: Delegation

"I think one area I could work on is my delegation skills. I am always so concerned about everything being done right and on time that I can get stuck in that mentality of thinking, 'If you want it done right, do it yourself.' Unfortunately, that's not always possible, and I've realized that I can slow things down if I am too controlling.

"I learned this recently when given the opportunity to manage the department's summer interns. I had never managed direct reports, so this was a hugely educational experience in many ways. It definitely taught me how to delegate, and my manager noticed the difference in my management style at the end of the summer. I know that I can benefit from additional development in this area, so I signed up for a management-skills training course and am always looking for opportunities to manage projects for our group."

Why it works: This is an excellent example for a junior-level employee in a role in which delegation abilities aren't critical. Please note that the last sentence in the first paragraph ("Unfortunately . . .") is important because it acknowledges how the weakness can be a problem and why it's worth working on.

The weakness is acknowledged and described, but the emphasis is more on how the candidate has sought out ways to improve.

Keep in mind that this isn't such a terrific answer if you're applying for a job that requires you to manage people.

Example 2: Too direct

"Sometimes I can be a bit too honest when I provide feedback to coworkers. My personality is naturally straightforward and to the point, and most of my colleagues value that aspect, but I have learned that there are times on the job when more diplomacy is required.

"I took a training class on conflict management, and it really opened my eyes to the need to communicate differently with different people. So now I am much better at providing constructive feedback, even if it doesn't always come naturally."

Why it works: This weakness is described well. The candidate notes how directness has been a weakness while also making clear that they don't behave like a raging jerk to their coworkers.

In the second part, the candidate talks about concrete steps they have taken and how they have improved.

Example 3: Public speaking

"Honestly, I would say that public speaking is an area I could work on. I tend to feel nervous when asked to present to a large group of people. In small team meetings, I'm the first one to stand up and present. But put me in front of a big group and I can become flustered.

"I spoke to my manager about this, and we set it as one of my development goals for this year. I took an internal presentation skills class and attended some meetings of Toastmasters, a networking group for people who want to practice public speaking. With some practice, I started to feel more comfortable. Last month, I even volunteered to represent our team at a division-wide town hall. I only had to present for 10 minutes, but I did it and got great feedback! It was actually kind of fun, so I plan on continuing to seek out opportunities to improve in this area."

Why it works: Fear of public speaking is a common fear. In this sample answer, the candidate makes it clear that they have no trouble communicating in general (which could be a red flag). It's just getting up in front of a big group that scares them.

The person goes on to describe how they identified the weakness, spoke with their manager about it, and then took proactive steps to improve. They even share a little triumph at the end.

Chapter 9

"Where Do You See Yourself in Five Years?"

"Where do you see yourself in five years?" Don't worry. This interview question isn't designed to test your psychic powers.

It's a ridiculous question, really, just begging for a fake answer. After all, who can possibly say where they will be in five years? And, even if you could, why would you share your hopes and dreams with a stranger in a job interview?

But this question is still asked regularly, and your interviewers aren't clueless — they have their reasons. By understanding their perspective, you can turn this cliché question into an opportunity to show your fitness for the job.

Understanding Why They Ask

Don't take the "Where Do You See Yourself in Five Years?" question too literally. No interviewer expects you to be able to accurately describe what you will be doing in five years.

A lot can happen in five years. You could raise a kindergartener in that time frame. You could complete a new degree, discover new passions, learn new languages, or change jobs multiple times.

When it comes to work, industries and jobs evolve quickly these days. Very few career paths have a predictable 5-year outlook.

So, why do interviewers insist on asking this question?

Nobody wants to hire an applicant who is halfhearted about the job. It's like dating someone who is only tolerating you until someone they're *really* attracted to comes along.

Your response to "Where do you see yourself in five years?" is your opportunity to sell the interviewer on your commitment to the career path and the position.

To evaluate whether you're a good fit for the job, many interviewers want to learn a bit about your career goals and how the position fits into your plan. They care about your career goals because they want to hire someone who will be motivated to stick around and succeed in the role after being hired.

If the role is an important part of your long-term career path, you're much more likely to be an engaged employee and to perform well.

TIP

You may also hear one of these similar/related questions that aren't quite as cliched as that old chestnut "Where do you see yourself in 5 (or 10 or 15) years?"

>> What are your long-term career goals?

>> How does this role fit with your career plan?

>> What is your ideal job at this stage in your career?

>> What are you looking for in your next role?

>> What is your dream job?

For every employer, the goal is to hire someone who is truly excited about the job — someone who sees it as an outstanding career move and will work hard to do a good job. It should come as no surprise, then, that a key part of the hiring manager's job is to spot red flags related to a candidate's long-term potential. A lot of work goes into recruiting, hiring, onboarding, and training a new employee, so no interviewer is going to invest all that time and effort in someone who is already planning to leave for something better as soon as it comes along (whether it's a job that's a better fit, grad school, your own business, or a trip around the world).

If you're hired and don't perform because of a lack of engagement, it's a management fail. Your manager will absolutely be judged, and maybe even penalized, when it comes to bonus or promotion consideration. If you're hired and leave prematurely, it's another management fail. Again, this will reflect on your manager's skills and judgment. Either way, your employer will have to start over with the tedious process of finding someone new. So it makes sense that managers are sensitive to any red flags related to your interest in the role.

Discussing Your Career Goals

The good news is that it's fairly easy to answer the question "Where do you see yourself in five years?" in a way that doesn't raise red flags — and even makes you a more attractive candidate.

Let's be clear: You should never lie during a job interview. However, that doesn't mean you must be 100 percent candid about all your goals and interests.

First, in a job interview, this question is always about where you see yourself *professionally* in five years (or whatever time frame the interviewer asks about). I have heard clients bring up personal and relationship goals — don't do it. First, your personal life isn't relevant to your ability to do the job, and it should *not* be considered in the hiring decision. Trained interviewers should not ask you about your marital status, family responsibilities, age, or health status (among other factors, including race, national origin, and sexual orientation). Legally, they cannot make hiring decisions based on any of these factors.

Unfortunately, conscious and unconscious biases influence hiring decisions. An interviewer may make unfair assumptions if you bring up future plans to get married, have kids, move, or retire. They shouldn't, but sometimes they do. That's why laws have been passed to discourage asking for this information in interviews.

Any discussion of future goals should focus on your career aspirations, not on your personal life.

Keeping things general (for once)

I tend to advise my clients to be specific when answering interview questions. Don't give them boring generalizations when you can impress them with memorable details.

The question "Where do you see yourself in five years?" is the exception that proves the rule. If you're too specific here, you risk raising doubts. You don't want to mention plans that don't align with how the manager sees the future of the role.

I'm not suggesting that you accept a position that doesn't have long-term potential that excites you. You don't want to get stuck in a dead-end job, especially if growth is an important work value for you. During the interview process, you will ask questions and learn more about possibilities and limitations.

However, early in the interview process, the danger lies in raising concerns before they know you well enough to love you.

Make your answer truthful, but broad enough that it doesn't trigger any doubts about your fit.

REMEMBER

Stress your interest in a long-term career at the company (especially if you have short job tenures on your resume). Your interviewer wants to know that you're ready to settle in and grow with the firm.

The truth is that anything can happen. The company could go out of business, you could be laid off, or you could be lured away for a better opportunity. However, remember that the organization will invest considerable time, energy, and money in hiring and training someone for this job. You must at least show an honest intention to stay long enough to be a good investment. If you have some job-hopping on your resume, it's particularly important to make the case that you're now ready for a long-term role.

Express your enthusiasm for the job as an exciting next step in your career. Talk about the career goals you can see yourself achieving as part of the organization.

Avoiding red flags

In some situations, your answer to this question will be particularly important. If you're making a career change or this position doesn't seem like an obvious next step based on your resume, your interviewer may be suspicious about whether you're *truly* committed to this field or just need to make a few bucks until something better comes along.

Suppose that you were recently laid off after working in academia for five years and are now interviewing for a job in biotechnology management. To be seriously considered, you need to be able to describe why you're excited about making the switch and building a career in biotech. You don't want to leave the impression that this would be only a temporary diversion until something opens up for you in your "real" field of interest.

This advice is also relevant for new grads. If your major and internships are in a totally different area than the job, be prepared to talk convincingly about why you want to build a career in the new industry.

REMEMBER

If your answer makes it clear that you don't see yourself working for the company in five years, that's a red flag from their perspective. If you share that your 5-year goal is to transition into investment banking, it will seem obvious that your heart is not in this accounting job at an advertising agency.

Many job seekers have long-term visions of going back to school or starting their own business. These are admirable goals, but there's no need to share them with your interviewer, especially if you're still weighing the possibilities. Of course, if you've already committed to full-time grad school or another path that will conflict with your ability to perform in the job, it's only fair to be open about that.

There are also some career paths that require advanced degrees or other additional training. For example, many finance and management consulting career paths require an MBA. In these cases, it's expected that your 5-year plan will include more schooling.

Don't sound unsure of yourself

In reality, you may be considering a few different potential career paths from here. It's smart for you to keep your options open, especially early in your career or if you're starting to feel like you need a change. However, you don't have to advertise this in your job interviews.

A job interview is not a session with your career coach. You want to give the impression that you're focused and have a plan (even if it's not the only plan you're considering).

TIP

Even if you're truly interested in the position, the wrong detail can hurt you. At the interview stage, you probably don't know a lot about the vision for the position or the typical career path at the company. Don't declare that you want to transfer to London within the year, be promoted to CFO within two, and retire to the Greek Isles in five.

Don't overthink it

"Well, that's a very hard question to answer. I don't know what I'll be doing in five years. Hmm, that's tough."

In my work with individual clients, I've seen this mistake a million times. It's great that you take the question seriously, but you aren't being evaluated based on the accuracy of your answer. Use your response to reassure the interviewer that you're invested in this career path.

Sample Answers

To help you outline your own answer, I've included some sample answers that communicate genuine enthusiasm without too much detail. As with the other sample answers in this book, these are based on real answers that have worked well for past coaching clients.

Example 1: Building a career

"My goal right now is to find a position at a company where I can grow and take on new challenges over time. Ultimately, I'd like to assume more management responsibilities and get involved in product strategy.

"But, most importantly, I want to work for an organization where I can build a career."

Why I like it

This answer offers some insight into the candidate's goals and interests (becoming a manager, being involved in product strategy), so it's not too generic. This response also strongly expresses a desire for a long-term career with the company.

Example 2: Learning and development

"I am driven to be the best at what I do, and I want to work somewhere where I'll have opportunities to develop my skills, take on interesting projects, and work with people I can learn from.

"Some of the most innovative thinkers in the industry work here, and that's a big reason why I would love to be part of the team and develop my skills and knowledge here."

Why I like it

With this answer, the candidate is emphasizing their focus on learning, performance, and achievement. They are also complimenting the company and its reputation for hiring quality people (including the interviewer, perhaps?). The reference to "building a career here" indicates an interest in sticking around and actively contributing.

hunting

Chapter **10**

"Why Are You Looking for a New Role Now?"

This question will *definitely* come up in your next job interview — because it comes up in every interview. If you're looking for a new role, that means either you've left your previous position or you're seriously considering a change.

Your answer to the question will tell your interviewer a lot about both your current career goals and your most recent work experience. In some cases, your reasons are straightforward, and you may not even need to read this chapter.

However, for many job seekers, this is a tricky question that requires discussing layoffs, toxic bosses, or other sensitive topics.

Understanding Why They Ask

Employers want to know why you're interested in leaving your current position — or why you already left your last position without another job lined up. This information helps them understand your motivations and whether it's a risk to hire you.

Your interviewer is asking this question to help them understand your current situation and probe for possible red flags, including these:

>> **Did you leave for a good reason?** If you left on a whim or for an odd reason, can the interviewer trust you to be reasonable and committed?

>> **Did you leave voluntarily?** If you were let go, was it due to performance, attitude, or integrity issues?

>> **Did you leave on good terms?** If you left due to conflicts or burned bridges, can they trust you to be a reliable team member?

>> **Are your work values a fit?** Your reasons for wanting to move on can say a lot about you. Is the open position really a better fit?

I know this explanation sounds cynical. People have plenty of reasonable and even positive reasons to leave a job. However, it's part of the hiring manager's job to make sure you're not hiding anything.

When you understand their concerns, you can answer in a way that makes it clear there's no reason to doubt your motives or capabilities.

Accentuating the Positive

Answering the "Why are you looking now?" question is easy if you're moving on for logical reasons that anyone would understand. If you've been with the same organization for a number of years, it may be enough to say you're ready for a change or looking for a role with more long-term potential.

In all cases, the key is to focus on the positive reasons for making a change, such as your desire to grow or to face new challenges. If you're fleeing a bad situation, don't dwell on it too much.

My clients have found that some dating analogies are helpful for understanding the interviewer's perspective. If you ask your date why they're having dinner with you, do you want to hear that it's only because their last partner was a nightmare and they need a change? No way. You want them to tell you how fascinating and intriguing you are. You may empathize with a bad ex story, but not if it's the only thing your date can talk about.

It's the same thing with job interviews: You want to put the emphasis on what you're seeking, not on what you *don't* want — even if the truth is that a bad situation prompted you to start looking.

In some situations, you have to address negative circumstances that influenced your decision. If you were laid off or left abruptly, it strains credibility to claim you were just "looking for new challenges." Just don't brood aloud on your misfortune — redirect the discussion to your excitement about this role, which is clearly a better long-term fit.

Answering the Question

This section describes some best practices to help you find the right balance when dealing with the "Why are you looking now?" question, even in tricky situations:

>> **Prepare your answer in advance.** As with any other potentially awkward question, it's easy to stumble and send the wrong signals if you haven't thought it through. This is particularly important if you're concerned about being misjudged — either because you're between jobs or because you haven't been at your current job for long. Planning helps you find the right words to explain your situation without raising red flags.

>> **Avoid sounding negative.** This can be difficult if you're escaping from a nightmare job or you were blindsided by a layoff. Many toxic and unreasonable managers lurk out there, but you can't be candid about your terrible, very bad boss in an interview. Negativity is generally interpreted as unprofessional. Your best bet is to find a positive or neutral way of describing your reasons for leaving, even if it means not telling the whole story.

>> **Give enough detail.** Some candidates are so focused on *not* being negative that they end up giving an overly general and vague answer that comes across as hiding something. This is particularly true in more unusual situations — such as if you left a job after three months or were let go.

Again, you don't need to tell the whole story. However, you should provide enough detail to make a convincing case for why you left.

For example, if you're looking to leave your current position after only a few months, it's hard to believe it was only because you "need a change." On the other hand, you can't say that you found yourself working for a new boss who is a sociopath.

REMEMBER

You want to find a balance. Be truthful but selective. For example, you might mention that a major reorganization led to significant changes in the job description and the team. Then be prepared to answer follow-up questions diplomatically.

TIP

>> **Offer credibility indicators.** Bad jobs happen to good people, and it might be hard to make your departure sound 100 percent sunny and positive. Do your best to describe it in a neutral way, and then back up your story with credibility indicators. For example, if you have a history of long tenures on your resume, you can mention them to show that your current three-month gig is a fluke.

If you were laid off and are between jobs, you can confidently say you left on good terms and have excellent references to make clear there was no performance issue. Don't be defensive, but use your positive experiences to help counter any concerns.

Handling Common Challenges

The "Why are you looking now?" question is much tougher to answer when you have a complicated situation to explain. Let's talk tactics for the most common scenarios.

When you're currently employed

Generally, it's easier to answer this question when you're still employed. You're just exploring your options, so there's no departure to explain.

However, you may inadvertently invite questions if you've been in your role for only a short time. In this situation, the interviewer will expect an explanation of why you're looking to move on so soon. You risk coming across as flaky — and thus a flight risk or unreliable. Most likely, you're ready to move on because some aspect of the work or the company changed or the situation was misrepresented to you when you accepted the job. Think about the proper language to describe the situation in a neutral way.

You may also want to convey that decision was difficult to make and then make clear that you're looking for a long-term position. (You might refer to previous roles to reinforce that this short stint is an exception to your usual pattern.)

Your interviewer wants to feel that their company is wooing you away from your current employer. The ideal answer from their perspective: You're thinking about leaving only because this new opportunity — *and the company offering it* — is just *so* awesome. Maybe you weren't even looking. Maybe you're content in your current role but just couldn't resist this interview because the position is your dream job.

Obviously, you want to avoid laying it on too thick and sounding insincere. You should never lie in a job interview. However, your best bet is to focus on the positive as much as possible.

Always make it clear that you would stick around and be reliable if hired for the new role.

REMEMBER

When you're not employed

If you're not currently employed, you will be asked why you left your previous role.

In this situation, you may face more scrutiny about your performance because it likely wasn't 100 percent your choice if you left without first lining up a new position.

Some people do choose on their own to leave. For example, someone might find that focusing on the job search may be too difficult when working full-time, or they may have relocated to a new state or taken a short sabbatical.

In any case, be prepared to talk about your departure in a neutral or positive way, avoiding defensiveness but also giving enough detail to explain your logic.

These days, it's sadly quite common to be let go through no fault of your own — due to layoffs, for example. Almost everyone in today's workforce has been through at least one round of layoffs, so hiring managers tend to be understanding if the rest of your resume is solid.

Another common scenario is someone leaving after a reorganization of some kind. This can be due to new management coming in with different goals and management styles — sometimes a reorganization leads to a whole different strategy for the team, leading to job descriptions changing dramatically.

When this happens, people sometimes feel that the fit is no longer there and choose to move on. In other cases, a new manager may want to bring in their own people and look to push out existing employees.

Most hiring managers won't question a layoff if you describe it well and don't raise red flags about your job performance or ability to work well with others.

REMEMBER

When you've been out of work for a while

If you've been between jobs for several months or longer, you can bet you will be asked both why you left and why it's "taking so long" for you to find a new role.

In terms of why you left without lining up a new position, the approach should be similar to the one I describe in the previous section. However, you can also expect follow-up questions about what you've been doing since then, so you may want to proactively address this issue in order to preempt those questions and address any suspicions that there's a negative reason for the gap.

Even when you're a stellar candidate, it can sometimes take a while to make the perfect match. This is especially true as you progress in your career — senior-level roles are more specialized and typically involve longer hiring processes.

In general, it's best to frame a long search as taking the time to find the right fit. Hopefully, this is true even if it's not the whole story. If you have endured a long stretch, this may not feel like a full explanation for some interviewers.

In some cases, you may have taken a bit of time off before getting serious about the job search. Maybe you wanted to travel, spend time with family, or simply recharge after many years of working around the clock.

If you talk about this break in the interview, keep it brief and make it clear that it was a purposeful, short break and that you are now 100 percent committed to finding the perfect next gig.

TIP

Avoid delving into too much personal detail when talking about work sabbaticals. In all cases, you want to also be able to show that you have been keeping your skills and industry knowledge fresh. You don't want to be perceived as out of the loop. You can talk about classes, projects, volunteer work, and other ways you've been staying current.

REMEMBER

I guarantee that you will be asked this question — and probably similar questions about why you left your previous position. The trickier the situation, the more important it is to prepare and practice. Be prepared to answer in a way that focuses on the positive and counters any concerns. This advice also applies to answering variations on this question, like these:

>> Why do you want to leave your current role?

>> Why did you leave your most recent position?

>> What inspired you to make a change?

Sample Answers to "Why Are You Looking Now?"

Let's look at a few sample answers to give you a sense of what a good answer to the "Why are you looking now?" question might look like.

Sample answer 1: Seeking a bigger role

"I have been at my company for three years now and have learned a lot from working with some amazing salespeople.

"I worked my way up to regional sales manager 18 months ago, and my region has exceeded our sales projections by at least 25 percent each quarter since then.

"However, I am starting to feel like I need some new challenges. This new position appeals to me because it would allow me to manage a bigger team and sell more innovative products."

Why I like it

First, this candidate reminds the interviewer that they have had a respectable tenure at their firm and have been promoted. This person talks about their success in the role. (It's always good to look for opportunities to discuss your accomplishments.)

Next, they share a positive reason for wanting to leave — they want to take on new challenges and stretch professionally. The candidate follows up on this statement by talking about how the position at hand would be an exciting challenge for them.

REMEMBER

Some candidates get this answer halfway right — they say that they're looking for new challenges and leave it at that. Without offering some detail about how you've conquered past challenges and why the new job would present exciting new ones, you can come across as being too general and unconvincing.

Sample answer 2: Leaving after nine months

"I have loved my time at Acme Financial and am truly proud of the successful marketing campaigns I have conceived and managed.

"However, I think the time has come for a change. We are in the midst of management changes right now, and a lot of projects are on hold.

"I have been thinking for a while that I'd like to work for a bigger company with more opportunities for growth. This position seems like a great fit because of my successful background in online marketing and my experience in running a team."

Why I like it

Again, the candidate starts by acknowledging positive aspects about their current position and organization.

They briefly address their company's internal turmoil in diplomatic terms, but they don't overexplain or sound defensive. This person puts the emphasis on their interest in the open position and their qualifications.

REMEMBER

Your interviewer might ask questions about any of the career transitions on your resume, even going back a few years. Be prepared to address your reason for leaving each position.

Sample answer 3: Layoff

"Unfortunately, my company's biggest client went out of business at the beginning of the year, and that had a major effect on our revenue.

"As a result, the company had to eliminate a number of positions, and I was among the five most recently hired in our department.

"I am proud of the work I did there. I earned stellar performance reviews, and my former manager is one of my strongest references.

"Though I didn't choose this situation, it has given me some time to think about what I want to do next. I feel like this role is a great fit, the job plays to my strengths, and I'm excited about the idea of working for a larger company with more diverse project opportunities."

Why I like it

This answer makes it clear that the candidate lost their job for reasons beyond their control. They explain that it was a matter of seniority and not performance.

They also make clear that they can provide a glowing reference from the job to back up their claim. Reasons are provided, but the answer is still concise.

They also bring the answer back to their interest in the position and how it fits with what they want to do next.

Sample answer 4: Let go

"After some management changes, it became clear that the new department director had different expectations for the role that didn't quite mesh with my strengths.

"Ultimately, they decided to bring in someone from their previous organization who had more sales experience.

"The experience taught me that my true talent lies in account management and customer service, and I know I would be a major asset in a role like this one, which focuses on improving the customer experience.

"Would you like me to tell you more about my experience in that area?"

Why I like it

This is a tough situation to explain. The candidate was terminated, but there were extenuating circumstances.

They keep the answer concise and the language neutral. The situation is described without negativity or defensiveness.

The candidate then cites a lesson learned and redirects attention to their strengths.

Chapter **11**

Mastering Behavioral Questions

Most companies now include behavioral questions in the interview process. If you're not familiar with the concept, behavioral questions are all of those fun ones that start with "Tell me about a time . . ." or "Give me an example . . ." or something similarly open-ended.

Some people dread these questions, but I'm here to tell you that they are opportunities in disguise. This is where you can use your storytelling skills to stand out from the competition. You just have to know how to prepare yourself for your time on the storytelling stage.

Understanding Behavioral Questions

To make the most of behavioral questions, you first need to understand the logic behind why they're asked so often. I promise that your interviewers aren't trying to torture you. Let's look first at behavioral questions from the hiring manager's perspective.

Defining the "behavioral" in behavioral questions

By definition, *behavioral* interview questions are any that focus on your past behaviors as indicators of future performance. These questions ask you to share examples of situations you've faced in the past and your behavior in response to them.

Knowing why they're asked

Most job interviews include behavioral interview questions. They are widely regarded as the most effective type of interview question in terms of getting useful information about a candidate's fit. They're not perfect by any means, but they have a number of advantages from the interviewer's perspective.

First, hearing about past behavior is the best way to gain a sense of how you might respond in similar circumstances in the future. A story provides a realistic look into how you approach your work and handle challenges. An interviewer can rely more on a real-life example than on a hypothetical discussion of what you might do.

They also know it's difficult to fake a good behavioral answer. Not many candidates can make up a behavioral example that's believable and holds up under follow-up probing. A good interviewer will spot a liar easily.

Another important factor is that behavioral questions help to focus the interview on the most important topics. The hiring manager can plan the best behavioral questions in advance and use the same ones with every candidate to keep the process consistent and fair.

Finally, behavioral questions are versatile. It's possible to come up with a behavioral question for just about any requirement in the job description — hard skills ("Tell me about a challenging Excel project you worked on"), soft skills ("Tell me about a time you dealt with a communication challenge"), cultural fit ("Tell me about your experience working in a fast-paced environment"), and more.

Making behavioral questions work for you

I told you that these questions are opportunities — and I meant it.

TIP

The secret to success in answering these questions lies in storytelling. By telling an engaging story about a past victory, you can stand out in a field of qualified competitors.

Human beings are much more likely to feel engaged with information when it's presented in the form of a story. Stories also engage the right side of the brain and trigger the imagination. That makes the listener feel like a participant in the narrative, which means more connection. Research even shows that people remember information more clearly when they hear it in a story.

Storytelling is the best way to stand out in interviews. That means you have to learn to craft stories (true stories, of course) that show you at your best, prove you're a great fit for the job, and (obviously) make quite clear that you are a pure delight to work with!

REMEMBER

It's difficult to come up with this kind of compelling story spontaneously in an interview. You're under pressure to answer quickly so the most common mistake is to blurt out the most recent example you can think of and it's usually not the best one. Even if you come up with a decent example, it's hard to remember all of the most impressive details if you haven't prepared. Worst case scenario: You go blank and miss the opportunity to demonstrate your abilities.

Preparation is the key with these questions. I'll teach you exactly how to prepare, but first, it's important to become familiar with the behavioral questions you'll be answering.

Analyzing Common Behavioral Questions

If you search online, you'll find endless lists of behavioral questions. You can easily get overwhelmed. Luckily, you can ignore most of those lists. One good thing about behavioral questions is that they're fairly predictable. Sure, you'll occasionally get a curveball from an interviewer trying to be edgy, but most behavioral questions can be anticipated.

TIP

If you analyze the competencies in the job description and get familiar with the most commonly asked behavioral questions, you'll know what to expect. This knowledge will help you prepare the examples you need in order to shine in all your interviews.

With that goal in mind, let's review the behavioral questions that come up most frequently in job interviews.

Examples by competency area

The most common behavioral questions are the ones that correlate with the most in-demand job competencies and skills. These can vary greatly based on industry, role, and experience level. However, you'd be surprised at how often the same behavioral questions come up — regardless of job type.

This is because certain core competencies are essential to success in most jobs. Also, to be brutally honest, most interviewers aren't exactly creative. They tend to reuse the same behavioral questions they've heard and asked in the past, especially if those questions have worked well.

I have been studying job interviews for more than 15 years at this point. I have heard interview field reports from thousands of hiring managers and job seekers.

Based on this experience, I've identified the most common behavioral question categories to be familiar with.

Teamwork

The most common behavioral questions tend to be about teamwork. In almost every job, you need to collaborate and work well in a team environment. It's also difficult to evaluate this competency based purely on the information in a resume. Here are some frequently asked teamwork questions:

Tell me about a recent team project.

Tell me about a time you had to deal with a challenging team dynamic.

Describe a project that required input from people at different levels in the organization.

Share a rewarding team experience.

Tell me about a time when you worked with a difficult team member.

Leadership

Expect leadership questions when interviewing for senior-level roles or any positions that require leadership potential. Think about your responses to these common leadership questions:

Tell me about a time you took on a leadership role.

Tell me about a time that you took the lead on a difficult project.

Who have you coached or mentored to achieve success?

Give me an example of a time you had to lead a team that wasn't performing well.

When have you delegated effectively?

Communication

Communication skills are important in just about every job. Different roles require different types of communication abilities, but this soft skill is frequently a focus of behavioral interviews. The following are some popular communication questions:

Give me an example of a project that required strong communication skills.

Tell me about a time you had to adapt your communication style to produce results.

Tell me about a communication failure.

Tell me about a writing project you worked on.

Tell me about a time you had to communicate a complex idea simply.

Tell me about an important presentation you've made.

Conflict management

Many jobs require the ability to manage conflict and disagreement professionally. Though conflict management depends on communication and teamwork skills (see the earlier sections "Communication" and "Teamwork," respectively), it can also be an important requirement in its own right. Here are several examples of conflict management questions:

Tell me about a time you had to deal with conflict on the job.

Give me an example of a project that required you to work with a difficult person.

Tell me about a time you had to deal with an irate manager, customer, or client.

Tell me about a time you had to work closely with someone with a very different communication style.

Tell me about a time you disagreed with your manager.

Analytical skills

Analytical skills include the ability to problem-solve and make decisions by collecting and analyzing information. Some hiring managers also use the term *analytical skills* as shorthand for the ability to work with numbers and data or to navigate Excel like a pro. Here are some common questions for jobs that list analytical skills as a requirement:

Tell me about a time you had to interpret a lot of data/information to form an opinion.

Give me an example of a time you broke down a complex problem into manageable parts.

Tell me about a time you had to make a data-driven decision.

Give me an example of a time you were able to diagnose a problem based on analysis.

Tell me about a project that required analytical skills.

People management

Managing people requires organization, diplomacy, decision-making abilities, coaching, and many other skills. Good management can make or break a department or even a whole company, so it's an important competency to ask about. To evaluate your management skills, interviewers may ask these questions:

Give me an example of a tough management decision you had to make.

Tell me about someone you coached to be more successful.

Tell me about a time you had to manage someone who wasn't performing.

Give me an example of a people problem you've had to handle.

Tell me about a time when team conflicts came up and describe how you handled them.

Project management

As with managing people, managing projects requires a great deal of organization, adaptability, multitasking skills, and attention to detail. Many roles require project management, even if it's not in the title. Here are some questions that might come up if you see project management or multitasking in the job description:

Tell me about one of the most challenging projects you've managed.

Describe one of the most interesting projects you worked on this year.

Give me an example of a time you had to adjust your approach to a project.

Tell me about a time you had to make a tough decision to keep a project on track.

Tell me about a time you had to miss a project deadline.

Work ethic

For most employers, the term *work ethic* means not only working hard but also having a track record of delivering on work commitments, even when it's challenging. To evaluate your work ethic, an interviewer may ask you these questions:

Tell me about a time you went above and beyond to get things done.

Tell me about a project that required a lot of work and dedication.

Give me an example of a time you stuck with something when you were tempted to give up.

Tell me about a time you had to meet a tough deadline.

Describe a situation that required persistence.

Trending behavioral questions

Behavioral questions about the classic competencies continue to be the most commonly asked. However, changes in the work world have also inspired new questions and topics.

Diversity and inclusion

More organizations are now prioritizing diversity and inclusion in all aspects of their hiring. That includes looking for candidates who value diversity, work well on diverse teams, and connect with the organization's values related to inclusion. You might hear related behavioral questions such as these:

Describe a time you promoted diversity, equity, and inclusion in a previous position.

Tell me about a time you worked with team members with different cultural backgrounds.

Relate how you have fostered a sense of inclusion and belonging on your team.

Remote work

Over the past few years, remote work has become the new normal for many positions. Some roles are fully remote, some are partly remote. Managers must now be proficient in managing remote workers. Interviewers want to learn whether your remote work preferences and abilities fit with whatever the role offers. Here are some behavioral questions that might come up:

Walk me through your typical day working remotely.

Tell me about a communication challenge you faced while working on a remote team.

Tell me about a time you managed a remote team member.

Technology trends

Keeping up with technology trends that relate to your job is vitally important. You may be asked about your experience and comfort level with new technologies, even if they're not in the job description. For example, as I write this book, AI and machine learning are the hot trends, and technologies like ChatGPT are affecting many jobs. Related behavioral questions might include these:

Tell me about your experience with Technology/Software X.

What have you done recently to update your technical skills?

Tricky behavioral questions

Some tricky behavioral questions have also gained popularity in recent years. These are not based on specific competencies but are designed to probe for weaknesses and red flags in your background. Here are some examples:

Tell me about a time you failed.

Tell me about a mistake you regret making.

Tell me about a time you received negative feedback.

TIP

I have some special tips on how to answer these tricky questions later in this chapter.

Preparing for Behavioral Questions

So far in this chapter, you've had a chance to familiarize yourself with the behavioral questions that are likely to come up in your interviews. Now it's time to learn how to answer them. I've talked about the importance of storytelling to help you stand out in job interviews. Now I'm going to share a valuable tool to help you outline your stories.

Introducing the STAR format

The STAR approach has been used for years in many industries to analyze the examples that candidates offer in response to behavioral questions.

More importantly, the STAR format is an extremely useful way for job seekers to organize their thoughts and outline story examples that are both concise and impressive.

Let's start with an overview of what STAR stands for:

S is for Situation

T is for Task.

A is for Approach/Action.

R is for Resolution/Results.

These are the elements you want to cover in each and every story. This order also creates a story arc that's easy to follow and appreciate.

Many years ago, I started using STAR with my interview coaching clients, and it works like a charm to simplify and focus the narrative. I've taught STAR to thousands of clients at this point. People come back time and again, telling me about how much more confident they felt and how much better they performed once they had STAR stories to tell.

REMEMBER

It takes a bit of thinking to tell STAR stories well. Most interview examples are not naturally concise, bite-size stories that you can deliver in one to two minutes. Often, you're talking about a complex project that went on for weeks or even months. But don't worry: You don't have to be an expert storyteller. I'm here to walk you through the process of crafting your STAR stories step-by-step.

Crafting your greatest-hits stories with STAR

I have a step-by-step guide to help you craft your first STAR story (and many more after that).

Step 1: Identify your best story ideas

The first step in developing these brilliant STAR interview stories is to figure out what experiences from your past will make the best stories. I find the best approach is to start with your greatest hits.

REMEMBER

A *greatest-hits* story is a story about one of your most impressive, interesting, relevant projects or work experiences. These are examples that demonstrate important competencies and show you at your best.

If you try to come up with a story for every possible behavioral question out there, you'll get overwhelmed quickly. Instead, focus first on your best stories, because each of these can typically be used for a variety of behavioral questions.

What are your biggest wins? What are the biggest challenges you've overcome? When did you get glowing feedback or related recognition?

If you get stuck, try listing your proudest professional accomplishments. Think of the times when you truly excelled. Maybe you tackled a difficult task, negotiated a big deal, or resolved a critical customer issue. Perhaps you delivered impressive results, improved a process, solved a problem, or exceeded expectations. Each item on this list might be a story.

A greatest-hits story probably demonstrates multiple strengths. For example, you may have managed a campaign that required creativity, problem-solving, and attention to detail. That means that, as a story, it's quite versatile. You can use it to answer multiple types of behavioral questions. A greatest-hits story will also help you show more of your strengths in the limited time you have.

With those lovely greatest-hits stories in hand, you'll already be prepared for most of the behavioral questions you'll face. From there, it's also important to analyze the job description (see Chapter 4) to determine whether you need to prepare additional examples. For example, if you notice that presentation skills are listed prominently as a requirement and none of your stories touches on that capability, you'll want to brainstorm to identify a killer presentation to talk about.

Step 2: Outline your bullet points

Once you've identified the examples you want to talk about, it's time to bring the stories to life using that simple STAR format.

WARNING

Don't script your answers word-for-word or you risk sounding like a robot! The idea is to outline your bullet points so that you'll stay on track but still sound human.

PART 1: SITUATION/TASK

Naturally, we'll start with the first two letters — S and T, which stand for Situation and Task.

You'll begin your story by providing some context and a bit of background — just enough to set the stage for the rest of the story. Resist the temptation to delve into too much detail here. Your key goals are to clarify your role and ensure understanding of the difficulty, complexity, and/or size of the challenge you faced. What were you trying to achieve and why?

PART 2: APPROACH

Now let's talk about A for Approach. In this section, you should describe the actions you took to complete the task, solve the problem, address the issue, or improve the situation. You'll also want to touch on *why* you approached it the way you did, to show a bit of how you think on the job.

Here is where you should also mention relevant skills used and competencies demonstrated, especially those highlighted in the job description for the opportunity at hand. Talk about the strengths that helped you succeed. Don't be too modest — spell out your strengths in detail.

REMEMBER

Stay focused on key details and avoid going off on tangents. It's easy to get side-tracked, especially when discussing a complex project. Luckily, this process of outlining your bullet points will help you focus on the right issues and avoid rambling.

PART 3: RESULTS

Finally, it's important to end your story with Results. Every good story has a happy ending. To make a big impression, you should emphasize a positive outcome, not just to show that you get results but also to end your story in a crisp, confident way.

If you have tangible results to mention, don't hold back! For example, brag about revenue generated, costs reduced, time saved, promotions earned, new clients won, and existing clients saved. Interviewers love to hear proof of your victories.

However, some excellent examples don't come with concrete numbers. For those, highlight your anecdotal results. Feel free to talk about general improvement, even if you can't quantify it. You can also impress the interviewer by citing positive feedback from your manager or the client or the CEO. Don't forget to mention experience gained, skills learned, and relationships improved.

Many of my clients sell themselves short by forgetting the Results or keeping them too vague. Maybe it's modesty or maybe it's the challenge of coming up with stories on the fly.

TIP

Outlining your stories, and especially defining what your Results were, helps you ensure that you're highlighting your experience and accomplishments to your best advantage.

Step 3: Identify your story themes

Once you've defined your STAR, the next step is to note which competencies and strengths were demonstrated in each example. This will help you categorize your stories and know which examples are most appropriate for various questions.

Step 4: Practice

Once you've outlined your story, don't forget the last step: practice. Telling the story out loud is an important final component to help you get comfortable and build your confidence.

Practice will also lock in your key points in your mind so that you'll be sure to remember them when you're under pressure in the interview.

Taking a Closer Look at STAR Examples

If you've worked your way through this chapter, you now understand the basics of crafting remarkable stories. It's time now to look at some examples for inspiration. These should help you see how you can fit together all the story elements to create similar stories about your own experiences.

For each example, I've included some commentary to help you spot ideas you can borrow. These examples are based on real-life STAR stories that have worked well for my past coaching clients. Some identifying details have been changed.

I am presenting these in script form so that you can see how it all might flow together. I want to reiterate that there's no need for you to write out exactly what you're going to say. When you outline a story, it should be more of a rough set of bullet points, not a script. If it's too scripted, it won't feel natural or authentic.

Now, on to the examples.

STAR story example #1: Customer service hero

S/T: Situation/Task

"In my current role as an assistant account manager, I support my boss on a $2 million account, our company's biggest client.

"Last month, my manager was out of town when I received a frantic call from Steve, our client contact, saying that he was unable to log in to our system to run reports that he needed by the end of the day.

"Now, this was a Friday at 3 p.m., and my boss was on a plane to London.

"Steve was freaking out, and I knew I had to figure out a way to help him or else the situation could get ugly."

WHY I LIKE IT

This situation description jumps right into the action and avoids going into a lot of detail about who Steve is or the history of the system — nothing that's not relevant, in other words.

Another good aspect of this story is that it has some nice urgency and drama. If you can inject that into your stories, that will help you keep their attention.

A: Approach

"The first thing I did was apologize to Steve for the inconvenience.

"I gave him a chance to vent a bit and reassured him that I would do whatever was humanly possible to resolve the problem for him.

"I called our help desk, but the technician told me that the issue would have to go into the queue, and she was very busy.

"I knew I had to escalate the issue, so I went directly to waiting outside the office of our customer support director (this particular technician's boss) until he could see me.

"I explained the situation and expressed how important it was for us to find a solution as soon as possible for our number-one client.

"I then set up a conference call with Steve and our customer support director so that he could see we were taking his issue seriously.

"Working together, we were able to identify the cause of the problem, which was related to the security settings Steve's own company had put in place."

WHY I LIKE IT

This is a pretty good overview of the actions taken, with a focus on competencies demonstrated.

First, client communication skills, and then a sense of urgency, proactive problem-solving, and persistence.

Finally, taking the lead while the boss was away and focusing on getting things done is good stuff.

R: Results

"We adjusted the security settings right there while we were on the phone, and Steve was able to run his report and meet his deadline.

"Later that day, Steve sent an email praising me for my quick response and cc'ing my boss and the CEO of our company.

"He said I had saved the day for him with my persistence and excellent customer service skills.

"Our CEO called me to congratulate me on my quick thinking and tell me to keep up the good work."

WHY I LIKE IT

Lots of good stuff here: Our hero solved the problem, made the client happy, and received excellent client feedback that makes for a memorable greatest-hits story.

TIP

If you're someone who is more humble by nature and you have a hard time describing yourself in glowing terms, quote other people saying wonderful things about you.

To me, this story presents this candidate as someone who's a strong fit for a job that requires customer service and good communication and problem-solving skills. This candidate also demonstrates quick thinking and a proactive mindset.

STAR story example #2: Leadership challenge

S/T: Situation/Task

"When I was at ABC Company, we survived some company-wide layoffs.

"The team of five that remained in the department had to absorb the duties of the two that left."

"As a result, people were overworked and morale suffered.

"At the same time, more mistakes were being made because attention was so scattered.

"As the manager, it was my job to get performance back on track."

WHY I LIKE IT

In this example, the candidate quickly paints a picture of the challenge faced. This person had to motivate a team of people who were stressed out, overworked, and seeing things in a negative light. This scenario obviously required strong leadership skills.

REMEMBER

The Situation/Task discussion should always be the briefest part of your answer. Avoid getting bogged down in too much detail. You don't need to fill the interviewer in on the reasons for the layoffs, how individual team members responded, or exactly what mistakes were made.

A: Approach

"I realized we had to make some changes, and I scheduled a meeting of the full team to discuss strategies.

"First, I communicated my appreciation for all their hard work during a challenging time for the company. I wanted to make sure they knew how much I valued them and that I was there to support them.

"I asked for their assistance in identifying ways for us all to be more efficient — including me!

"I made it clear that this was a brainstorming meeting to come up with options — that no idea was silly and that it was a safe environment for making suggestions.

"I went with this approach because I knew we were all feeling powerless and I wanted to give them some ownership over solving the current challenges. They responded positively and had some excellent suggestions.

"We spent an hour capturing ideas on a white board and then voted on the five with the most potential. I then assigned each person to do more research on how we might implement one of the ideas."

WHY I LIKE IT

In this example, the candidate gives us a step-by-step breakdown of her leadership strategy. This person empowered the team to help solve the problem, asked for constructive feedback, and made everyone feel valued and heard.

REMEMBER

Managing a team doesn't necessarily make you an outstanding leader. It's important to choose a story that demonstrates *true leadership* by stepping up to motivate or take initiative — ideally, in challenging circumstances.

R: Results

"My team loved being empowered to help find a solution. Rather than complain, they channeled their energy in a more productive way once they knew that they would be heard.

"Right off the bat, we identified two ideas that could be implemented quickly and save us a lot of time.

"One idea was to eliminate one of our weekly reports. This freed up eight hours each week — including two hours of my time and three hours for my top account manager.

"Another was to train Penny, our administrative assistant, to take on some of the tasks that were burdening our account managers.

"We also decided to incorporate brainstorming and idea evaluation into our staff meetings each month.

"We are now more efficient and morale is way up.

"My boss even asked me to help him roll out this process to the other departments in our division."

WHY I LIKE IT

This is a completely happy ending. The candidate covers a number of positive outcomes, including these:

- » Boosted employee morale
- » Improved efficiency
- » Kudos from the big boss, who wants other departments to follow the candidate's approach

See how awesome anecdotal results can be? Don't be discouraged if your story doesn't end with a bang and a million-dollar deal. Leadership skills can be demonstrated impressively and effectively in many ways.

Chapter **12**

Answering Tricky Questions

t's time to talk about the trickiest questions. If you've had a chance to follow along with me from the beginning of this book, then you know that I've covered plenty of challenging questions already, though the ones in this chapter require some special diplomacy.

First on the agenda are questions about potential red flags in your background. These include gaps between jobs and job-hopping and other career moves that can be perceived as unusual.

These days, it's rare for anyone's career path to be completely smooth and predictable. Hiring managers and recruiters know that. However, they also know that gaps and job changes are sometimes indicators of problems in previous roles.

They are trained to ask about these gaps — and I'm going to train you to answer in a way that makes it crystal-clear you're not a risky hire.

Then I'll switch gears to prepare you for another tricky topic: compensation. Many job-seekers are uncomfortable talking about money — but avoiding the subject or saying the wrong thing can cost you. I want you to feel confident asking for what you're worth.

Finally, I give you some tips on what to do in the interview if, despite your preparation, you encounter a question you can't answer.

Talking About Resume Red Flags

If you've been called in for an interview, you've already passed the first test. They like your resume, and they don't see any major deal-breakers in your background.

If you're not getting calls for interviews, you may need to make over your resume. For advice on rewriting your resume like a pro, check out *Resumes For Dummies*, 8th Edition, by Laura DeCarlo (published by Wiley).

The interview phase is designed to identify the best candidate among several qualified finalists. That means getting to know you and asking questions about anything on your resume that could be a red flag.

Most hiring managers have been burned by candidates who talked a good game in the interview and later proved to be misrepresenting their work experience.

During the first round in particular, interviewers are looking for reasons to eliminate candidates.

You need to understand what their concerns might be and make it clear that they have nothing to worry about.

Often, these are details that are awkward to talk about. That's why I highly recommend preparing your bullet points and practicing until you're comfortable discussing even the toughest topics.

Let's talk about the best strategies for addressing the most common resume red flags.

Explaining gaps

Has it been a few months since you left your last job? Did you take some time off between your current job and the previous one?

Recruiters and hiring managers are trained to look for gaps between positions on candidates' resumes. Of course, they know that candidates have plenty of good reasons for a gap, especially during times of daily layoff announcements in the media.

However, they also know that a gap sometimes means a candidate was fired for cause or otherwise left under negative circumstances.

You can bet that they will ask about any recent gaps and will listen closely to your explanation.

Taking a look from the interviewer's perspective

What are some issues that an interviewer might be worried about? The biggest concern is that a gap indicates some kind of performance issue.

The logic is that you would have lined up a new position first if you had left the old one voluntarily. Does the gap mean you were let go or forced out for performance reasons?

If you did leave voluntarily and are now unemployed, what's the story there? Are you flakey or unreliable or maybe just don't know what you want?

The longer the gap, the more they wonder. Why is it taking so long to find a new job? Is there something wrong with you?

Then there are those special situations when your gap has stretched for several months or even years. Many people make a choice to take time off for personal reasons, like raising children, caring for family members, recovering from illness, or going back to school. In these cases, the interviewer may be concerned about whether you've kept your experience and knowledge fresh or whether you're truly committed to returning to full-time work.

I am not judging you here. I'm just playing devil's advocate for your benefit. If you know the biases you're up against, you can counter them more effectively.

You may want to curse these interviewers for jumping to negative conclusions, but keep in mind that a bad hire will make them look incompetent and cost the company a lot of money and time. They're just trying to ensure that they don't overlook a red flag.

This person called you in for an interview, so they likely *want* to believe there's a good reason for the gap. Everyone knows that layoffs happen due to budget cuts, reorganizations, and other reasons beyond employees' control. In other cases, new management comes in or a job description changes significantly, leading the candidate to make an understandable decision to move on.

If you address your gap well, an interviewer can check that concern off their list and move on.

You want to address the person's fears without sounding defensive or like you're trying to avoid the question.

Finding the right words

Finding the right words can be tricky even if you have nothing to hide. Interview etiquette dictates that you should never speak negatively about your previous employer or manager. Even if you left because of a toxic work environment or a nightmare boss, you shouldn't say that.

On the other hand, you want to be absolutely clear that you were not at fault.

Why is negativity such a no-no? First, the interviewer doesn't know you yet. A job interview provides just 30 to 60 minutes to form an impression, so every minute counts. You want to avoid coming across as negative, complaining, disloyal, or difficult. Diplomacy is a useful skill in most jobs, so why not demonstrate it in the interview?

This task is more challenging if you've left a job for complex or unpleasant reasons. Sometimes the pain or anger is still fresh and that can come out in your words, your tone, or your body language if you don't prepare.

Though I'm generally not an advocate of scripting interview answers word for word, it can sometimes be useful when the right wording is important to prevent misunderstanding.

It might be enough to script a few go-to phrases to describe messy situations in a neutral way.

Answering direct questions about a gap

First, be prepared for direct questions about the gap, especially if you're now in the gap or it's very recent. Here are some common questions that might pop up (with some more confrontational than others):

» Why did you leave without finding a new role first?

» Can you explain this gap on your resume?

» You were with your last employer for only *x* months — why is that?

» Why have you been out of work for so long?

» What were you doing between *x* and *y*?

» Why did you decide to do *x* (if you chose to take a temporary job or consulting gig or job outside of your career path)?

» Were you fired?

For all these questions, the best approach is to outline a few bullet points to cover: 1) why you left the role 2) what you were doing during the gap and 3) what you want now.

For point 1, briefly describe your reasons for leaving the role. See Chapter 10, which covers how to answer the question "Why are you looking for a new role now?," for detailed advice on how to talk about transitions, even when the reasons are complicated, and some sample answers to inspire you.

Point 2 is most important if the gap is long. A gap of a few months after a layoff doesn't require a lot of explanation. It can take time to find a new role. However, with a longer gap, you should speak briefly about why you left the workforce and then describe how you kept your skills current.

REMEMBER

You don't have to provide a lot of detail about personal reasons for taking time off, especially if you're worried about discrimination. It's enough to say you took time off for personal or family reasons and leave it at that.

Legally, interviewers are prohibited from making hiring decisions based on protected classes, which include disability and familial status. They should know better than to grill you for details about a personal reason for time off.

To show you've been productive during the gap, talk about taking classes, working on consulting or freelance projects, using your skills in volunteer work, or even just keeping up on industry news — any activities that show you'll be able to jump right back in.

Then, in point 3, make it clear that you're now fully committed to returning to full-time work.

Choosing a proactive approach

In some cases, you may not want to wait to be asked about the gap. You may prefer to be proactive about owning and explaining the gap.

If you have a logical and easily explained reason for the gap, it can be beneficial to address it early in the interview, get it out of the way, and allow everyone to focus on your fantastic skills.

The proactive approach can also be helpful with interviewers who shy away from asking directly (but may still be wondering about it).

A few common interview questions provide useful openings to explain a gap without making it a big deal.

TELL ME ABOUT YOURSELF

You can head off questions by weaving the gap into your career story in the "Tell me about yourself" statement. This strategy might make sense if you're between jobs and you know they're wondering why. It shouldn't be the first thing you talk about. However, you can include it in the last section of our 3-part model for answering "Tell me about yourself."

TIP

See Chapter 6 if you need a refresher on our 3-part model for answering "Tell me about yourself."

REMEMBER

Don't get caught up in too much detail. However, you can share a confident, positive statement about your reasons for leaving to make it clear you have nothing to hide.

For example, as you transition from part 2 to part 3 of your "Tell me about yourself" story, after giving the highlights of your recent work experience, you might say something like this:

> Unfortunately, due to budget cuts in the marketing department, my position was eliminated, along with several others on the team. Although I had a great experience there, I realized that I was ready to move on to a new challenge with more long-term growth potential, and this role seems like a great fit.

TIP

If the gap is old news (not within the past year or two), there's no need to mention it in the "Tell me about yourself" overview. You can get to it later, if necessary.

If the story is complicated, it may be best to avoid explaining your gap in your "Tell me about yourself" response. You don't want to put too much emphasis on the gap and distract from your career highlights.

WHY DID YOU LEAVE YOUR LAST JOB?

You're certain to get this question, gap or no gap.

However, your answer is particularly important if you're not working now and they perceive that as a gap.

Chapter 10 goes into detail about how to frame your departure in a positive or neutral way, even if it was an abrupt or messy exit.

Discussing job-hopping

Here I'm defining a job-hopper as someone with a history of multiple short employment tenures. The term still has negative associations for some people, even though shorter job tenures have become more typical over the years.

Looking from your interviewer's perspective

Many hiring managers are biased against job-hoppers because they view frequent employment changes as a sign of flightiness or unreliability. It's a somewhat out-dated perspective, but it's still out there.

People change jobs more frequently these days than in the past. In a turbulent business environment, employees are more often forced out due to layoffs, restructurings, and business failures. Professionals also hop more often by choice, looking for ways to develop skills and experience and avoid dead-end positions.

Because of all of this, most of today's employers are more open to considering an applicant with a short tenure or two on their resume. However, keep in mind that a history of job-hopping (staying less than 2 years and especially less than 1 year) can affect your chances of getting hired.

REMEMBER

It's your interviewer's job to spot red flags and avoid hiring someone who won't stay long enough to contribute. If you leave abruptly, whether willingly or because you can't perform, it affects their reputation (and maybe their bonus or promotion potential). Plus, they then have to spend more time and company dollars to hire and train your replacement.

That means it's in your best interests to reassure them that you're a great hire with long-term potential. When it's time to interview for a new job, you must be prepared to discuss your reasons for leaving shorter-term positions in a way that shows you're not flaky or unreliable.

Explaining your hopping history

Let's talk about exactly how to ensure your job-hopping won't hurt you.

The key is to 1) explain why and 2) redirect to the positive.

I recommend preparing a few bullet points in anticipation of direct questions about job-hopping. For example:

>> **Why did you leave Position X after such a short time?** They will be most concerned about recent positions with short tenures (especially if it's your most recent position that was less than a year).

You're less likely to be grilled about a short stint early in your career, especially if it's your only one and/or you've had long-term roles since then. You should still be prepared to discuss an older position if they ask, but it will rightfully be not as big of a concern for most interviewers.

>> **Why have you moved around so much?** It gets trickier when you've had a few short-term positions in recent years and it looks like a pattern.

One time is easier to explain as a fluke. When you have multiple short tenures (especially recent ones), your interviewer may need more convincing. In this situation, it's even more important to prepare your response thoughtfully. If you don't explain enough, they may think you're hiding something. If you go into too much detail, you risk derailing the conversation and putting too much focus on the hopping.

TAKING A PROACTIVE APPROACH

As with a gap, you might want to present your hopping history in your "Tell me about yourself" spiel.

For example, if your most recent gig was a short one, it makes sense to address it early and get their concerns out of the way.

Don't lead with job-hopping, of course. You don't want to start on the defensive. Please see Chapter 6 for my advice on answering "Tell me about yourself" with our three-part model and leading with your strengths.

As you move from part 2 to part 3 of your "Tell me about yourself" overview, you could briefly touch on the recent short-term role before stating why you're excited about the opportunity at hand.

For example:

> Most recently, I worked as an HR coordinator for XYZ Corp., which was a great learning experience while working on rolling out their new benefits plan. Unfortunately, my role was eliminated in a company-wide layoff, which led me to look for a new opportunity. I'm excited about this role because I see it as a great long-term fit.

If you have multiple hops in recent years, there may be a way to weave them into your "Tell me about yourself" career narrative. I advise caution here, however: Too much explanation can give too much weight to the job-hopping.

TIP

If your job-hopping story is complicated, save it for later, after you've already wowed them with your strengths and accomplishments.

KEEP IT POSITIVE

Nobody takes a permanent position with plans to leave after just a few months. It usually happens because things went wrong in some way, and you may still be feeling salty about it.

However, negativity or blaming can raise concerns that you have trouble getting along in a work environment. I know that's not always fair. After all, there are plenty of bad bosses in the world.

In a job interview, though, it's best to remain neutral and diplomatic when discussing reasons for leaving a position (especially if you have multiple departures to discuss over the past few years).

For example, avoid this: "The new head of operations was totally incompetent and just didn't like me because I didn't kiss up to him properly."

Even if this is true, saying it makes you look gossipy and self-serving.

Try a more neutral version: "A new head of operations came in and the department changed drastically, to the point that I didn't see opportunities for me to continue taking on new challenges in the position."

Explain the situation as diplomatically as you can, and then redirect to any positive outcomes you can mention. For example:

>> You learned a lot in the role.

>> You developed valuable relationships (It's always helpful to be able to say you left on good terms with your manager and coworkers).

>> You realized what's most important for you in a long-term role (and, of course, the job you're interviewing for has all those qualities).

Focus on the positive as much as you can, but don't try to completely sugarcoat a tough situation. Don't pretend you were delighted to be blindsided by a layoff after two months or try to play off a short tenure with a vague excuse that you were "seeking new challenges."

WARNING

Don't make it all about the money. Implying (or saying outright) that you left a job to pursue a higher salary will raise red flags.

There's nothing wrong with expecting to be paid what you're worth, but nobody wants to hire someone who can be easily lured away for a few more dollars.

The key is to put the focus on the opportunity and the work, not the paycheck. Saying that you switched jobs primarily for higher pay can make you look disloyal.

TALK UP YOUR STABILITY

Go beyond answering the direct questions and look for opportunities to reinforce that you're not a job-hopper by nature.

Emphasize the longer-term positions on your resume to show that you're reliable and committed. When asked about what you're looking for or your 5-year plan, be clear that you're seeking a long-term role at an organization where you can grow and contribute over time.

These strategies can help you reinforce that you're a good bet for a long-term hire, someone who will stick around and grow with the company.

Addressing unusual career moves

By unusual career moves, I mean significant career changes and especially any move that could be viewed as a demotion or a step down.

These moves are important to address if they're recent and especially if they raise any doubts about your fit for the position at hand. For example, if you recently made a career change out of accounting and are interviewing for accounting roles again, hiring managers may wonder whether you're truly committed to the career path. If you were in a project coordinator role and then moved to an assistant position with less responsibility, it could raise doubts about your performance.

REMEMBER

Be prepared to talk about any job transition on your resume, including your motivation for making the change. They may not ask about all of them. However, hiring managers know to look for unusual moves that could raise red flags (as with gaps and short tenures, discussed earlier in this chapter).

"Unusual" isn't always a negative. You have to look at the job description and think about it from the hiring manager's perspective. If a transition could raise doubts about your interest in the role or your ability to perform, prepare some bullet points to explain and, ideally, reassure.

Curious about what kind of answer might work in just such a situation? Check out the following example:

After three years of working in accounts payable, I was offered an opportunity to try something new in our HR department. It seemed like a good fit at the time, and I did learn a lot, especially with the opportunity to step up and manage a small team for the first time.

However, after a year in HR, I have realized that my long-term career interests are in corporate accounting and I'm looking for a role that leverages my passion for accounting as well as my management and communication skills.

Remembering to practice

I don't want to be repetitive, but I also hate to miss the opportunity to remind you how highly I recommend practicing out loud to improve your interview skills. It is particularly important to practice answering tricky questions that require extra diplomacy.

If you're nervous about how to present a resume red flag, practice is critical. Practice helps you become more comfortable with your thoughtfully crafted bullet points and makes it easier to remember your answers when the pressure's on.

Fielding Questions About Compensation

Money is notoriously an uncomfortable subject. In job interviews, you may have the added pressure of worrying that saying the wrong thing will hurt your chances of negotiating an attractive offer.

I want to help you make more money in your next job. Let's talk about how to handle interview questions about salary and compensation.

Preparing for compensation questions

Why do interviewers ask candidates salary questions? Ultimately, they want to know whether they can afford you before they invest time and resources in courting you to come to work for them.

Traditionally, the salary question has been one (or both) of the following:

>> What are you looking to make?

>> What are you making now?

In recent years, many states and localities have passed laws that discourage asking about current salary or salary history in interviews. These laws are designed to encourage fair pay. (The idea here is that it's not fair to those who are stuck in an underpaid position if future offers are based on that low salary and not the fair market rate for their skills.)

As a result, you may find that fewer interviewers will ask you what you're making now. However, you're still likely to hear questions about your salary requirements during the interview process.

Questions about compensation can come up early on, as part of the screening process, or pop up later, after you've made it through a couple of interview rounds.

Your mission? Expect these salary interview questions and have plans in place to address them before going into the interview.

Talking strategically about money

So, how do you address a direct question about your salary requirements?

It seems like an innocent enough question. It makes sense that potential employers would want to know a ballpark figure for your expectations, right?

Not so fast. First, why should you be the one who has to name a number first? An employer that values transparency should be upfront about the compensation range from the beginning. It's easier for everyone to avoid wasting time or playing games.

But many companies are not upfront about salary ranges early in the hiring process. If they name a range, it may be such a wide range that it doesn't help you much. Then they want you to be the first to name specific numbers.

Negotiation experts agree that the first person to name a number is at a disadvantage. Your best bet is to avoid stating your specific salary requirements as long as possible.

Benefiting from waiting

Why wait? The biggest issue is that, early on, the company isn't sold on you just yet. They're still feeling you out and "comparison-shopping" between you and the other candidates.

You'll have better leverage to negotiate later, so it serves you best to avoid naming a specific number too early. In fact, a high number can price you out of contention before you've even had a chance to make a good impression.

On the other hand, if you're nervous or insecure, you might blurt out a number that's too low just to improve your odds of moving forward to the next round. Going too low can put you in a position where you feel forced into accepting a salary that you can't live comfortably on. This rarely leads to a happy work situation.

Okay, now you're convinced that you should defer the question as long as possible. What's next?

Crunching the numbers

Before you plan your response, it's important to know the going rate for jobs in your field and in your job market.

You can research salary ranges online on websites like www.payscale.com, www.glassdoor.com, and www.salary.com. You'll find market salary ranges for hundreds of job titles — taking into account factors such as the size of the company, its location, and your experience level.

You will probably find some conflicting information and broad ranges in some places, but you'll develop a general sense if you look at a few sources. Your goal is to arrive at a reasonable salary range that seems fair based on both market value and your own experience.

You should also think a bit about your priorities. Is there a salary offer that would make you say yes on the spot? What salary would you immediately walk away from?

REMEMBER

Go in with knowledge so that you can confidently name a number if pressed.

Redirecting the question

Let me specify now how to postpone naming your number and do it diplomatically. One way is to elevate the conversation.

For example, you could say:

> Salary is not my top consideration right now. I'm more interested in finding a position that's a good fit for my skills and interests. I'm confident that you're offering a salary that's competitive in the current market.

You're letting them know that you're confident in your abilities and respect your-self too much to sell yourself short. By doing this, you're tactfully letting them know you're not desperate and expect to be compensated appropriately for your time and talent.

Naturally, some interviewers will press further for a specific number. Here's where your research comes in handy. At this point, if it's hard to keep deflecting, you can say something like, "Well, because of my research and past experience, my understanding is that $45,000 to $60,000 per year is typical based on the role and requirements."

TIP

This frames the number as "Here's my understanding of what's competitive" as opposed to "Here's what I want."

If you've done your research, you'll be able to quote a reasonable range and then they can respond.

Discussing your current salary

What if you're asked about what you're making now?

As mentioned earlier in this chapter, many states have laws prohibiting questions about your current salary or salary history. However, you may still hear this ques-tion at some companies. Often, interviewers ask this question believing that offering a salary 10 percent to 15 percent higher than your current salary will be sufficient to lure you away from your current position.

This question can be tricky for candidates who feel they are either underpaid or overpaid in their current roles. Others may be making a career change or moving from commission-based to salary work, or otherwise be in a situation in which the comparison just isn't valid.

If you're making too much, the interviewer may feel that they can't afford you or that you're overqualified. However, it's far more common for someone to be underpaid and worry about the perception that there's something wrong with them for that reason or that they're only worth a lowball offer.

Many people choose jobs with lower salaries for good reasons like bonus, com-mission incentives, flexibility, location, or learning opportunities. You don't want to let the decision to work for a less-than-stellar salary in the past derail your opportunity for a competitive salary in the future.

In any of these cases, deflection can be your best bet, but you eventually have to address this question. You'll be in a much better position if you can deflect until they already love you and you have more leverage to negotiate.

When pressed to give your current salary when you know it will sabotage your chances, consider the following tactic to delay the question a little longer, if not put it off altogether — something like this:

> Since this position is not exactly the same as my current job, I think it makes more sense to talk about a fair salary based on the responsibilities and requirements for this job. I'm very excited about the position . . .

If you feel you must reveal your low salary earlier than you would like, don't forget to mention the contributing factors as well. For example, employers understand that a job in Iowa pays less than a job in New York City.

After the offer

In some cases, the toughest salary discussions come after the offer.

Congratulations, we want to hire you — it's great news until you see the lowball offer.

The offer is simply that: a starting point.

Sometimes, the offer is even a test. The way you respond to the offer can change everything.

When negotiating a job offer, start by showing gratitude for the offer and enthusiasm about the potential of the position before you dive into negotiating mode.

Second, make your counteroffer one that is fair, well-reasoned, and thoughtfully presented.

Try countering with a salary range instead of a concrete number. Surprisingly, some companies shy away from offering the bottom-range number to avoid seeming impolite. Providing a salary range also gives the employer the impression that you're flexible and willing to work with them.

Be willing to walk away if the offer isn't right for you.

It's hard to do, especially in a competitive job market, but if you're not desperate to put food on the table, it may be better, in the long run, to wait. It can be tempting to accept just so that you can stop job-hunting already. But if you've taken the time to research the market and think about what's most important to you, you'll know when it pays to wait.

Keep in mind that some companies may have a cap on salaries, but that doesn't mean they can't sweeten the deal in other ways. If you get pushback on a higher salary, try negotiating for other benefits that could make the offer more appealing for you. Performance bonuses, signing bonuses, future pay raises, additional vacation days, company stock, retirement contributions, health benefits, flexible work hours — you get the idea.

Staying Cool When You Don't Know the Answer

To complete this chapter about answering tricky questions, let's talk about what to do when you just don't know the answer.

My interview coaching clients worry about this situation a lot. If you prepare and practice, I don't expect this to be a major problem.

But every once in a while, you might be thrown a curveball question, and there are techniques you can use to handle this stressful situation with grace.

Buy some time if you draw a blank

In some cases, all you need is a little more time to come up with an answer. It's perfectly okay to ask for a moment to think.

Many job seekers struggle with this idea because they feel like every instant of silence drags on forever in a job interview. The first instinct is to panic, making it even more difficult to come up with an answer. Or, nerves may lead you to blurt out your first thought and it's usually not a brilliant response.

However, most interviewers appreciate a thoughtful answer. It's natural to take a moment to think, especially if it's a complex question or a request for a specific example.

Take a deep breath and a moment to consider the question. If you need more time, try asking the interviewer to repeat or clarify the question. This can buy you a little more time to think, and the repetition or rephrasing may help inspire an answer.

You can also say something like this: "That's an excellent question. Let me just take a moment to think about the best example. . . ."

This answer helps reframe the silence as thoughtful and takes a little pressure off.

Reframe and redirect

If you just can't directly answer the question that's asked, even with time to think, you can try to connect it to a related topic that you *can* speak knowledgeably about.

This strategy is a little risky because, if you don't do it well, it can come across as dodging the question. However, in some situations, it can work well.

For example, if the interviewer asks you to share an example of a time when you disagreed with your manager and you draw a blank, you could try to reframe a related example of handling a disagreement with a coworker.

If you can think of a way to address the intent of the question, that can be enough to satisfy the interviewer.

Try the honest approach

In some cases, there is just no way to reframe. For example, you may be asked an unfamiliar technical question or about some experience you just don't have.

In these situations, honesty is the best policy. Acknowledge that you don't know the answer to that question. The key to recovering is to then assert your desire and ability to learn. You can do this by talking about your experience in similar areas or your general ability to get up to speed quickly.

For example, when talking about experience you don't have, you can say, "I haven't worked with that software in the past, but I have been reading up on it and am looking forward to learning more. It seems similar to XYZ Software, which I was quickly able to teach myself to use in my previous position."

TIP

Don't lie to try to impress anyone. The risk of getting busted is too high. You'll earn more respect with honesty.

Or, when confessing that you're not familiar with an industry development they ask about, you might say: "I'm not an expert on that particular deal, but I've seen some coverage in the press and would be interested in learning more, as I've worked on similar transactions in the pharmaceutical space and was able to get up to speed quickly on the complex regulatory issues."

Recover from a flub

If you blurt out a weak answer or are forced into saying "I don't know" and then recover from your brain freeze later, you can always circle back to the topic. Look for a natural opening or wait until the end of the interview and revisit the question.

For example, you could say, "Earlier, I was caught a bit off guard by your question about the bond market, but I wanted to come back to that and answer it more thoughtfully . . ."

You may also have an opportunity to bring it up at the end of the interview after you've asked at least a few questions. When the interviewer asks if you have more questions or anything else to add, you can raise any important topics that you flubbed and reiterate your sincere interest in the position.

If you don't recover your composure until after the interview, you can even use your thank-you note to circle back and revisit a missed opportunity — a question you didn't answer well or a key point you didn't make effectively.

Do not panic

Even if you flub a question completely, all is not lost unless you panic. I've had many clients who were able to recover from a terrible answer and go on to win the offer.

Try these techniques and do your best to come up with the best answer you can in the moment. But then *move on.*

Don't get distracted by mentally kicking yourself or replaying the terrible question over and over.

REMEMBER

It's just one question. It doesn't have to be a big deal. If you overthink it, you're likely to underperform during the rest of the interview or completely lose your confidence.

Don't over-apologize or be too self-deprecating. Focus on doing your best with the rest of the questions and ending the interview strong.

Even the greatest athletes make bad plays. Your overall impression is much more important than answering every question perfectly.

Often, these curveball questions are not the most important questions in the interview. They're random tangents or attempts to see whether you can think on your feet. If your answers to the core questions are strong, the positive impression will easily overshadow any judgment about your curveball prowess.

Chapter **13**

Asking Smart Questions

I n the normal course of events, after the interviewer is done peppering you with questions, it's your turn.

"What questions do you have for me?" they will ask.

That doesn't mean the interview is over and it's time to relax (not just yet!). Now you get to ask your own questions — and they had better be good.

Asking the right questions helps you gain valuable information about the opportunity. Even more importantly, your choice of questions tells the interviewer a lot about you and your fit for the job.

I'm going to help you understand the interviewer's perspective so that you can ask questions that present you as a capable, intelligent, engaged candidate — and move you one step closer to a job offer.

Recognizing the Power of Good Questions

You might logically assume that the point of asking questions is to find answers, to gather information. However, this is just one of your goals when it's your turn to be the interviewer. Naturally, you want to seize this opportunity to learn what you need to know to make a decision if offered the job.

But there's another important consideration that many job seekers miss. By asking thoughtful questions, you show your interest in the interviewer, the company, and the opportunity.

This can give you a real edge over other candidates.

REMEMBER

Research shows that first impressions and last impressions tend to be the most memorable. Because you typically ask your questions at the end of the interview, choosing good ones is more crucial than you might assume. Think about your favorite concerts: the artist always saves a showstopper for the final encore so you walk out feeling exhilarated (and ready to get your tickets to the next show).

It only takes a few minutes to prepare and ask smart questions, but they communicate a lot, including these aspects:

>> **Your overall interest in the opportunity:** Research shows that top-performing employees are highly engaged employees. Employers are looking for enthusiasm and drive. They want to hire someone who will be motivated to excel in the position and stick around long enough to make a difference.

>> **The factors you care most about:** They will assume that your questions reflect your values. What parts of the job excite you? What intrigues you? Where do you have concerns?

>> **How you operate:** When you ask thoughtful questions, you show that you cared enough to do your homework. You can truly see yourself in the role and want to learn as much as you can. You're proactive and curious, not someone who just sits back and hopes for the best.

The best questions do double duty: They help you assess the opportunity, and they make a positive impression on your interviewers.

Asking (at least two) questions

You should always ask at least two questions at the end of the interview.

That means preparing three or four in advance for every interview, just in case you need spares. Sometimes, one or more of your planned questions gets covered during the conversation and you don't want to be left with nothing to ask (or look silly by asking about something that's already been discussed).

I recommend listening closely during the interview to identify additional questions you can ask to follow up on topics of interest that come up. Often, these make for the best questions because they're authentic and organic and show that you were listening.

TIP

Interviewers hear the same questions over and over again from candidates. If you can come up with something a little bit different or personal, it can help you stand out. However, it's not necessary to steer clear of commonly asked questions. In many cases, they are asked a lot because they are about important topics.

Keep in mind that you will meet with multiple people for most opportunities and that you'll need questions for each interview. You should tailor your questions for each individual. For a screening interview with an HR representative, you'll likely want to focus on general questions about the position requirements and the company. With a hiring manager, you can delve into more specific questions about the day-to-day work and team structure. If you meet with the CEO or another senior exec, you might think more about the big picture and ask about company culture and goals.

TIP

I'll clue you in on a question type that's reusable, one you can ask in more than one interview — even at the same organization. Just focus on asking individuals for their personal opinion on an important aspect of the job or the company. You will likely hear different perspectives from different interviewers. For example: "What do you think are the biggest opportunities for the company this year?" or "What do you see as the team's greatest strengths?"

Keeping a closing statement in mind

Have you ever found yourself in an interview that went off track? Maybe the interviewer monopolized the conversation, or maybe they didn't ask good questions and just wanted to chitchat. Whatever the reason, you can tell that the interview is wrapping up and you never got a chance to talk about why you're a great fit for the job.

This is where a brief closing statement can make all the difference. Consider preparing a closing statement just in case you need one.

I mention this topic here because the most natural time to bring up your closing statement is when you're asking your questions. First, ask a few smart questions (I give you more specifics on how to do this shortly).

That's when they usually ask, "Any other questions?" or "Anything else?"

Rather than ask another question or offer a fumbling reply of "I guess that's it," you bring out your closing statement. A good closing statement is short and conversational but sums up your key selling points and your interest in the position.

For example: "Thank you. I think you've covered all of my questions. I have to say I'm even more excited about the opportunity after hearing more about the team and the exciting product improvements coming up this year. I feel like the role is a great fit for me, given my experience with similar product launches and my international marketing background. I'd be happy to answer any other questions that come up."

Preparing Informed Questions

Now it's time to get specific about what makes a smart question — and what types of questions to avoid!

Whether you're planning questions in advance or coming up with them on the fly, it's helpful to be familiar with the types of questions that have been consistent winners with interviewers. All these questions work well across various industries and job types.

Asking about the day-to-day work

It's important to learn as much as you can about how you would spend your days on the job. Sure, the job description provides a long list of responsibilities and requirements, but how does that translate into your daily routine?

This information helps you determine whether you would be happy in the role. You may also get some additional information about which skills are *most* important (so that you can be sure to mention them as strengths).

By asking about daily responsibilities, you also show that you are imagining yourself in the role and are excited to learn more.

Here are a few sample questions:

>> Can you tell me more about a typical day on the job?

>> How does the person in this role collaborate with the rest of the team?

>> Can you provide more information about the project management aspect of the job you mentioned?

Asking about priorities

You can go beyond the day-to-day work by asking about priorities. This strategy shows that you're thinking critically about where to focus and how you can make the most impact.

The answers may also help clarify the interviewer's expectations for the role.

Here are some sample questions about priorities:

>> What do you consider the top priorities for the role in the first six months?

>> What are some of the team's critical goals this year?

>> How will you measure success for this position?

Asking about challenges

You can also ask about challenges. These questions show that you're not the kind of person to shy away from demanding tasks and you're already thinking about how you can help.

The answers may also help you form a more realistic picture of the job, including the tough parts.

Sample questions about challenges include these:

>> What's the biggest challenge facing the team right now?

>> Are there any processes that you'd like to improve?

Asking about work culture

When you run out of questions about the work, you can always ask about the company or team culture. These questions show that you're seriously evaluating the work environment and considering how you'd fit in.

Many organizations like to talk about the work culture and the organization's values on the company website, but you'll form a much clearer perspective by asking a human being who works there.

You can learn more about company culture by asking these questions:

>> How would you describe the company culture?

>> What do you like about working with this team?

>> Which company values stand out for you?

Asking for their perspective

Here we have those reusable questions I mentioned. Ask for personal viewpoints on key aspects of the job or the work environment.

These questions can bring up "hidden" requirements that aren't clear from the job description! The answers can give you a crystal-clear picture of the job and whether you'd be happy in it.

By asking the interviewer for a personal opinion, you also show that you value their perspective and respect their expertise.

Helpful questions in this category include:

>> What do you think are the most important qualities to excel in this position?

>> What is your favorite part of the job?

>> What made you choose to join the team?

Read on to the end of this chapter for more sample questions you can borrow, adapt, or use for inspiration.

Avoiding the Wrong Questions

Keep in mind that there are some questions that are known to raise red flags with the interviewer. By asking one of these questions, you end the conversation by prompting concerns or negative feelings, which can sabotage your chances even if the rest of the interview went beautifully.

Don't lead with money or benefits

Of course, you want to know all about compensation and benefits (including time off, insurance options, and employee discounts). Ideally, the company rep is transparent from the beginning about compensation range and key benefits and you don't have to ask about them in an interview.

Whatever you do, don't lead with these questions in your first interview with someone new. Make sure your first questions demonstrate your interest in the position. If you zoom straight into quizzing them about time off or parking space, they may assume that's all you care about.

REMEMBER

You'll be more likely to negotiate a better deal if you wait to talk details until later in the process. Wait until they love you and you'll have more leverage to ask for some extra vacation days or whatever else you need.

Don't be negative

Steer clear of questions that focus on problems. You don't want to come across as a negative person. If there's an issue you're concerned about, wait until you've established rapport (and asked some positive questions) and then find a way to phrase your question in a neutral way.

If you've heard there's been turnover in the department, don't ask, "What's up with so many people quitting?" Be diplomatic and ask, "Why is the role open now?"

TIP

Avoid yes-or-no questions. It's hard to get a conversation going with a closed-ended question. Don't ask, "Does the company offer training?" Instead ask, "Can you tell me more about the training and development opportunities here?"

Don't put them on the spot

It's also hard to have a good conversation if you stump your interviewer with a question they can't answer! Don't ask a long, meandering question that in reality consists of multiple questions. You'll only confuse them. Don't ask broad, challenging questions about the future of the industry or the world. Don't get too personal. Definitely don't ask questions about controversial topics (politics, religion).

If you ask a question that puts them on the spot, you'll create an awkward moment instead of wowing them with your interest and intelligence.

Don't ask this question!

I want to single out one specific question that you should never ask. I'm salty about this one because I know that a lot of the advice floating around out there tells people to ask this question at the end of an interview.

That question is, "Is there anything about my background that you have concerns about?" There are also related ones, like this: "Is there any reason, based on what you know about me now, that you wouldn't offer me the job?"

These are prime examples of questions that put interviewers on the spot (as discussed in the previous section). I have spoken with many hiring managers about this question and never met one who recommended it.

So, why do these supposed experts recommend it? It's based on sales psychology: In sales, when you're meeting with a prospect and trying to close the deal, you want to counter their objections.

You might ask a question like this: "Do you have any concerns that would prevent you from buying?" Then the prospect brings up their objections and you can address them.

This tactic works in sales, but it doesn't work in job interviews. It only makes people uncomfortable and ends the interview on an awkward note.

First of all, most interviewers need some time to process after an interview. They typically review their notes, fill out a scorecard, and discuss with colleagues how you compare with other candidates. So, in that moment, when you haven't even finished the interview yet, it's too soon to come up with any kind of informed judgment. They are still processing everything you've told them.

Even if they have some concerns in mind, they're not going to be honest with you about them. Most people hate to deliver bad news. It's uncomfortable to critique someone you don't know. Interviewers don't want to deal with the effort or the awkwardness — even if they have clear opinions.

Also, in most companies, HR has trained managers to not give feedback to candidates in interviews. There are too many potential risk factors in terms of managers saying something inappropriate.

Finally, studies have concluded that the last part of an experience has a huge impact on how the overall experience is remembered. First impressions are critical, but last impressions are also vital. If an interview ends on a positive note, the overall memory of the experience is strong for the interviewer (and for you, too).

In other words, you don't want to end by asking the interviewer to think about all your shortcomings.

My Go-To Questions List

I've covered the best practices, the types of questions that are most effective, and some questions to avoid. You now have everything you need in order to come up with stellar questions to ask in any job interview.

But, as your interview coach, I also want to provide you with some additional sample questions that you can steal on those days when you're short on time or struggling for inspiration.

Questions to ask hiring managers

The hiring manager will know the most about the position and have the most say in the hiring decision. If you're hired, they will be your boss and have tremendous influence over your work life and future prospects. You can ask questions about the details of the job, the team dynamics, and how success will be evaluated.

>> Can you tell me more about the day-to-day responsibilities of this job?

>> What are your goals for this position over the next six months?

>> How do you see the responsibilities for this role evolving over the next six months to a year?

>> What would it take to exceed expectations in this role?

>> What would you say are the biggest challenges the team now faces?

>> Can you tell me more about the onboarding process?

>> What is the most critical skill to succeed in this position?

>> How would you describe the team's collaboration style?

>> Why is this position open?

>> How would you describe your management style?

>> Can you share information about common career paths in the department?

>> What advice would you give someone starting in this role?

Questions to ask any interviewer

Some questions are appropriate for just about anyone:

>> What makes this a great place to work?

>> What do you see as the most important skills for someone stepping into this role?

>> How does the company support career growth?

>> How would you describe the company culture?

>> How does the company prioritize diversity and inclusion?

>> What is the most interesting project you've worked on recently?

>> What are some of the most interesting changes you've seen at the company in the past year?

>> How does the company stay ahead of competitors?

>> What makes someone a good culture fit here?

4
Pulling Everything Together

Chapter **14**

Your Interview Success Plan

My plan for this book was to pack it full with all the information you would need to achieve job interviewing success. However, it's easy to feel over-whelmed by all this information if you don't have an actionable plan. This chapter outlines a plan you can use again and again, each time you have a new opportunity to interview.

First, I outline the step-by-step plan. Then I delve into detailed advice on how to execute it. I do talk about the importance of preparing your bullet points and prac-ticing in Chapter 2, but now I'd like to go deeper into how to do it properly.

As part of this process, I spend some time giving tactical advice on overcoming two of the most difficult interview challenges that come up at this stage:

» First is learning how to become better at "selling" yourself in interviews. I talk about why this is important in earlier chapters, but understanding the importance doesn't always translate into knowing *how* exactly to adjust your approach.

» Second, I offer guidance to help you reduce your interview anxiety so that nerves don't get in the way of making your best impression.

Read this chapter and follow the plan to prepare for your upcoming interview. You'll see references to other chapters for more information on topics covered elsewhere, which is perfect if you haven't had a chance to read all the previous chapters (or if you just need a refresher on anything).

Then, bookmark this chapter and return to it every time you schedule a new interview.

Creating Your Prep Strategy

Let's start with an overview of the steps that will get you ready to ace any interview, whether you're an experienced pro or totally new to interviewing.

If you haven't done so already, I recommend reading the previous chapters so that you have more context for executing your plan. However, if you're in a rush, look for the recommended chapters under each step and go straight to the information you need when you need it.

Step 1: Analyze the job description

The process begins with analyzing the new job description. In some cases, if you're targeting one type of role consistently in your job search, this will be a quick review to note minor differences between the new role and the opportunities you've interviewed for previously.

There are always some variations. Perhaps the required skills won't change much, but you'll see that some positions emphasize different aspects of the job or specific culture-fit qualities. Often these differences provide clues to the hiring manager's priorities and likely interview questions. For example, if you notice multiple references to communication skills, you can plan ways to emphasize communication as one of your strengths and prepare examples to demonstrate your abilities.

REMEMBER

See Chapter 4 for step-by-step instructions to help you analyze the job description and identify where you're a great fit and where there are potential gaps. This way, you'll be prepared to highlight your most relevant strengths, and you'll be ready if someone asks a tough question about an area that can be perceived as a weakness.

This particular step is even more important if you're exploring multiple career paths and types of opportunities. This is a common scenario for many new graduates, anyone considering a career change, and those looking to take on a bigger role with more responsibility.

Some people like to feel interview-ready before they start applying for jobs. They like the idea of knowing that they'll feel confident saying yes as soon as they receive that first call to come in for an interview.

If you like to plan ahead, search for a job description that's similar to the one you're seeking, even if you're not yet ready to apply. Look for similarities in the requirements and job duties — as well as the industry or type of company. This analysis will help you identify which questions/topics to focus on in your preparation.

Then, once you get that call, you'll be ready to roll, with maybe a few additional topics to consider based on the actual job description.

Step 2: Research the company

I also recommend researching the company early in your preparation, especially if you aren't familiar with the organization and/or the industry. This research will help you prepare a relevant reply to the question "Why do you want to work here?" (It's a question you'll hear in just about every interview.)

Your research may also identify other important questions that are likely to come up. For example, if you're interviewing for a job in a different industry, you're sure to get questions about your knowledge of that field and about why you're interested in making a change. If you're interviewing with an organization that's quite different from your previous employers (think startup versus large company, nonprofit versus public corporation, creative versus buttoned-up), you'll likely be asked about your ability to thrive in the new environment.

This company research is also key in evaluating whether you'd enjoy working for the organization.

See Chapter 4 for tips on conducting company research. You'll also find advice on researching the industry and your future interviewers, which can also be helpful.

Step 3: Anticipate questions

Based on your research, you'll be able to anticipate the majority of the interview questions. As the expression goes, forewarned is forearmed. You can prepare for the trickiest questions and avoid getting caught off-guard.

As I discuss in Part 3 of this book, many interview questions are predictable for those of us who have done our homework. A core set of questions is common in job interviews regardless of industry, level, or job type.

I cover these questions and how to prepare for them in the following chapters:

>> **Chapter 6:** "Tell Me About Yourself"

>> **Chapter 7:** "Why Do You Want to Work Here?"

>> **Chapter 8:** "What Are Your Strengths and Weaknesses?"

>> **Chapter 9:** "Where Do You See Yourself in Five Years?"

>> **Chapter 10:** "Why Are You Looking for a New Role Now?"

>> **Chapter 11:** Mastering Behavioral Questions

You'll be able to anticipate additional questions based on the job description and your background. Consider the following types of questions:

>> **Job-specific questions:** You can expect some questions based on your ability to perform the essential duties of the job. In most cases, the interviewer will want to know about your experience in the tasks required.

For example, in an interview for a technical project manager position, they might ask a behavioral question like this: "Tell me about the most challenging project you managed in your previous role."

They could also ask a more general question about your experience. For example, "Can you give me an overview of your experience in managing technical projects?"

Usually, the most important job duties are listed first in the job description section headed Responsibilities, Duties, About the Role, or similar wording. Review these bullet points and prepare how to describe your experience in each aspect of the job (along with examples).

TIP

One way to prepare is to ask yourself what questions you yourself would ask to determine whether a candidate would be able to perform these duties well.

If you lack direct experience in any key job responsibilities, prepare to talk about related experience and your ability to learn quickly on the job. In some cases, lack of direct experience isn't a dealbreaker. There's a learning curve for every job, and some organizations prefer to train you to do it "their way."

REMEMBER

If you've made it to the interview stage, they like your overall background and may be willing to overlook lack of experience if you demonstrate drive and teachability.

There will likely be some overlap between job-related questions and technical questions (see the following bullet point), as most roles have technical requirements.

>> **Technical questions:** Most interviewers will want to evaluate your technical skills and knowledge. For highly technical roles, answering these questions convincingly is critical. In fact, you may be asked to complete a technical assessment or a take-home project to demonstrate your technical abilities.

The job description typically lists the technical requirements, including knowledge of certain software programs (whether basic or advanced) and the ability to perform specific tasks using those programs. You can expect to be asked about your proficiency, whether via a general question ("Tell me about your experience using Excel") or a behavioral question ("Tell me about a complex financial model you created using Excel").

For developer and coding jobs, candidates will eventually be asked to complete a coding interview. This might be before or after a fit interview to discuss overall qualifications. In a coding interview, the interviewer assigns you a coding challenge and you write the code in real-time — generally, using a physical whiteboard (for most in-person interviews) or a shared online tool (for video and phone interviews).

During coding interviews, you must also be prepared to talk through your solution and answer questions about your choices. As with other interviews, practice is the key in preparing for coding interviews. Some platforms allow you to practice solving coding problems in a wide variety of programming languages. The following practice tools can be useful if you're new to coding interviews:

- **LeetCode** (https://leetcode.com) provides lessons and coding interview simulations using questions commonly used by top technology companies. You can access some articles and practice questions for free; others require a premium membership.

- **HackerRank** (www.hackerrank.com/dashboard) also offers practice problems as well as coding contests and skill certifications. Some recruiters use HackerRank for assessing candidates during the interview process.

>> **Tricky questions:** Be prepared for questions about any potential red flags in your background. For example, if you have a recent resume gap, you will almost certainly be asked about it. If you have short-term stints at past jobs (less than a year), interviewers like to inquire to ensure that, if hired, you're not a job-hopper or likely to leave abruptly. If you're making a career change or an unusual career move (for example, interviewing for a more junior position than your previous one), your interviewers will want to learn more about your motivations and transferable skills.

In Chapter 12, you can learn more about why interviewers ask these red flag questions and how you can answer in a way that neutralizes their concerns.

You can also read about how to answer other tricky questions in Chapter 12 — including compensation questions and curveball questions that are difficult to prepare for ("If you could have any superpower, what would it be? What is your spirit animal and why?").

Step 4: Outline your bullet points

Once you have your list of likely questions, it's time to get busy outlining your bullet points for each answer. In some cases, you may already feel confident about how to respond and you won't need to prepare speaking points. For example, if you're a tech expert, you may already feel comfortable discussing your recent projects with a fellow developer. If the job is a perfect fit with your career goals, you may not need to prepare much for answering "Why are you interested in this opportunity?"

However, I highly recommend outlining bullet points for any complex or tricky questions. I don't mean scripting your answer, but simply outlining the key points you want to make to ensure that you don't sell yourself short or, even worse, go blank or blurt out the wrong thing.

In Part 3 of this book, I review best practices for answering the most common interview questions. These chapters can help you outline strong answers and stand out from the competition. I provide models to organize your ideas into concise answers and give you sample answers for inspiration.

You could debate which questions are tricky — it may vary a lot based on your background. However, I recommend that everyone outline bullet points for the following questions:

>> **Tell me about yourself (see Chapter 6):** This is the first question in many job interviews, and you want to start strong. It can be a difficult question because it basically requires an elevator pitch: a concise overview of your career story so far.

Unprepared candidates fall into the trap of rambling until the interviewer tunes out. Others rush through generalities and miss out on the chance to make a powerful first impression.

My 3-part model will help you organize your story into a 1- to 2-minute overview that emphasizes your most relevant qualifications.

» **What are your greatest strengths/Why should we hire you? (see Chapter 8):** You'll get some variation of this question in most interviews, and you should view it as a valuable opportunity to sell your fit for the role. Most job seekers are not used to "bragging" about their strengths, so preparing bullet points is the key to being able to put your best self forward in an authentic way.

My approach to such questions, as spelled out in Chapter 8, helps you identify your most compelling strengths and sketch out proof points to add credibility.

» **What is your greatest weakness? (see Chapter 8):** Questions about weaknesses are still pretty common out there (if a bit less so than in the past). Weakness questions are awkward and can throw you off your game, so I recommend that everyone prepare an answer in advance.

My 3-part model will help you describe a weakness in a way that doesn't raise red flags with interviewers.

» **Why do you want to work here? (see Chapter 7):** This question comes up in every interview. To make an impression, you must communicate your interest in the organization as well as the day-to-day work of the role. Variations include "Why are you interested in this opportunity?" and "Why do you think this role is a good fit?"

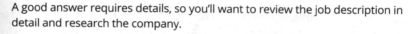

A good answer requires details, so you'll want to review the job description in detail and research the company.

TIP

» **Behavioral questions (see Chapter 11):** Finally, I recommend that every job seeker prepare a set of at least three to five greatest-hits stories that they can use to respond to behavioral questions ("Tell me about a time . . .").

Start with the examples that illustrate your most impressive accomplishments. These will be versatile and can be reused for answering various types of behavioral questions. Then you can expand your stories as needed based on the job description. For example, if an opportunity calls for process improvement as a key competency and none of your existing stories focuses on that, outline a new story to add to the collection.

You can use the STAR format to outline these stories and keep them concise and focused. See Chapter 11 for more on STAR, including instructions and examples.

REMEMBER

Step 5: Practice round 1

When it's time to start practicing, you're unlikely to remember all those great bullet points if you don't practice them out loud.

The first time through, it's fine to keep your bullet points in front of you and reference them as needed. This initial run-through is an important step in seeing how your answers flow and starting the process of committing them to memory (not word for word, but rather the general shape of the answers).

The best way to do this is in the form of a practice interview that's as similar to a real interview as possible. For example, the Big Interview practice tool features hundreds of mock interviews with question sets customized for various jobs, industries, and experience levels. Each set includes 8 to 12 interview questions with the ability to pause, skip ahead, and try again as many times as you like. As mentioned in the introduction to this book, I am offering a free Big Interview trial for buyers of this book; you can give it a try at `https://www.dummies.com/go/bigInterview/`.

TIP

I recommend eventually recording your practice answers. However, you don't have to record in round 1 if you're not ready yet. Some people prefer to ease into it.

Another option is to put together a list of your anticipated questions and ask a friend to play the role of interviewer so that you can practice out loud. Finally, in a pinch, you can just practice out loud on your own. It won't feel as realistic, but it will still be beneficial in developing a comfort level with delivering your answers.

In the second half of this chapter, you'll find more tips for making the most of your practice interviews.

Step 6: Refine and adjust

If you find yourself stumbling over certain phrasings or transitions when you practice the first time, make notes on where adjustments are needed. Keep in mind that you will probably feel awkward practicing out loud the first time — even if your answers are perfect.

If your answer feels too long and rambling, you can pare them down. If your wording feels too stiff or scripted, you can edit your language.

REMEMBER

You don't talk about yourself in quite this way in any other interactions. It probably won't flow naturally at first. That's why practice is important. If you can find the right flow during practice, you'll feel and sound more confident in your actual interviews.

Step 7: Hold a dress rehearsal

After you've made your adjustments and feel good about your answers, practice again. Keep practicing until your answers flow naturally.

Just before your interview, plan a dress rehearsal. If possible, dress for the interview and record yourself. This will refresh your memory if it's been a while since your last practice. You'll warm up your memory, voice, and body language. You may also identify some answers that need a bit more refinement or practice.

If you're preparing for a video interview, your dress rehearsal can also be a tech check to make sure your setup, lighting, background, and connection speed are perfect.

REMEMBER

See Chapter 3 for my guide to acing video interviews.

TIP

If you'll be interviewing in person, make sure you have your wardrobe ready, you have directions to the interview location, and you have set your alarm.

Step 8: Step up on interview day

If you've prepared well, you won't have a lot to worry about on interview day. Dress your best (see Chapter 15 for more on that topic), schedule your day to ensure that you can get to your interview (or connect via video conference) on time.

If you're not doing your dress rehearsal on interview day, take the time to at least run through an answer or two out loud immediately before the interview. This warm-up will help you shift into interview mode.

TIP

If you get nervous, try one of the breathing exercises or other relaxation tips in the last part of this chapter.

Keep your bullet points handy so that you can read them one last time as you're waiting for the interview to begin.

Then let your training and preparation take over.

Step 9: Take a moment for post-interview analysis

As soon as possible after the interview, jot down what questions were asked and a few notes about what went well and any areas for improvement.

In the immediate aftermath of the interview, you probably won't want to do this. You'll be riding an adrenaline high or just feeling eager to take a break from thinking about interview questions. However, capturing a few notes can help you in perfecting your approach for next time (whether it's the next round for this opportunity or a different job altogether).

Then reward yourself for putting in the work and completing the interview. You've done everything within your power to ace it.

Now enjoy an expensive coffee, a walk in the park, or whatever else gives your brain a break and your spirits a lift for a few minutes at least.

Step 10: Follow up

Don't forget to follow up! See Chapter 2 for advice on thank-you notes and how to stay connected after the interview.

Bonus step: Refresh the plan

After you've implemented the plan once, future interview prep will be much easier. You will already have advanced knowledge on how to interview, though you may need to refresh your memory on certain topics if it's been a while.

You have already outlined bullet points for many of the key questions. However, it pays to start with Step 1 each time, analyzing what's different about the new opportunity so that you can customize the following steps accordingly.

You will always need to prepare a new answer for "Why do you want to work here?" You will anticipate additional questions based on the various job requirements. You may need to customize existing bullet points to highlight different strengths.

If you return to the plan after a year or more, that probably means you have new job experience and/or education to incorporate into your speaking points for "Tell me about yourself" and your behavioral stories.

If you prepare well the first time, it should all come back to you pretty quickly. Much of the work on outlining answers will be done and you'll have developed a comfort level with talking about these topics in interview mode.

Outlining Your Key Speaking Points

As you dive into outlining your answers, keep in mind some key best practices. These will help you make the most of your prep time and develop answers that truly resonate.

You're not writing an essay here — think of the outlining process as creating a checklist of the topics you want to cover in each answer.

Focusing on "selling" yourself

In many chapters of this book, I preach the importance of actively promoting your strengths and accomplishments in job interviews. You can't count on interviewers to see your best qualities — you must show them.

I also frequently mention that promoting personal strengths and accomplishments is one of the biggest challenges for my coaching clients. Even the most accomplished have trouble with it.

So now you know it's important, but that doesn't mean you'll magically do it.

It's at this stage in the interview preparation process that you need to put it into practice. If it doesn't come naturally, I have some techniques to help you proactively turn up the volume on your accomplishments in your interviews.

It can be useful to approach this task as a marketing challenge. Amusingly enough, some of my most modest clients have been marketing executives who were brilliant at marketing but struggled with applying this knowledge to promote themselves.

Completing the necessary market analysis

To approach your interview like a marketer, you must start with market research. Ask yourself the following questions:

>> Who is your target audience (hiring manager)?

>> What are they looking for (priorities for the position)?

>> How can your product (you) solve their problem(s) and/or improve their life?

>> How do you fit their top requirements for the position?

>> What sets you apart from the competition?

To position yourself well for the role, you must understand what they care about most.

For detailed advice on how to do this kind of market analysis effectively, see the section on evaluating your fit in Chapter 4.

Pitching your product

Based on the analysis you've carried out, you should be able to identify your key selling points for the job. However, you may still struggle with how to translate them into compelling bullet points.

Let's look at some common questions that provide useful openings for discussing your strengths and successes.

>> **Tell Me About Yourself questions:** Most interviews open with this question or a variation thereof. (Walk me through your resume/background, and so on.) This is an opportunity for you to start strong and steer the interview discussion toward your key experience and areas of strength.

   See Chapter 6 for tips on crafting an informative answer that incorporates your selling points.

>> **Strengths questions:** Any question about your strengths is an invitation to share your selling points. Variations on "the strengths question" include these:

   ● Why would you be a good fit?

   ● Why should we hire you?

   ● What makes you stand out from other candidates?

   Chapter 7 can help you identify your key strengths and outline a concise but impressive answer.

>> **Behavioral questions:** Most interviews include some behavioral questions (any questions that start with "Tell me about a time . . ." or otherwise prompt you for specific examples from your past).

   I work with all my coaching clients to prepare at least three to five strong stories that showcase their achievements and competencies.

   I always start by having them identify their greatest-hits stories and using the STAR format to outline the key details.

   Your greatest-hits stories are perfect opportunities to "brag" about your biggest accomplishments and most glowing feedback.

REMEMBER

   See Chapter 11 for step-by-step guidance on writing your own greatest-hits stories.

   Your stories can then be used for answering behavioral questions, but they can also be woven into the conversion in other ways. For example, if the interviewer asks what you did in your last role, you'll have success stories ready to illustrate your experience.

You can't count on interviewers to ask the right questions. However, rest assured that they want to hear about what you can do. Don't hold back.

Using self-promotion hacks for the modest and shy

If you continue to struggle with crafting selling points that feel both authentic and comfortable, I have some tricks you can use:

>> **Stick with the facts.** Rather than state an opinion about yourself (which can feel awkward for modest types), present objective facts that demonstrate your point.

Rather than say

I'm a very strong writer

try this:

I've been published by Publications X and Z and I was excited to be selected for Writing Prize ABC during my senior year.

>> **Quote somebody else.** Sometimes it can feel less "braggy" to quote someone else's positive opinion of you. In fact, this approach can lend additional credibility, even if you're perfectly okay with tooting your own horn.

How would your manager, coworkers, or clients describe your strengths? Just don't quote your mom. (We all know she's biased.)

Rather than say

I'm a very effective project manager.

try this:

I was honored when my manager told me that I'm the most efficient project manager on the team. In fact, the CEO specifically requested me to lead our highest-profile client engagement this quarter.

>> **Push yourself out of your comfort zone.** Give yourself permission to brag. Try writing your bullet points as if you were a brazen self-promoter. Purposefully be as over-the-top as possible.

You can always dial it back if the results feel obnoxious. However, I have seen many clients benefit from forcefully pushing through their modesty.

TIP

This approach will also serve you well in preparing for future performance reviews and discussions about raises and promotions.

>> **Solicit feedback from a trusted (and objective) advisor.** How do you know if you're selling yourself properly? You may find it difficult to be objective about whether you're finding the right balance between confident and modest.

For help with this, look for an advisor with some knowledge of the interviewing process. (Some of your friends and family members likely have experience interviewing candidates.) Ideally, you also want someone who can maintain some objectivity about you. Often, a parent or significant other will have trouble with this aspect. You need feedback that's both candid and constructive.

Validation is a powerful thing. My coaching clients often just need to hear, "No, that doesn't sound like bragging" or "Yes, that's a convincing example/detail." They can stop second-guessing themselves and go into the next interview with confidence.

REMEMBER

Candidates worry too much about coming across as arrogant. I would argue that if you're worried about sounding arrogant, you aren't in danger of actually crossing that line. I've had only a few coaching clients whom I advised on toning down their self-promotion. Every other client has benefited from turning up the volume on their accomplishments.

Working on your bullet points

Now it's time for a lesson on how to write effective bullet points. Read on.

Prepare an outline, not a script

I mention this point earlier in this book, but it bears repeating:

Do outline your key ideas in an order that flows logically.

Don't write a script and memorize it.

If you try to force yourself into an exact script, it's a lot more work and you'll sound rehearsed.

The process of writing your bullet points offers many benefits:

>> Writing down your thoughts helps you focus them.

>> When you write the words and then read them back and then speak them out loud, they're more likely to stick in your memory.

>> When you capture your ideas in writing, you can easily revisit, edit, and customize for future interviews.

Keep it concise

I mention this point elsewhere, but your interviewers have short attention spans. You must keep your answers focused and concise if you want to engage them.

If you could spend all day with interviewers who have endless patience and interest, you could let the conversation flow naturally. However, the weird and time-sensitive nature of the job interview makes bullet points the best format.

I'm not saying this is easy. Even professional writers struggle with being concise. It's much easier to write three long, stream-of-conscience paragraphs than to craft a single concise one. Trust me: I just deleted several sentences from this section because my first rough draft rambled and repeated.

TIP

You can use a rough draft approach when it comes to formulating your bullet points. Set a timer and then jot down the list of topics you want to cover with whatever level of detail feels right. If writing isn't a strength, try speaking your rough draft out loud. Record it and then transcribe it (Zoom has a transcription option) or just play it back and jot down what you hear.

In my practice interviews with my coaching clients, I often record their answers while also jotting down the key points of what I'm hearing. Then I give them feedback on what worked well, what I would add to make it stronger, and where it dragged on or lacked focus. This helps you create a refined set of bullet points.

Once you have your thoughts on paper, you can expand, cut, and rearrange.

WARNING

I know it's tempting but be cautious about using ChatGPT to help you outline your bullet points: I have experimented with it and found the results lacking. Usually, I get a lot of generic fluff that sounds like a robot wrote it. I've also seen a lot of accuracy issues. For example, ChatGPT tried to write a STAR story about a product design challenge and got most of the details wrong about what a product designer does.

That said, if you know how to write good prompts, ChatGPT can help you construct a rough draft if you get stuck. Just make sure you review and edit it so that your draft is accurate *and* sounds human.

Speak powerful language

The words you use make a big difference in how you're perceived. Positive, confident language presents you as a more capable and engaging candidate.

That doesn't mean you should try to wow them with obscure vocabulary. This isn't an eighth grade book report.

You should always use conversational, accessible language in your interview answers. However, think about where you can incorporate words that show your confidence, enthusiasm, and initiative. This is particularly important when interviewing for senior-level positions and roles that require advanced communication skills.

If you feel that your answers fall a bit flat, consider the following ideas:

>> Can you use more *I* and *we* statements with action words to show your accomplishments?

- "We developed the new approach . . ."
- "I solved the problem . . ."
- "We increased efficiency . . ."

>> Can you incorporate more enthusiastic language to show that you enjoy what you do and are a pleasure to work with?

- "I love a fast-paced environment . . ."
- "I learned so much on this project . . ."
- "I was really proud of my team's work on that . . ."

>> Can you cut negative or self-deprecating language? The following phrases, for example, should never show up in your bullet points:

- "It turned out okay, I guess . . ."
- "I think I'm pretty pleasant to work with . . ."
- "I struggle with time management sometimes . . ."

TIP

Don't be shy about featuring your results in your bullet points. Take inspiration from resume writing and spell out how you delivered. Include result numbers, positive feedback, lessons learned, and other results-focused language (such as *innovative, award-winning, under-budget,* and *on deadline*).

This is particularly important in your behavioral examples. Remember that the *R* in STAR stands for *results*.

Save time by using templates

If you read the chapters in Part 3, you'll see that I've developed helpful models for outlining strong answers to the toughest questions. These models (see the list below) will save you time and headaches by providing structure and rules for what to include (and what to avoid):

>> STAR model for behavioral examples (Chapter 11)

>> 3-part model for Tell me about yourself (Chapter 6)

>> Strength/proof point model for selling your strengths (Chapter 8)

>> Weakness/improvement model for describing a weakness (Chapter 8)

>> Address + redirect model for answering tricky questions (Chapter 12)

In Big Interview, we have Answer Builder tools to guide you through using these models to outline your bullet points. However, you can also do it in a Google doc, your Notes app, or with a pen and paper.

TIP

Once you have used a model to outline an answer, you can then use that document as a template for future answers. This makes it easier to customize answers for different interviews and to make additions and improvements in the future.

Practicing Like a Pro

Once again, it's important not to skip the practice step.

Just as you would practice for an important speech or a big performance, you must practice for your interview.

Most people have heard this advice, but my experience shows that few candidates actually put time into effective practice.

To make sure you can deliver your bullet points in a compelling and natural way, you'll need to speak those selling points out loud — first with your notes at hand and eventually without them.

I can't emphasize the value of practice enough, though I know that the process of practicing can feel awkward.

In my early days of interview coaching, I noticed that my clients did not practice. I didn't understand what the holdup was. They knew it would help them, and they wanted to improve, but they still didn't practice on their own.

They waited until our sessions because they felt awkward trying to practice with a friend or even in the mirror. This is one of the reasons I chose to develop the online Big Interview practice tool for them. (Okay, I hired smart developers to build the tool for me. I just want to be clear about the *we* and the *I*.) It allows users to easily practice at home by themselves and work out the kinks *before* they walk into an interview.

If you prefer to practice with a friend, that can also be very effective in improving your delivery and building confidence.

As you practice, you'll likely make tweaks to the content and how you deliver it. Your answers should come out a little bit differently each time, but still cover the selling points that you've identified as most important in your bullet points.

Practice will also make you more comfortable with making positive statements about yourself out loud and help you own your strengths in your own voice.

Finally, practice will make it easier to remember what you want to say — even if your nerves act up when the pressure is on in the interview.

Starting practice NOW — just do it!

Start practicing before you feel ready. Don't expect that you'll perform flawlessly the first time. The first practice round is part of the process of learning your part and finding your voice.

You don't have to have perfect hair or the right outfit or your answers memorized. You don't have to record yourself or ask anyone else for feedback until you're ready.

However, the sooner you start practicing, the faster you'll become comfortable with Interview mode.

Assessing how you come across on camera

When you're ready, I recommend recording yourself. (Lots of tools — Zoom and Google Meet, to name just two — can help with that task.) You can even limit yourself to recording just the audio if you're camera shy.

The goal is to gather feedback to help you improve. Even if you've had a chance to look at only a few chapters in this book, you should know enough to be able to spot mistakes you're making if you play back the recording.

In particular, recording video will help you evaluate and refine your delivery and your nonverbal communications. See Chapter 15 for more on improving your presentation — including eye contact, body language, filler words, speaking style, and more.

I know it's hard to evaluate yourself objectively, so consider sharing the recording with a coach or trusted friend for feedback if you need input on how you're coming across.

Eliminating nervous habits

Practice, even without recording yourself, will help you smooth out nervous habits and refine your nonverbal communications. Over the years, I've found that practice is the best cure for common issues like the excessive use of *um*, a lack of eye contact, talking too fast, and fidgeting.

Again, see Chapter 15 for help in identifying if nervous habits are detracting from your overall presentation, along with tips on how to control any distracting behaviors.

Another way to eliminate nervous habits is through reducing your anxiety, which I cover in the next section of this chapter.

Reducing Interview Anxiety

It's natural to get nervous before a job interview. Someone is about to scrutinize your appearance, mannerisms, what you say, and how you say it.

And the stakes are high. If they like you, it can mean a job offer, a sweet salary, and maybe even the corner office. It could change your life. No pressure.

Even the most confident candidates tend to feel a little anxiety, especially when they *really* want the job.

Some people truly struggle. Their nerves sabotage their performance on interview day and limit their career opportunities. When you're nervous, you're more likely to go blank or blurt out the wrong thing. Anxiety also prompts nervous habits like fidgeting, talking too fast, and saying *um* and *uh* too much.

Luckily, certain techniques can help you control your anxiety before and during job interviews — allowing you to put your best self forward and making the whole experience much less painful.

Recognizing what's scary about a job interview

High stakes can certainly lead to anxiety. However, that's not the only issue for many people.

Another fear factor in a job interview is that someone else is in control. You don't know what your interviewer will ask or how they will treat you. You don't know whether you'll be facing a friendly professional or a demanding grump. For many (especially Type A overachievers), the lack of control can lead to additional stress and anxiety.

Finally, an interview pushes you out of your comfort zone. It's a different kind of conversation than you're used to.

You'll be called upon to promote yourself, which most people don't do well. You're expected to "just be yourself," as they say, but you're also under pressure to convey all your best qualities while simultaneously being likable and engaging — all within about 30 minutes spent with a total stranger. It's a lot to think about.

TIP

If you haven't interviewed much in the past, or if it's been a while, being out of practice can make it even more difficult.

Preventing your nerves from becoming a problem

Some people are fortunate enough to be naturally calm under pressure, or at least better able to manage their nerves and "fake it until they make it."

For others, interview anxiety can lead to serious interview mistakes and inadvertently raising red flags with the interviewer. In the worst-case scenario, the interviewer will be so distracted by your nervous habits that they won't even remember your strengths and qualifications.

I can't promise to completely eliminate your interview jitters. In fact, it's probably a good thing to be a little bit nervous — that small burst of adrenaline can keep you at the top of your game.

However, I can give you some proven techniques to combat feelings of stress, awkwardness, helplessness, and anxiety.

Curing interview anxiety

It all starts with the motto that any Boy Scout learns early: Be prepared.

Preparation is the best way to overcome interview nerves. If you do your homework, preparation will lead to more confidence — and confidence puts you in command. Confidence can also help you channel your nervous energy into a positive force.

It's similar to the way an athlete trains to be in peak condition on the day of the big game. The more you prepare and practice, the more confident you'll feel when your career aspirations are on the line in the job interview.

This confidence will help you eliminate distracting nervous habits like repeatedly saying the words *um* and *uh*, fidgeting, rambling, and making dodgy eye contact. You will feel more in command of your answers and your body language.

I have seen it hundreds of times: An interview coaching client comes in for a first session and that initial practice interview is a mess. It's all shifty eye contact, slouching, fidgeting, and stumbling over words.

Then, magically, after a session or two and some homework, I see a transformation. There's no magic trick to it. It's a result of working on their interview approach and then practicing out loud until they start to feel natural in Interview mode.

REMEMBER

Interview mode takes place when you shift into that version of you that's irresistible to employers. It's not a fake persona; it's just a more polished and confident and professional version of you, a version that isn't afraid to talk about how great you are.

So, how can you prepare in a way that empowers you and helps you minimize interview anxiety? Read on for my advice.

Practice

Practice is the most important thing you can do to reduce anxiety and nervous habits. In the previous section of this chapter, I talk about the most effective way to practice for job interviews, so I won't rehash that here. However, it's worth reiterating the value of practice in developing more interview confidence.

REMEMBER

With practice, you grow accustomed to talking about yourself out loud in Interview mode so that it doesn't feel weird on interview day.

Accentuate the positive

The self-help gurus are right: It pays to think positive, at least when it comes to job interviews. The job search can be brutal and it's easy to become cynical — even the best candidates face repeated rejection and rude behavior.

But insecurity and negativity can truly hurt you. It can prevent you from seeing your key selling points clearly and expressing them well in your interview.

Prepare and practice with the attitude that you can ace this interview. Fake it until you make it — it's a cliche, but it's based in truth.

Many studies have shown that acting a certain way can lead to your brain rehearsing a new way of thinking — you can change your own thinking and the perceptions of others. Putting a smile on your face can make you feel happier — and in turn, others are likely to respond more positively.

Psych yourself up

On interview day, make time to get yourself into the right frame of mind.

First, don't skip dress rehearsal. Even if you've practiced a lot and feel pretty good, do a run-through of a practice set right before your interview. It's a good way to get your brain, voice, and body language into Interview mode.

Try relaxation and confidence-boosting techniques

If you're still feeling jittery, you can apply additional techniques that can help you calm those nerves — before or during the interview.

Different techniques work for different people. These are some of the most effective:

>> **Breathing:** There are effective anxiety-reducing breathing techniques that help you center yourself before the interview. The simplest is just to sit, close your eyes, and complete a series of deep breaths, taking at least a few seconds for the inhale and a few for the exhale.

If you make a habit of doing this breathing exercise regularly, you can train your body to respond quickly to it. Then, once you're in the interview, a pause and a simple deep breath can do a lot to calm jitters or a sense of panic.

The science behind this strategy is that anxiety leads to quick, shallow breathing, which can affect your body language and your voice. Sometimes, people forget how important it is to just stop and slow down their breathing.

>> **Visualization:** Some people swear by the power of visualization, and I know it has helped me in some stressful situations.

There are a few ways to use visualization techniques to reduce interview anxiety. First, a simple calming visualization can be useful. Close your eyes and imagine yourself relaxing on the beach — or anywhere else that you feel calm and serene. Try your best to imagine that cool breeze in your hair and feel your body relaxing.

It may also calm your anxiety to visualize a successful interview. Picture yourself in the interview room making a fantastic impression. Most importantly, try to vividly imagine yourself feeling a strong sense of positive confidence as you nail it in your imaginary interview.

Visualize your interviewer smiling and nodding. You can even try to picture getting the job offer and imagine how excited and proud you feel in that moment.

TIP

You'll get the best results if you combine the visual with the strong positive feeling and associate the two. It's a fast and easy way to focus your thoughts and feel a burst of confidence.

>> **Power posing:** There has been some debate about Amy Cuddy's work on what she calls *power posing*. Her theory is that posing like a superhero for two minutes can boost your confidence and reduce your stress, literally changing your body chemistry.

Some researchers have disputed the idea, but in my anecdotal experience, power posing has been useful for some of my clients before a job interview.

I've tried it myself to get amped up before speaking to a large group. In my opinion, it's worth a try if you're still feeling nervous as the interview approaches.

You can go with Wonder Woman or Superman and simply stand tall and strong with hands on hips and legs confidently slightly apart for a moment or two and feel the power. Just remember to do your posing in private before the interview — not during.

>> **Pacing yourself:** Once the interview begins, if you feel your heart start racing and find yourself stumbling over your words, it's likely that your anxiety has taken over and you're talking too fast.

Nerves tend to make you speed up your mannerisms as well as your speech. They can also lead to the temptation to speak before you consider the question properly.

Slow down and don't be afraid of the pause. If you race to fill every silence, you're likely to blurt out something you'll regret.

TIP

Avoid self-conscious thoughts about pausing. Interviewers expect you to pause and think before answering complex questions.

If your pause starts to feel awkward, it's okay to say something like this: "That's a great question. I just need a moment to decide on the best example to share."

Putting it into perspective: No matter how desperately you want the job, try to remember that it's just one opportunity. Your entire future is not dependent on landing this particular job.

You don't even know that much about the position yet. Sure, it looks good on paper, but it's not your only option.

You're there because they liked your résumé and/or the impression you made in the earlier interview round.

No matter what happens, this interview will be a learning experience that will make you a better job candidate and a savvier professional in the long run.

Focus on projecting confidence and putting all that preparation to use.

REMEMBER

Preparing for curveballs

If your nerves are due to fear of the unknown, it can help to have a game plan for dealing with unexpected questions — just in case you get a tricky one. Let's talk briefly about what to do when you just don't know the answer to a question.

My interview coaching clients worry about this situation a lot. If you prepare and practice, it won't happen often.

But every once in a while, you might be asked a curveball question, and you can use certain techniques to handle the situation with grace.

This section presents some good approaches for dealing with a question that stumps you. Pick the ones that work best for your circumstances and the question at hand.

Buying some time

In some cases, you can come up with an answer with just a little bit of time to think. It's perfectly okay to ask for a moment.

Many job seekers struggle with this notion because they feel that every instant of silence drags on forever in a job interview. The instinct is to blurt something out — or panic, making it even more difficult to come up with an answer.

However, most interviewers appreciate a thoughtful answer.

REMEMBER

It's natural to take a moment to think, especially if you're answering a complex question or fielding a request for a specific example.

Try taking a deep breath and waiting a moment to consider the question. If you're still drawing a blank, ask the interviewer to repeat or clarify the question.

This can buy you another few beats to think — and the repetition or rephrasing may help inspire an answer.

You can also say something like this: "That's a great question. Let me just take a moment to think about the best example."

This helps reframe the silence as thoughtful and takes some of the pressure off.

Reframing the question

What if you just don't have an answer for the question and you know that you won't come up with one, even with time to think?

If possible, try to connect the question to something related that you *can* speak knowledgeably about. This is a little risky because, if you don't do it well, it can come across as dodging the question. However, in some situations, it can work very well.

For example, if the interviewer asks you to share an example of a time when you disagreed with your manager and you draw a blank, you could try to reframe a related example of handling a disagreement with a coworker.

This isn't a perfect answer, but it addresses the goal of the question: to evaluate your ability to deal with conflict.

REMEMBER

If you can think of a way to address the intent of the question, that can be enough to satisfy the interviewer.

Being honest

In some cases, there is just no way to reframe — if you're asked an unfamiliar technical question or about experience you just don't have, for example. In these situations, honesty is the best policy.

Acknowledge that you don't know the answer to that question. The key to recovering well from this is to then assert your desire and ability to learn. You can do this by talking about your experience in similar areas or your general ability to get up to speed quickly.

For example, when disclosing experience you don't have, you can say, "I haven't worked with that software in the past, but I have been reading up on it and am looking forward to learning more. It seems similar to Other Software that I was able to teach myself very quickly in my previous position."

Or, when confessing that you don't know the answer to an industry-related question, you might say, "I'm not an expert on that particular deal, but I've been following it in the press and would be interested in learning more because I've worked on similar transactions in the pharmaceutical space and was able to get up to speed quickly on the complex regulatory issues."

Circling back

If you blurt out a weak answer or are forced into saying "I don't know" and then recover from your brain freeze later, you can always circle back to the topic. Look for a natural opening or wait until the end of the interview and revisit the question.

For example, you could say, "Earlier, I was caught a bit off guard by your question about the bond market, but I wanted to come back to that and answer it more thoughtfully . . ."

You can even use your thank-you note to circle back and revisit a missed opportunity — a question you didn't answer well or a key point you didn't make effectively.

Refusing to panic

Even if you flub a question completely, all is not lost unless you panic. I've had many clients who were able to recover from a terrible answer and go on to win the offer.

Try these techniques and do your best to come up with the best answer you can. But then *move on*.

Don't get distracted by mentally kicking yourself or replaying the terrible question over and over.

It's one question. It doesn't have to be a big deal. If you overthink it, you're likely to underperform during the rest of the interview or completely lose your confidence.

Don't over-apologize or be too self-deprecating. Focus on doing your best with the rest of the questions and ending the interview strong.

Even the greatest athletes make bad plays. Your overall impression is much more important than answering every question perfectly.

Chapter **15**

Mastering Nonverbal Communications

Your interviewer will start forming opinions about you before you say a single word. In a job interview, your nonverbal communication plays a critical role in your first impression — and how you are evaluated throughout the hiring process.

We can all agree that what you say in a job interview is important. Many of the tips I've shared throughout this book deal explicitly with how to best put your skills, experience, and goals into words. In this chapter, however, I have another lesson to impart: How you say what you say is also important.

You have only a few seconds to make that first impression and a lot of it is subconscious. Eye contact, body language, the quality of your voice, the tone of your voice, how you move — all these little aspects work together to form an immediate impression and then add credibility to what you're saying as you interact with the interviewer.

To be clear, I don't support the act of judging candidates negatively based on how they look or sound or on minor presentation issues. Hiring decisions should always be about the ability to do the job.

However, possessing strong presentation and nonverbal communication skills can give you a major edge in connecting with your interviewer and conveying confidence and authenticity.

A frequently cited study claims that 65 percent of your daily communication happens through nonverbal means. This chapter is all about helping you send the right messages.

In my years of experience working with both interviewers and job-seekers, I have witnessed how certain habits can draw attention away from even the most eloquent interview answers. I've also seen how practicing and making minor adjustments can dramatically improve overall impressions (and boost internal confidence at the same time).

In this chapter, I cover the nonverbal communication elements that tend to impact interview communication the most — why they matter and how you can make them work for you. These include wardrobe, eye contact, and body language. I'm also including some important factors that aren't technically nonverbal, because they're about your speaking style. These include your pace of speech, your tone, and your use of filler words (those annoying instances of *um* and *uh* and similar).

I cover them here because they're more about communication style than about the words you choose. They're also similar in that issues are often caused by nerves and speaking style improves greatly with practice.

Dressing for the Job You Want

Let's start with wardrobe. Your choice of attire can make a big difference in the impression you make, especially that all-important first impression.

Luckily, dressing to impress for job interviews is easy once you know the guidelines.

A common tip is to dress for the job you want. This is a smart approach when it comes to job interviews. You want your interviewers to be able to picture you as an employee.

In most cases, they're not hiring you for your fashion sense. (If you're interviewing at *Vogue* magazine, that's another story.) Your experience and abilities are what matter most. But don't kid yourself: Interviewers do judge by appearances to some degree, often subconsciously.

Your appearance should convey professionalism, polish, and confidence, but that doesn't mean you have to cater to outdated or biased ideas of professionalism.

Be yourself, but show that you made an effort. Wear something that makes you feel great, that puts a little swagger in your step. Just avoid choices that might distract from someone noticing your brain power and your capabilities.

General guidelines

I suggest dressing just a bit more formally than the company's basic dress code stipulates. As a rule of thumb, aim to dress like an employee would dress on a day they were making a major internal presentation to the CEO, for example.

This strategy shows that you're polished and professional and care about making a good first impression.

Hopefully, this advice goes without saying, but good grooming is key. Make sure that your hair and nails are clean and groomed and that your clothing is clean and wrinkle-free. Get your suit dry-cleaned. Iron that shirt.

What to wear

The standards for what to wear vary quite a bit based on the company culture and the job. In some industries, a buttoned-up suit is still preferred, especially for client-facing or senior-level employees. In many others, wearing a formal suit will make you seem too formal; it might even signal that you don't fit in.

You need to do your research on the organization and its dress code if you're not already familiar with industry norms. When in doubt, it's better to be a little too formal than to come across as too casual.

Some of these guidelines are relevant only to an in-person interview. For a video interview, you won't have to worry about shoes or a briefcase, for example. However, some job-seekers find that it helps to dress for the part completely, even on a video or phone interview. The look helps them channel their interview confidence.

I'm not going to dictate a universal set of interview wardrobe guidelines. Luckily, company dress codes are much less rigid these days than in the past. However, certain choices can help you elevate the professionalism of your look — and some choices may make the wrong impression with certain interviewers.

Sometimes, the options can feel overwhelming and it's nice to have some guidelines. For example, it's hard for any candidate to go wrong with a dark-colored business suit paired with a white or solid-colored shirt. You can dress a suit up or down. For more conservative environments (think law firm or bank), keep the blazer, wear a power tie, maybe add a classic piece of jewelry.

WARNING

For more informal work environments, a suit can make you stand out in a bad way. In fact, some companies tell candidates *not* to wear a suit. Appearing too formal can read as being out of touch or even uptight in some crowds.

To make it more casual (think startup or creative agency), lose the blazer and/or choose a shirt that's more laid-back or colorful. Add some personality with an accessory.

REMEMBER

Nice-looking shoes are definitely a plus. You'll walk a little taller. They don't have to be designer shoes or expensive — just professional and well-maintained. If you spring for a new pair, make sure you break them in before the interview. (I know I find it hard to project swagger when I'm limping in pain.)

Finally, if you're carrying a bag (a briefcase, purse, or backpack), choose one that looks sharp. In an in-person interview, your bag will be quite visible to the interviewer. It might even end up sitting between the two of you on a desk or a table. You may be pulling your resume out of the bag as part of your first impression. Make sure you carry one that looks professional — and keep in mind that the standards will be different at an investment bank than at a preschool.

What not to wear

If all this fashion advice sounds a bit boring, that's because it is. The goal is to avoid being discriminated against based on appearance or personal style. That means keeping the focus on your ability to do the job and represent the organization.

REMEMBER

It's fine to show some personality, but unless you're in the fashion industry, don't try to make a major statement with your wardrobe at the interview. You can always dress more creatively after you get hired. However, personal style is subjective, and it's better to keep it fairly neutral until you've wowed them with your qualifications. Your clothes and style shouldn't overshadow what you have to say. Keeping your look understated keeps the focus on your skills and expertise.

Here are some specific choices to avoid, at least until you get to know your interviewers better:

» Dramatic makeup looks

» Heavy perfume/cologne

>> Showing too much skin

>> Jeans

>> Athleisure

>> Anything that reads as beachwear or clubwear

>> Overly casual shoes (beat-up sneakers, flip-flops)

>> Clothing that doesn't fit well (too tight or oversized)

>> Clothing with visible wear and tear (stains, pilling, loose threads)

>> Clothing that shows perspiration (especially if you tend to sweat when you're nervous)

TIP

Keep your hair simple. Don't try a new or uncomfortable style on interview day. If you tend to play with your hair when you're nervous, consider pulling it back to prevent temptation.

Bottom line: Never underestimate the confidence–boosting power of an interview outfit that makes you feel like a million bucks.

It can be worth it to splurge on something that makes you stand just a little taller and radiate a little more confidence.

And, when in doubt about what to wear, choose the option that you feel best in.

Gender presentation

In the past, interview wardrobe advice was generally separated into tips "for men" and "for women." More recently, a greater understanding of the complexities of gender identity and expression has led to some rethinking of these outdated "rules."

Gender presentation (or *gender expression*) is defined as the external display of one's gender, through clothing, hair, makeup, demeanor, social behavior, and other factors. It is an important aspect of identity, but gender presentation does not always align with gender identity.

You should never feel pressure to change your gender presentation for a job interview. You deserve to feel comfortable and authentic.

Many organizations have strong commitments to diversity and inclusion. They invest in training for managers to minimize both conscious and unconscious bias in the hiring process. Researching the company (see Chapter 4) and its reputation for inclusive hiring may help you feel more comfortable going into the interview (or at least know what to expect).

REMEMBER

Unfortunately, you may still encounter interviewers with bias (unconscious or conscious) against candidates who don't conform to the gender norms they're used to.

The wardrobe suggestions in this chapter can be adapted for anyone, regardless of gender identity.

Many candidates prefer gender-neutral clothing for job interviews. For example, pantsuits and button-up shirts tend to work well for everyone. However, you can also opt to express yourself as you wish. The response of your interviewers will tell you a lot about whether you could work comfortably in that environment.

Based on recent legal interpretations of Title VII of the Civil Rights Act of 1964, employers should not discriminate against candidates based on gender identity or sexual orientation. However, employers are permitted to set dress codes in some situations, provided that the dress requirements are reasonable and serve a legitimate business purpose. (Examples include safety, brand image, and visibility.) Dress codes should also be enforced consistently and not favor or affect one gender over another.

If you feel that an interviewer has discriminated against you based on your gender presentation or gender identity, consider reporting the situation to the organization's HR department or contacting the Equal Employment Opportunity Commission. Of course, it's always your call on whether you feel comfortable making a report. Some organizations take these complaints very seriously, but others may not be receptive.

REMEMBER

It's your right to be evaluated fairly based on your qualifications, not on your gender presentation.

Improving Nonverbal Communications

Now that you have your wardrobe planned, it's time to talk about the many other factors that influence your nonverbal communications and ability to connect with your interviewers. These include eye contact, facial expressions, body language, and nervous habits.

When it comes to job interviews, nonverbal communication plays a crucial role in conveying confidence, professionalism, and authenticity. The way you present yourself through your body language, eye contact, and other nonverbal cues can significantly impact the impression you make on interviewers.

Before I get to the detailed advice about each of these factors, I want to provide some high-level guidance that will help you with improving all forms of nonverbal communications.

The challenge of self-analysis

Many of my interview coaching clients come to me with severe anxiety about what they're doing "wrong" when it comes to nonverbal communication. Sometimes, they know they have issues with one habit or another (most often, overuse of filler words, avoiding eye contact, and/or talking too fast). In other cases, they just feel awkward or have received feedback that they seem nervous or unengaged and they're not sure exactly what to work on.

Part of the problem is that it's difficult to analyze your own nonverbal communication. The first challenge is that it's impossible to accurately evaluate yourself in general. You can't see or hear yourself from an outside, objective viewpoint. That can lead to hypercritical self-consciousness or, in other cases, false feelings of confidence that you sound "fine" because you're used to your own bad habits.

It's even more difficult to evaluate your own performance in an interview. During the interview, you're busy juggling a long list of mental tasks. You're taking in the interviewer and the environment, you're trying to anticipate questions, and you're mentally running through your speaking points. On top of all this, you're trying to manage your eye contact, facial expressions, body language, and delivery. It's a lot.

WARNING

Many clients tell me it's all a blur after it's over. They have trouble remembering the details of the questions, let alone the quality of their eye contact or number of "ums."

However, it's important to have a realistic sense of your nonverbal communication strengths and weaknesses. The easiest way to do this is to record yourself and review the footage. Some shy away from this idea, and I don't blame them. I detest watching myself on video, too.

I forced myself to get over it (or at least to tolerate the discomfort), and you can, too. You don't have to learn to love watching yourself on video. You might only need to record and view a few answers to get a good idea of how you're coming across in interview mode.

TIP

Remind yourself that you won't be perfect on the video, especially if you're not used to interviewing. The goal here is to see where you need to improve. I guarantee that you're already doing many things right, and maybe more than you realize. If you're still a bit rough around the edges, you can fix that. Knowing what to work on will help you focus your time in the right way.

Even after recording, some people have trouble watching objectively and spotting what's working and what's not. Again, objective self-analysis is difficult! One approach that might help is to request objective feedback from a friend, mentor, or coach. Share with them a video recording you've made, and then pick their brain for feedback on your nonverbal communication (as well as your answers while you've got them paying attention).

Recently, new technology has emerged that can help with objectively appraising presentation skills through video analysis and artificial intelligence. My team at Big Interview created our Video AI tool to help automatically evaluate nonverbal communication habits that are most important in job interviews (including eye contact, pace of speech, use of filler words, vocabulary, and others). There are similar tools designed for judging general communication skills for students and public speakers and the technology continues to evolve and become more useful.

WARNING

Listen to feedback with respect but remember that opinions will vary. Don't let one person's negative critique dash your confidence. Consider all perspectives, but remember that not everyone is an expert and not everyone is good at constructive criticism.

With all of these methods, recording yourself has the added benefit of forcing you to practice. Practice is the best way to refine your nonverbal communication. Actually, it's the *only* way.

The value of practice

As I mention in earlier chapters, my mantra for succeeding in job interviews is "prepare and practice." When it comes to presentation and delivery, practice is the key to improving both your skills and your confidence.

You undoubtedly know the value of practice from other aspects of your life: Practice makes perfect in sports, public speaking, performing, and learning a new language.

Your nonverbal communication becomes automatic, even when nervous, when you have enough practice. However, you must practice in the right way to make sure you're internalizing proper behavior.

TIP

I came across a relevant quote about practice that's attributed to the legendary golfer Sam Snead. Snead said, "Practice puts brains in your muscles." I loved it so much that I had to look up Sam Snead. (I had never heard of him, though he was apparently the Tiger Woods of the 1950s and 1960s.) The idea behind the quote helps to explain how practice has a miraculous effect on how you carry yourself.

Practice isn't just about learning your "lines" (or familiarizing yourself with your bullet points when it comes to interviewing). Practice helps you develop a comfort level in an unfamiliar scenario or when performing in an unfamiliar way. You get used to the physical aspects of sitting in an interview and engaging with a stranger asking you questions. You learn how it feels to make good eye contact, sit confidently, and speak eloquently. Then it starts to feel more natural and requires less control — or even consciousness.

REMEMBER

The familiarity and comfort allow you to relax and feel more confident — that means you can focus more on what you're saying and on making a true connection. (I have seen many clients go from nervous and fidgety to graceful, sometimes after just a practice round or two.)

In the following sections, you'll see that I recommend practice to improve on every common nonverbal communication challenge I discuss. You'll need to practice the right behaviors, so read on for the specific advice. However, know that a single mock interview can help you accomplish many goals — from refining your answers to mastering your eye contact and body language to eliminating filler words and nervous habits.

Making Eye Contact

I'm starting with eye contact because it's such a powerful part of your nonverbal communication. Making comfortable eye contact with a stranger can be difficult, especially when you're out of practice. (Many of us experienced that feeling of uncomfortable eye contact when first coming out of COVID isolation.)

I want to spend a little time explaining why eye contact is vital in job interviews. It's not just a random etiquette rule; there are deeply ingrained reasons that humans respond to eye contact, and there are also some common misperceptions. Then I'll cover how you can evaluate your own eye contact and work on making it more effective.

Recognizing the importance of eye contact

In theory, eye contact sounds easy enough. You probably do it subconsciously multiple times per day. However, if you've ever felt awkward about making eye contact in a job interview, you're not alone.

There's something very personal about gazing into someone's eyes. In an interview, you're meeting a stranger — a stranger who, let's be honest, is there to judge you.

It's normal to subconsciously shy away from eye contact in this scenario, feeling like it's forcing too much connection too soon. Eye contact can feel especially vulnerable when you know you're being evaluated.

There are also cultural differences in how eye contact is perceived. In some cultures, prolonged eye contact can be seen as aggressive or disrespectful. If you grew up with this perspective, "good eye contact," as it's defined in the United States, can feel particularly uncomfortable in a job interview.

In anthropological terms, the United States is a low-context culture, meaning there is more emphasis on the individual than on the group as well as a decided preference to get down to business quickly (instead of spending more time on establishing trust). In high-context cultures, including many countries in Asia and South America, social trust must be earned first, and situations and relationships are more important than the actual words spoken. This cultural context affects how eye contact is perceived.

Eye contact is also more difficult for people who are shy, introverted, or on the autism spectrum. Research has found that many people with autism consider eye contact to be invasive, distracting, and even physically uncomfortable. Though many adults with autism know that eye contact is deemed important in situations like job interviews, that doesn't make it easy to change their behavior.

TIP

If you notice that your interviewer isn't making consistent eye contact, it doesn't mean they don't like you or aren't paying attention. Your interviewer may have grown up in a high-context culture, they may be a person on the autism spectrum, or they may just be an introvert. You should still make your best attempt at good eye contact, but don't be too aggressive about it.

One of my missions in life is to educate hiring managers on what eye contact really means and stop them from judging candidates based on bias and outdated assumptions. However, it's surprising how many people still jump to the conclusion that lack of eye contact means the candidate is dishonest, unreliable, or uninterested.

On the other hand, plenty of research out there shows that eye contact is a powerful way to connect and communicate. Even if interviewers know not to associate eye contact with honesty, they can still be persuaded with eye contact. Some people also make subconscious positive associations with good eye contact. If you can learn how to maintain confident eye contact, it can give you an advantage in standing out from your competitions.

Let's look at four proven ways that eye contact can help you in interviews:

1. **Conveying confidence:** Steady eye contact communicates confidence, which helps to establish trust. When someone shies away from eye contact, it can make them seem unsure. This is a big deal in job interviews, especially for more senior roles. In the short time frame of the job interview, you can't possibly "prove" that you're reliable. Interviewers are always taking a chance when they make an offer (just as you're taking a chance in deciding to accept an offer). If you seem confident, it gives them more reassurance that you are who you say you are — and a good bet as a hire.

   This is where the expression "fake it until you make it" comes from. When you seem confident in your abilities, you're more likely to inspire confidence in others as well.

TIP

   A study at King's College London found that people associate higher levels of eye contact with stronger leadership abilities and higher intelligence, among other positive qualities.

2. **Showing interest:** Eye contact communicates attention and interest, which helps you show respect for the interviewer and enthusiasm for the opportunity.

   Making eye contact signals to the other person that you're paying attention to what they're saying. People like to feel that they're heard and that their perspective is valued.

   Meanwhile, showing curiosity about the opportunity is critical. Every hiring manager wants an engaged employee. If a candidate seems zoned out or uninterested during the interview, it raises immediate doubt about the fit.

3. **Being memorable:** Eye contact also has a positive impact on how people remember you. A series of studies conducted since 1980 found that listeners were more likely to retain information delivered when making eye contact with the speaker.

   In fact, a recent study found that this effect extends to eye contact made during a video call. Participants retained more of the information from the call when more eye contact was involved.

4. **Making a connection:** Finally, eye contact is a vital part of establishing a meaningful connection with someone. You know this from other aspects of your life. When you look into someone's eyes, it helps you establish rapport.

   People associate steady eye contact with honesty, trust, and openness. In a job interview, you don't have a lot of time to convey these qualities, so good eye contact can be a shortcut to a stronger relationship.

   At the same time, looking into your interviewer's eyes can help you understand them and their perspective. You'll be better able to read their reaction to you and their feeling about various aspects of the job and organization.

Improving your eye contact

There's no perfect amount of eye contact that's applicable in every situation. In fact, "good eye contact" can vary significantly based on culture and personality.

In a job interview, the goal is to aim for natural, consistent eye contact. That includes briefly looking away or down at times as you gather your thoughts, but always coming back to reconnect.

Communication experts recommend maintaining eye contact for 50 percent of the time while speaking and 70 percent of the time while listening. It is also recommended to establish and maintain eye contact for approximately 3 to 5 seconds at a time before looking away.

REMEMBER

You don't need "perfect" eye contact. Just don't let your level of eye contact become a distraction for the interviewer.

Most people err on the side of making too little eye contact, which means the interviewer notices them looking away or looking down frequently. It's easy to fall into this habit when you're nervous.

Unfortunately, as discussed, making too little eye contact can be interpreted as a lack of confidence or even dishonesty by some interviewers.

WARNING

Too much eye contact can also be off-putting. If you gaze into someone's eyes intensely for long periods, they can become uncomfortable pretty quickly.

Good, natural eye contact means establishing eye contact confidently when you first meet someone, holding it for a few seconds, and then consistently coming back to it as the conversation continues.

The best way to improve your eye contact — and to make eye contact feel more natural — is to practice. The following sections present some tips for practicing your eye contact.

Video practice

For some people, it's more comfortable to start by practicing with a face on the screen. One option is to use an online video practice tool, where you see and hear a recorded actor asking the question and then respond. Practice looking into the eyes of the actor on the screen. They can't judge you. For an example of an online interview tool, check out my company's Big Interview platform; I am offering free access for readers of this book to try it out at https://www.dummies.com/go/bigInterview/.

This strategy helps you get accustomed to eye contact without having to worry about what the other person is thinking. It may sound silly, but it works.

TIP Video practice can also help you when it comes to making natural eye contact during video interviews (whether live or prerecorded). See Chapter 3 for more advice on excelling in video interviews. You don't even have to record yourself at first. However, when you're ready, start recording yourself so that you can play back the video and see how you would look to an interviewer.

TIP Similarly, you can try practicing eye contact by looking at a photo or a paused video on your screen. Pick a photo of your favorite actor or actress, if you like. Then at least you enjoy looking at the photo and may even find some extra inspiration.

Practice with a friend

Another strategy is to practice with a trusted friend. This allows for a more realistic approximation of an in-person interview.

You don't have to focus on just eye contact. If you can convince somebody to practice with you, you want to get all the feedback you can on all the aspects of your answers and delivery. However, if you know that eye contact is a challenge for you, consider asking your practice partner to pay special attention. On the other hand, if you don't mention it, you will probably get a more objective evaluation.

Eye contact hacks

If you continue to struggle with eye contact, you can try these strategies to consciously train yourself to make — or at least fake — eye contact:

>> **Count down:** As you practice, try forcing yourself to maintain eye contact for a count of 3 to 5 seconds. Count "one Mississippi, two Mississippi," and so on, so that you can get an accurate sense of how long that period is. (It may feel much longer than you expect.) After you count to 5, allow yourself to look away and take a breath, and then go again. It will start to feel more natural after a bit. You may want to try this with a video interviewer first.

>> **Not-quite eye contact:** Try looking at the space between the person's eyes or just above their eyes. This may not translate exactly as eye contact, so experiment. You may find that starting with not-quite eye contact will ease you into the real thing. Just be careful not to look too high or low or else you may just make your interviewer self-conscious about their nose or their hair.

>> **Break with a gesture:** If you need to break your eye contact, try nodding, looking up pensively, or jotting down a note. These gestures can make breaking your gaze feel more natural and not highlight that you're simply uncomfortable with the eye contact. Just don't rely too much on the same gesture, because that can become distracting as well.

>> **The triangle technique:** Some experts suggest that you imagine an inverted triangle connecting your interviewer's two eyes and mouth. Then, every 5 seconds, you rotate which point of the triangle you're looking at. To me, this sounds like a lot to remember on top of everything else, but it may be worth a try if the other techniques aren't helping.

Editing Your Body Language

Now let's talk about the importance of body language. Awkward body language can distract from all the wonderful things you're saying about yourself.

In an interview, you must project confidence with your body as well as your words.

TIP

Body language is important in every interview, but it becomes more crucial as you start to advance to interviewing for more senior roles that require executive presence. (Read more about conveying executive presence in Chapter 16.) Even if you're just launching your career, it's not too early to start developing some executive presence.

Nervous body language, like nervous eye contact, can send the wrong messages. So let's get specific about the elements of body language that make the biggest impression — and how you can adjust your physicality to show you're a strong candidate.

Posture

The first thing to consider is your posture. Yes, your mom was right to tell you to stand up straight. Standing or sitting up straight and looking straight ahead communicates confidence. Compare this with the message sent by someone slouching, slumping, or reclining.

Most likely, you'll be seated for the interview itself. However, for an in-person interview, you will walk to the interview location and perhaps stand to meet your interviewer if you're seated when they enter the room.

REMEMBER

You're being observed throughout the experience, not just during the Q&A. Remember your posture, and stand and walk with confidence. If you're asked to wait somewhere before or between interviews, maintain a professional posture. You don't want your interviewer to walk into the lobby and be treated to a first impression of you hunched over in a chair, jiggling your leg nervously, and scrolling the content on your phone.

When it's time to take your seat for the interview, sit up as straight and tall as you can. This confident, engaged posture says you're interested and trustworthy.

Keep your back straight and your shoulders slightly relaxed to avoid coming across as too rigid. You want to come across as confident but natural, not frozen. Sometimes when you're nervous, you tense up without realizing it, and it can look to the interviewer like you're bracing yourself. If you find yourself tensing up physically in interviews or other nerve-wracking situations, make a conscious effort to take a deep breath and relax your shoulders as you get settled.

TIP

Try leaning forward slightly, especially when listening to your interviewer speak. This conveys engagement and interest in the conversation.

Be careful to avoid slouching. Slouching says you're not taking this interview seriously and makes you look less polished and professional. At an extreme, you might look like an annoyed teenager forced to chat with a distant relative. This isn't the vibe you want in an interview.

Another bad posture habit is hunching over. Some people naturally hunch into a protective posture when they feel they are in a vulnerable situation. To the interviewer, this can read as defensive or insecure. When you hunch over, you're taking up less space and that can make you look and feel less confident.

For many of us, assuming a powerful posture can translate into feeling more powerful. That means faking confident body language can actually make you feel more confident.

TIP

Some studies have claimed that "power posing" changes your body chemistry and leads to better performance in job interviews (and other stressful situations). The original research on this topic inspired a viral TED Talk, but more recent studies have disputed the findings. However, based on my experience with clients, some people do feel more powerful when they try a brief Wonder Woman or Superman pose before walking into an interview. It may all be in their heads, but if it works, it works! Give it a try if you need an extra dash of confidence.

Now, what are you supposed to do with your hands? The key is to use open body language to signal engagement and friendliness. Avoid crossing your arms — this makes you look defensive and closed-off.

When seated, your best bet is to keep your arms relaxed at your sides or resting on the table in front of you. This gives you a nice base position that is both confident and natural. From there, you can gesture with your hands, lean forward, nod, and otherwise use body language to respond to the conversation. (Read the later section on nervous habits for advice on how to avoid gestures and movements that will detract from the confident image you're trying to project.)

If you're not sitting at a table, you can keep your hands on your knees or in your lap. It may take a little experimenting and practice to find what feels comfortable for you. Again, avoid crossing your arms and legs in this position, because it can read as defensive. It's fine to cross your legs if that's how you feel comfortable, especially if you're wearing a skirt. If you do, make sure you're using other forms of open body language (arms, gestures, facial expressions) to make it clear that you're open and engaged.

TIP

In a video interview, you don't have to worry about any body language below the camera frame. In phone interviews, they can't see you at all. However, I recommend following the body language advice in this chapter for video and phone interviews as well. Your posture will look great on video, and the added confidence will likely make you sound more eloquent.

CLIENT CASE STUDY: MATT

Matt was a recent college grad. His parents sent him to an interview coach because he was having trouble finding a job in the competitive finance field despite his academic accomplishments. He was a laid-back, likable guy and told me all his interviews seemed to go well, but he wasn't getting offers.

As soon as we started the practice interview, I could see that body language was a big part of his problem. He slouched down and leaned way back in his revolving office chair, spinning back and forth repetitively, jiggling his legs as he talked. His eye contact was sporadic and his answers short and perfunctory. At one point, he actually stretched his arms over his head and yawned. I really thought he was messing with me.

As you can imagine, the overall impression was that he didn't want to be there. I could see why interviewers would think he wasn't serious or invested. It was partly a defense mechanism: He was laid-back by nature, but he also tended to try to play it cool when nervous. In a job interview, playing too cool to care doesn't get you very far. Matt didn't realize how his multiple nonverbal cues (posture, gestures, eye contact) added up to an interview red flag.

We worked on changing his body language and controlling his nervous habits. We also worked on articulating his interests and strengths more clearly.

It took some practice for Matt to feel comfortable with his answers and with a more engaged posture, but he was able to shake most of his nervous habits and land a job offer.

Facial expression

Your facial expression is probably the most obvious form of body language. Every day, you use facial expressions to read how others are feeling: smiling, frowning, nose wrinkling, eyes widening, eyes narrowing, mouth tightening, jaw dropping.

In a job interview, you should maintain a neutral, friendly expression as your baseline. Many people do this naturally, but if you have a very expressive face, your nerves may show up as frowning, scrunching, or wincing. You may not even realize you're doing this.

Another common problem is RBF (also known as resting bitch face). Some individuals by default just always seem annoyed or unfriendly. It might be due to bone structure or eyebrow position or past conditioning. (RBF can be handy in warding off harassment in the subway.)

This effect can be difficult to change. However, if you know that you sometimes come across as irritated when you're not, you can neutralize the effect by making a point to act and sound friendly (see all other forms of nonverbal communication discussed in this chapter) and consciously smile more frequently.

In all cases, smiling helps significantly in making a positive impression. When you smile, your eye contact is warmer and more engaging. Smiling also conveys interest, enthusiasm, and friendliness. Sometimes, even the friendliest candidates are so focused on what they're saying and how the interviewer is responding that they forget to smile.

That doesn't mean you should grin with delight throughout the entire interview. Make a point of smiling when you first meet your interviewer. From there, smiling may come naturally for you, especially if the interviewer is pleasant.

CLIENT CASE STUDY: NATHAN

Nathan was an accomplished candidate who sought my help because he was attending many interviews and passing all the first-round phone screens but never receiving an offer. He worked in a competitive area of the finance industry, so he wanted to do everything he could to stand out.

It turned out that Nathan's main problem was his body language. We worked on his answers as well. (He was selling himself short in some areas.) However, the first thing I noticed in our first practice interview was his facial expression: As soon as he started answering, he gritted his teeth and tensed his jaw and looked like he was in pain. This was a big change from his natural friendly expression when we were chatting before the practice interview.

I had to choose my words carefully to give him the necessary feedback without insulting him, but he was grateful for the honesty. The cause was related to concentrating on remembering his answers, combined with a naturally expressive face and nerves. After a series of unsuccessful interviews, his confidence had taken a hit and the pressure to get it right had intensified.

Awareness was the biggest factor here. Then I asked him to practice consciously relaxing his face before answering. Practice in general also helped because he grew more comfortable with his answers and that reduced his anxiety.

Nathan went on to land a great job and later referred several friends for coaching.

However, if smiling doesn't come naturally for you, try consciously looking for opportunities to smile as the meeting progresses. For example, smile when talking about your interest in the opportunity, rewarding past experiences, or describing your interests.

Because most people rarely get to see your own facial expressions in action, I recommend practicing and recording yourself on video. Practice an easy question and then force yourself to practice a difficult question that you haven't prepared for. This will help highlight whether your face visibly changes when you're under stress.

Let's talk for a moment about *microexpressions*, those tiny involuntary expressions that occur in just $1/25$ of a second. You may have heard about the work of Dr. Paul Ekman, who has studied microexpressions in depth and written several books about them.

Some of these microexpressions are common sense — for example, wrinkling your nose shows disgust, and raising your eyebrows indicates surprise.

Others are less intuitive. For example, according to Ekman, if a right-handed person looks to the right when speaking, they are likely lying. The idea is that looking to the right reveals activity in the right hemisphere — the creative half of the person's brain. On the other hand, eyes pointed to the left suggest that the speaker is telling the truth by calling on activity in the rational, left hemisphere.

This is all very interesting, but it's unclear how much of microexpression theory is backed up by science. I can also tell you that I've never met an interviewer who was an expert on reading microexpressions, so don't waste time worrying about them during your interview prep — unless you're applying for a job with the CIA.

Fidgeting

People commonly fidget a bit in job interviews, especially when they're nervous. Some of us tend to move around a lot and talk with our hands (I definitely do this), which can sometimes come across as fidgeting.

From a confident base position, it's fine to gesture in a natural way, especially if that's how you talk. The problem is when gestures or movements become repetitive or distracting, taking the focus off your words and drawing attention to your nerves.

These are some of the common nervous gestures I see in interviews:

>> Touching the hair (adjusting, twirling)

>> Touching the face (itching nose, covering mouth, rubbing ear)

>> Fidgeting with an object (pen, piece of jewelry, clothing)

>> Shifting back and forth

>> Spinning or moving in the chair

>> Jiggling the leg

>> Tapping the fingers or feet

REMEMBER

Occasional shifting and gesturing are fine and can keep you from seeming too rigid. As with vocal fillers, nervous body language becomes an issue only if it's a distraction.

For interviewers, repetitive fidgeting can indicate excessive nervousness, discomfort with the topics being discussed, lack of presentation skills, or even a lack of professionalism, if taken to an extreme.

CLIENT CASE STUDY: ALEXANDRA

My client Alexandra couldn't seem to stop twirling her hair. It was her subconscious habit when she was trying to think of what to say next. With practice, she was able to greatly reduce this behavior, but she would occasionally fall back into the old habit when faced with a particularly difficult question or an intimidating interviewer.

Finally, we decided to try pulling her hair back. She resisted at first because she had lovely long hair and felt that it looked better down. However, this approach helped her to finally break her fidgeting habit.

As a bonus, she felt the hairstyle change made her look more polished and a little older, which was beneficial as a young candidate interviewing for management roles.

If you're not sure whether you tend to fidget to the point of distraction, it's important to get feedback. You can record a video practice interview and see for yourself or ask a trusted friend to observe and evaluate. Even friends who aren't interview experts can help with evaluating body language.

To reduce fidgeting, the key is practice. It may sound counterintuitive to practice in order to seem more natural, but it works. At first, you may have to focus on *not* fidgeting. After a bit of practice, however, most of my clients naturally stop (or reduce) these behaviors. This is because practice helps with nerves and gets you accustomed to speaking without fidgeting.

TIP

If you have trouble shaking nervous habits, try removing temptation wherever possible. For example, if you know that you subconsciously touch your long hair, pull it back. If you fiddle with your watch or rings, leave them at home.

Finding Your Voice

Now I want to cover some important behaviors that aren't technically nonverbal but are related to your vocal delivery. You might argue that these should fall under verbal communication, but I include them in the chapter about nonverbal communication because they're part of your presentation style and are usually linked to nerves and subconscious habits, much like your eye contact and body language.

I'm referring to your pace of speech, use of filler words and phrases (*um, uh, ya know*), pausing, and vocal variation.

Learning to master these aspects of your delivery will help you with all forms of communication, not just job interviews.

Pace

First, your pace of speech affects how you're understood and perceived. Speaking too quickly can make it difficult for your listener to follow along — and can make you appear overly nervous or unpolished. Slow speech can be perceived as low-energy or low-enthusiasm.

Based on research, the most natural and engaging speaking falls in the range of 115 to 180 words per minute.

TIP

For reference, professional narrators (for audiobooks, for example) tend to aim for a rate of about 150 words per minute.

This is quite a wide range — and that's because good speakers tend to vary their speed based on the subject and audience. The goal isn't to be a robot who speaks at the same rate at all times. An engaging and natural speaker varies their speed — speeding up a bit to show enthusiasm and then slowing down to emphasize a point.

The ideal range also takes into account some natural variations based on age, where you're from, and other factors.

Too fast

In job interviews, candidates commonly speak too rapidly, often due to nerves.

A rushed speech rate can make you sound anxious or unpolished. Even worse, speaking too quickly makes it hard for your listener to understand you.

First, your listener may not know what you're saying if you're talking too quickly to properly enunciate. This is even more of a problem for candidates who are soft-spoken or have an accent.

Even if they can make out what you're saying, they don't have time to truly take it in if you're already rushing to your next point.

Some people just naturally talk fast. On the positive side, a bit of speed can help you sound engaged and high-energy. But in a nerve-wracking situation like an interview, the pace can get away from you.

Too slow

I've also worked with a few clients who tended to speak too slowly in interviews, though this is less common. Taken to the extreme, a slow rate of speech can make you sound low-energy or indicate that you have trouble finding the right words in communication.

The right speed

Feedback can help you decide whether you need to slow down (or speed up) a bit. Record yourself or ask a trusted friend for their opinion.

REMEMBER

Evaluate yourself in a situation as similar to a real interview as possible so that you can identify how your pace changes when nervous.

The good news is that you can learn to adjust your pace, even when you're nervous. The best way to do this is to practice out loud with a conscious effort to maintain a pace in the ideal range.

Filler words

Most of my clients tend to use too many filler words during our first practice interview. It's a common nervous habit that's hard to shake.

Common filler words include *like, so, you know, basically, anyway,* and others. In addition to filler words, some speakers struggle with other "speech disfluencies," like repetition, stopping midphrase and restarting, and noises like sighing and throat-clearing.

Research has shown that these can hurt you when overused, leading to perceptions of the speaker as being unprepared, uninformed, unpolished, and/or even dishonest.

That doesn't mean you should try to cut every filler word from your vocabulary. In spontaneous speech, it's normal to hear disfluencies from even the most polished speaker. The problem comes when there are enough disfluencies to be distracting.

According to studies, the typical speaker has 6 disfluencies per 100 words. My own research shows that listeners start to sit up and notice when they hear more than 8 per 100 words.

And, unfortunately, many interviewers associate noticeable disfluencies with negative qualities in candidates. This isn't quite fair, because nerves and other neutral factors can prompt disfluencies.

On the other hand, some studies have indicated that answers with multiple disfluencies *do* correlate with the speaker hiding or misrepresenting facts.

Overuse of fillers can happen to even the best speakers. Many of us tend to drop the words *um* and *uh* subconsciously when we pause to think — or when we feel unsure about what to say next.

REMEMBER

A high *um* count is usually due primarily to nerves or feeling hesitant from a lack of practice. However, excessive filler words and vocal tics can undermine your credibility.

I want to make sure that your disfluencies don't make the wrong impression in your interview. The first step is to know whether your use of *um* and *uh* is excessive.

It's difficult to evaluate your own filler words as you speak. Friends and mentors rarely give us good feedback, either. They're unlikely to count your filler words unless your problem is extreme. Instead, they tend to interpret a few extra filler words as your being unprepared or nervous or rambling.

This challenge led me to the idea to create an *um* counter of my own, a special AI algorithm to automatically catch and identify these short sounds. Users can record their answers and automatically analyze the number of disfluencies per 100 words to determine whether they need to work on toning down their filler words. Try out free access at https://www.dummies.com/go/bigInterview/.

If you identify that you have a problem, try these techniques to sound more polished:

>> **Prepare thoroughly:** When you're prepared for the key questions, you don't need filler words. Most disfluencies come out when you're confused about what to say next or you lose your train of thought. I usually tell my coaching clients not to even worry about filler words until they've done their prep for the common questions. I often see clients eliminate filler words without even trying after they've prepared and practiced their answers.

>> **Take a moment when needed:** If you do get lost in an answer or stumped by a tricky question, pause instead of fumbling forward with filler words. Often, a moment is enough time to gather your thoughts and decide how to proceed. Pausing makes you sound more thoughtful than uttering a string of *um* and *uh* and talking in circles. Once you get comfortable with taking a moment when you need it, you'll be able to resist the temptation to buy time with filler words.

Pauses

Pauses are part of natural speech, and you should not try to eliminate them completely. In fact, pauses can make you sound thoughtful, help you emphasize your key points, and allow you time to gather your thoughts to answer more eloquently. When you don't pause appropriately, you can come across as overly rehearsed, robotic, or even deceptive.

On the other hand, excessive pausing can lead to interviewers thinking you're unprepared or you lack knowledge or confidence or you're dodging questions.

So, how do you know whether your pauses are excessive? After all, average pause length varies by language, culture, and context.

When in doubt, use the general rule of thumb that a typical pause in speech lasts 1 second or less. However, it's natural to pause a bit longer before starting a new answer or a new topic — for 2 to 3 seconds, depending on the context.

A pause of more than 3 seconds is considered noticeably long. However, keep in mind that a noticeable pause is occasionally okay. It's better to pause to think for a moment if you get stuck in an interview. You're better off pausing than launching into a knee-jerk response or falling back on excessive filler words.

TIP

When you find yourself pausing frequently, it's a good sign that you need more preparation. When you do the work of preparing for the most common and likely questions, you won't be caught off guard easily.

Sure, you can't predict everything, and curveballs come up sometimes, but good preparation will keep your pauses to a minimum.

Tone and vocal variety

Mastering tone and vocal variety can make you a more compelling speaker — in interviews and out in the real world.

I consider this the advanced level of finding your voice. After you eliminate obvious distractions in your speaking style, you can continue to refine your presentation by working on your tone and vocal variety.

Tone refers to the emotional content conveyed by your voice. What is the energy and meaning behind your words? For example, you can say, "That's great!" with joy and enthusiasm, or you can say it dripping with annoyance and sarcasm.

Excellent actors are brilliant at expressing emotion with tone. However, for the purposes of a job interview, you don't need acting chops to convey tone.

The goal is to put some energy and positive emotion into your speech. Your interviewers will be able to hear your interest and enthusiasm, not just in your words but in your tone as well.

Without this emotion, your voice is flat and often monotone. I'm sure you've met people with this delivery style. It's quite difficult to stay interested and engaged, even if their words are well-chosen. The overall impression is that they're low-energy, uninterested, or even boring.

I have worked with several clients who had to address their flat tone in order to land an offer.

TIP

This is particularly important when interviewing for roles that require motivating and persuading others.

When clients ask me for ways to eliminate that monotonous tone in their spoken presentations and thus make their tone more engaging, I tell them that the answer lies in expanding their vocal variety. In this context, vocal variety means emphasizing certain aspects of your speech through pitch, tone, volume, pace, and pauses.

REMEMBER

Vocal variety makes you more interesting to listen to. Think about the most boring professors you've had — I'd bet they tended to drone. Now think about your most interesting professors and your friends who are great storytellers — they use their voices to maintain your attention.

You can also use vocal variety to convey emotion and put emphasis on key ideas.

Some people have a naturally low-key delivery style, with pitch and volume that doesn't vary much. Others fall back on monotone delivery when they're nervous. I also hear it in clients who have tried to memorize answers word-for-word.

The problem is that a monotone delivery, or even just a low-key presentation style, can easily portray you as low-energy, low-interest, and low-initiative. Interviewers are also more likely to tune out if your words blur together and nothing stands out.

In my coaching, I've discovered that the most effective way to add vocal variety is through word choice. I help my monotone clients create bullet points for key questions that incorporate positive, enthusiastic language. It's much easier to put positive tone behind *amazing* or *fascinating* than behind neutral words.

For most of these clients, this language doesn't come naturally, because they aren't overly expressive by nature. That's why they have to plan and script a little bit to make sure their interest comes through in their words. The added benefit is that you'll at least be showing enthusiasm in your words, even if your tone doesn't change.

REMEMBER

I don't recommend scripting answers word-for-word. Reciting memorized answers is likely to sound *more* monotone rather than less monotone.

The idea is to script a few positive words into key answers. For example, add some enthusiastic statements early in your "Tell me about yourself" statement, in your answer to the "Why are you interested in this opportunity?" question, and in your greatest-hits behavioral stories.

I then encourage my clients to *emphasize* those words in practice. Once they hear the difference it makes, they start to look for other opportunities to add positive language, even spontaneously.

Sometimes, it takes some practice to get used to speaking with a more emotional tone. For those who struggle, I sometimes work with them to create a purposely over-the-top version, making it clear that it will sound ridiculous and that we will tone it down later. Often, their over-the-top version sounds perfectly natural and engaging and I play the video to prove it and reassure them.

TIP

If you struggle with a serious monotone problem, try reading aloud a children's story and hamming it up. Ideally, do this with an actual child. They tend to love over-the-top voices and narration. This will give you some practice with adding tone and vocal variety to language that isn't so personal to you and your background. And it might loosen you up a bit. Just don't use the Goldilocks voice in your interview.

CLIENT CASE STUDY: SIMONE

My client Simone was interviewing for senior-level accounting roles, looking to take the next step up to more of a leadership position in her field. She was getting lots of interviews and advancing through multiple rounds, but not getting offers.

In our first practice interview, I heard her shift into a semi-monotone delivery style that was quite businesslike but also quite dry. Combined with her modesty in her responses, this made her come across as competent but not executive material, as some business types like to say.

The executive roles tended to require more interacting with senior-level managers and clients, more motivating of teams. She was qualified but wasn't selling that aspect in her interviews.

We worked on her modest answers first, emphasizing her experience in presenting to the CEO and inspiring her direct reports. We incorporated some enthusiastic language to help her inject tone and variety into her delivery. And, of course, we practiced.

The difference was dramatic, and Simone was soon offered an executive-level job that excited her.

Chapter **16**

Overcoming Common Interview Challenges

After 15 years of coaching and more than 2,000 clients, I have found that several common situations call for interview skill intervention. These are the challenges that motivate people to call an interview coach, so I have a lot of experience in helping people overcome them.

You've probably dealt with at least one of them in the past — or maybe you're facing one right now.

I wrote this chapter to give you a shortcut to a focused plan for each of these common scenarios. I provide an overview of the key concerns and to-do items for each situation and then point you to additional chapters to go deeper into preparing for each essential topic.

"Help! My Interview Is Tomorrow and I Need to Prepare Quickly"

The good news is that you got that exciting interview invitation. Congratulations!

The bad news is that you haven't prepared and maybe you're freaking out a little. Maybe you just started your job search and haven't yet had time to freshen your interview skills. Maybe you weren't actively looking, but an amazing opportunity landed in your lap. Another possibility is that you've been interviewing, but it hasn't been going great and you know you need to rethink your approach for the next one, especially if it's a dream opportunity.

Whatever your situation, it's time to get you up and running quickly. With limited time to prepare, you'll need to be focused and work extra hard to get really good really fast.

Brush up on best practices

If you're already familiar with how job interviews work and what to expect, skip ahead to the next section.

However, if you don't have a lot of interview experience or you haven't had any training in the past and have been flying blind, I recommend that you review Chapter 1 and Chapter 3 to get a quick background in interview best practices and the different interviewers and formats you'll encounter.

Analyze your fit

Before you start preparing your answers, take a moment to review the job description for the new opportunity and analyze your fit, including your greatest strengths and any potential weaknesses or gaps you'll want to address.

Chapter 4 will walk you through this process and help you identify the most likely questions to prepare for.

Prepare for the most likely questions

Part 3 of this book focuses on the most likely and most critical questions to prepare for when you don't have a lot of time. It's inspired by the Fast Track curriculum I came up with on Big Interview with the help of my team — a curriculum we created for people just like you.

Each chapter provides an overview of why each question type is asked and how to structure impressive answers. I also give you handy models to help you quickly outline impressive answers.

If you have limited time, focus on the following topics first:

>> Tell me about yourself (Chapter 6)

>> Why do you want to work here? (Chapter 7)

>> What are your strengths and weaknesses? (Chapter 8)

>> Why are you looking for a new role now? (Chapter 10)

>> Mastering behavioral questions (Chapter 11)

>> Answering tricky questions (Chapter 12)

TIP

Review your resume before the interview, especially if it's been a while since you updated it or read it closely (which is often the case if you weren't actively looking and the opportunity popped up unexpectedly). No one knows their entire resume by heart, especially the older bits, so it's best to refresh your memory in case questions come up.

"I Haven't Interviewed in Years and I'm Rusty"

Has it been a while since your last job interview? Even if you rocked your interviews the last time around, you're probably feeling rusty if it's been a year or more. If it's been 5 years or longer since your last formal interview, you definitely need a full refresher course.

After all, talking about yourself in a job interview is a specialized skill. In real life, you aren't called upon to talk at length about your strengths, weaknesses, accomplishments, and career goals, so you fall out of practice.

WARNING

Most likely, you weren't perfectly prepared the last time around, either. Let's face it: Most of us were never taught how to interview well. We just tried our best to figure it out. Now you have an opportunity to learn to do it the right way and become a true ace.

Meanwhile, over the years you've been racking up new experience and accomplishments. You've never talked about these in an interview, and this recent experience will be the most relevant for your interviewers because it reflects what you can do now.

REMEMBER

Don't just fall back on your speaking points from the last time around, when you were less skilled and accomplished. I have seen this outlook trip up many coaching clients. They were interviewing from the perspective of their younger selves and not coming across as senior enough for the roles they wanted.

Identify what's new

First, let's consider what has changed since the last time around and see what the new challenge looks like:

>> **New job description:** Job description analysis is your first step. This new opportunity is likely quite different from the ones you last interviewed for.

You must analyze the job description thoroughly so that you can anticipate the most likely questions and how interviewers are likely to view your fit (both strengths and weaknesses). See Chapter 4 for advice on analyzing job descriptions.

>> **New experience:** If it's been a while, it's essential that you inventory your experience since your last round of interviewing.

For your last position (or the last few, if necessary), make a list of all your new skills and experience and accomplishments. It's important to remind yourself of how far you've come and how your skills and expertise have evolved.

You are certain to be asked detailed questions about your most recent position(s). Be prepared for questions along the following lines:

- Tell me more about your most recent or current role.

- What were your greatest accomplishments in your most recent or current role?

- What were the biggest challenges in your current or most recent role?

- Tell me more about a particular project or responsibility [from your resume] in your current or most recent role.

This inventory also prepares you for other important questions that are likely to come up, including these:

Tell me about yourself (see Chapter 6): Your most recent role should feature prominently in your elevator pitch.

What are your strengths? (see Chapter 8): Be sure to include the new and newly improved strengths that are most relevant for the position.

Behavioral questions (see Chapter 11): Be ready with STAR stories about recent accomplishments, especially those that demonstrate key competencies for the position.

REMEMBER

STAR is the acronym formed by these four words: *Situation, Task, Action, Result.* It's a model to help you outline your greatest hits stories and I have STAR advice and examples in Chapter 11.

>> **New goals:** Your goals and motivations have likely also changed. Think about the new answers to the following questions:

- Why are you looking for a new role now? (see Chapter 10)

- What are you looking for? (see Chapter 7)

>> **New world of interviewing:** Interviewing is constantly changing. If it has been a while for you, you may not be accustomed to video interviews. You may also not be prepared for new types of questions or new approaches to hiring.

Review Chapter 2 for an overview of what you need to know about recent trends in hiring and interviewing.

Ace common interview questions

Next, I recommend spending some time reviewing the chapters that deal with the most common (and trickiest) questions.

Here are my top picks for you:

>> **Tell me about yourself:** Again, this is the inevitable opening question that can make or break the interview within the first minute. This should be a 1- to 2-minute overview of your relevant career experience, and it's essential that you emphasize your most recent role and convey the right level of overall experience. See Chapter 6 for my 3-part model and sample answers.

>> **Why do you want to work here?:** This is a critical question in every single interview. If you haven't interviewed in a while, it's likely that you're now at a critical juncture in your career, whether moving on from a long-term employer, reentering the workforce after spending time away, or making a career change. This means it's even more crucial for you to be able to articulate why this job is the perfect next chapter for you. See Chapter 7 for more on answering this question.

>> **What are your strengths?:** You're likely to get at least one question about your strengths, so get ready to talk up your most impressive capabilities. You probably don't talk about yourself in this way outside of job interviews, so you're likely to be out of practice. However, it's important for you to sell your strengths in a way that feels authentic. It's also important that you don't fall back on outdated strengths from the last time around. You must present strengths that do justice to your current experience and skill levels. See Chapter 8 for more on talking about your strengths.

>> **Behavioral questions:** Those "Tell me about a time . . ." questions can be tough. If you haven't interviewed for a while, you have to outline your new stories and refresh your memory on those greatest hits from your past. See Chapter 11 for advice on outlining your greatest-hits stories using the STAR format.

>> **Tricky questions:** Prepare for any tricky questions that might come up based on your background and the job description. For example, if you're rusty because you were just abruptly laid off, you'll likely be asked to explain your departure. Chapter 12 has advice on answering the tricky questions that come up.

Now, practice!

Practice is especially important when you haven't interviewed for a while. Practice will help you refamiliarize yourself with Interview mode before you're under fire.

I know that interview practice can feel tedious, but it absolutely makes a huge difference when it comes to feeling (and sounding) confident.

REMEMBER

Practice doesn't mean memorizing a canned answer and reciting it. The idea is to sketch out your key speaking points and then practice delivering spontaneously until you feel comfortable with the basic outline of what you want to say.

Practice helps you become comfortable with your answers, increase your confidence, and eliminate nervous habits. See Chapter 14 for guidance on how to make the most of practice.

TIP

If you've been working for the same company for many years, it's important to demonstrate that you're up to the challenge of making a change and aren't stuck in a rut. Make sure you have a great answer to "Why are you interested in this role?" Emphasize your excitement about making a change.

"I Hate Selling Myself"

This is such a common issue that I address it many times throughout this book. Some people truly struggle with being self-promotional in job interviews. It's understandable that you're not accustomed to raving about your greatest accomplishments in everyday life, at least not to complete strangers. You may have also been conditioned to believe that bragging is bad form.

However, a job interview calls for some bragging. The interviewer wants to hear how you stand out from other applicants and what makes you the best person for the job.

It's impossible to form a complete picture of another human being in just 30 or 40 minutes. That means the interviewer will know only what you tell them. You can't count on them to read between the lines of your resume or understand the full truth behind your humble words.

For an in-depth guide to learning how to sell yourself in interviews, see Chapter 14.

"I Need to Convey 'Executive' Presence"

Interviews definitely become more challenging as you advance in your career and pursue more senior-level positions. On the plus side, you have more experience and accomplishments that you can talk about.

However, senior-level opportunities are extremely competitive. You'll be going up against other highly accomplished and impressive people.

In addition to looking for the right skills and experience, your interviewers will be looking for that mysterious quality called *executive presence.* People have varying opinions on exactly what this term means — and how one can convey it properly during a 30- to 40-minute job interview.

In my experience in working with both hiring companies and senior executive job seekers, executive presence is primarily about projecting confidence. You must demonstrate that you're someone who has not only the skills to lead and make important decisions but also the ability to inspire trust and credibility both inside and outside of the company.

There are different types of executive presence, of course. Some leaders are charismatic and extroverted, and others project more of a strong, silent confidence.

When people talk about executive presence, you often also hear the word *gravitas*, a word derived from Latin for *heavy*. A leader with gravitas conveys substance and authority.

Of course, a leader with executive presence must also come across as likeable and approachable. It's a balancing act, to be sure.

Even for those who easily project confidence on the job, it can be challenging to deliver that executive presence on demand in a job interview.

The three C's

You'll be happy to know that executive presence can be learned. Think about it as conveying the three C's: confidence, connection, and calm:

» *Confidence* shows that you're assured of your ability to excel in the role and that you're comfortable with taking on new challenges.

» *Connection* is important as well — someone can be confident to the point of arrogance and not connect with the interviewer. The interviewer needs to see you as someone who can motivate and inspire the team.

» *Calm* is linked to the gravitas I mentioned earlier in this chapter: Leaders need to be calm under pressure and able to make tough decisions in a thoughtful way. There's such a thing as being *too* calm, of course — you don't want to put anyone to sleep or come across as low-energy. But you also want to make clear that you can lead with authority without allowing nerves or emotion to get in the way of doing the right thing.

The next several sections give you some tips on how to project these three C's of executive presence — in job interviews and anywhere else.

Wardrobe

A big part of executive presence is looking the part. What you wear is a major factor in making a first impression.

For professional presentation, dress for the job you *want* to have. The typical senior-executive uniform varies a bit, based on industry. An expensive suit will serve you well in some fields, though in others, a formal suit will make you seem stiff or out of touch.

An interview calls for a little extra effort. You may dress just fine for your daily gig as a manager, but when you meet new interviewers for the first time, it's worth investing the time to look just a bit sharper.

Body language

Your body language can help you amp up your executive presence, but it can also sabotage your attempts at charisma.

In an interview, the stakes are high, and people feel that they're being judged (because they are). This tends to bring out nervous habits you may not even be aware of.

Nerves are normal, but *visible* nerves detract from executive presence. You want to come across as confident and unflappable. After all, in an executive role, you will be called upon to make tough decisions under pressure, to motivate others, and to represent the company.

This list describes various aspects of executive presence body language:

>> **Posture:** Sit up straight and project confidence. Don't slouch or take a casual stance. Don't hunch or cross your arms — it makes you look defensive.

>> **Eye contact:** Make eye contact confidently and naturally. Resist the temptation to look away or look down for long stretches. People tend to avoid eye contact — often subconsciously — when they're nervous and when they're distracted by thinking about what to say next.

>> **Facial expression:** Remember to smile and show that you're happy to be there. A natural, relaxed smile helps convey confidence and calm while making a connection with the interviewer.

>> **Fidgeting:** Fidgeting definitely doesn't help with gravitas! Some job seekers are fidgeters, especially when nervous. With clients, I see nervous hand gestures, shifting or spinning in their chairs, fiddling with their hair or a pen or their resume in front of them. Again, preparation and practice will help you eliminate these nervous tells.

Please see Chapter 15 for more advice on improving your nonverbal communications.

Vocal quality

A commanding voice can communicate confidence and gravitas even in those moments when your words aren't quite right. You don't need a perfect radio-announcer voice, but you should do your best to sound both confident and energized.

Your tone is a big part of it. Your vocal tone can undercut your gravitas. If you sound squeaky or unsure (as in the classic up-talk style, where you add that little upwards lilt at the end of sentences that makes it sound as if you were asking a question.), you'll have trouble conveying authority. However, a monotone makes you sound low-energy and boring.

REMEMBER

Pace also plays a role here. Speaking quickly comes across as feeling nervous — and can also lead to your interviewer missing your most important points if you talk too fast. However, speaking too *slowly* can read as having low energy or low enthusiasm.

The good news is that all these vocal issues can be improved with interview practice. Even if your natural vocal tone and/or pace isn't your best quality, you can easily improve with awareness and practice.

It's generally a combination of tone (a deeper tone tends to conjure more of a sense of gravitas), pace (too fast can read as nervous and too slow can read as dull), and inflection (enough warmth to read as enthusiastic and engaging).

Chapter 15 covers the specifics of how to make adjustments to your vocal delivery.

Language

Choosing your words carefully can help a lot with conveying executive presence.

In fact, word choice can compensate for weaknesses in other areas. Not everyone is born with the vocal talents of Morgan Freeman or the physical presence of a supermodel. The right words can also inspire more confident body language and vocal inflection.

If you review the chapters in Part 3 and develop compelling speaking points for all the critical interview questions, including your behavioral stories, you'll have answers that demonstrate your confidence and capabilities.

As you're working on those speaking points, keep executive presence in mind. Make an effort to use confident language that positions you as senior level. Use words like *strategy, vision,* and *results.*

Use action words such as *led, managed, initiated, created, solved,* and *succeeded.*

Make sure you add enough *I* statements among the *we* statements. This can be a shift in thinking for many leaders. You're used to talking about *we* and giving credit to the team. That's great. But in an interview, you also want to make clear where you played a key leadership role. Give yourself some credit — don't expect your interviewer to be able to read between the lines.

If you struggle with conveying enthusiasm, think about incorporating positive language to emphasize that you enjoy your work and are excited about the opportunity. You can use phrases like these: "It was a fantastic project . . ." "I loved having the opportunity to work on this project . . ." and "My favorite part of the job is XYZ . . . ."

Answering key questions like a boss

Certain common questions offer perfect opportunities to highlight your executive presence. Here's a sampling:

>> **Tell me about yourself (see Chapter 6):** The right answer to this ubiquitous opening question can establish you as a leader within the first minute. Even if you believe that you have a good approach, I recommend rethinking to make sure you're taking full advantage of this opportunity to highlight your senior-level experience and set the right tone for the whole interview. You want to make sure this answer is up-to-date and reflects your most recent accomplishments — people often fall back on their "old" entry-level or midlevel answers — answers that usually sell themselves short.

>> **Strengths (see Chapter 7):** You're bound to get some variation on the strengths question. These are some common variations:

   • "Why are you a good fit?"

   • "What would you bring to the role?"

   • "Why should we hire you?"

REMEMBER

At this stage in your career, you're going up against other candidates with impressive experience, so it's harder to stand out. You must take the time to choose the best strengths to highlight and back them up with detailed examples.

>> **Behavioral questions (Chapter 11):** When you get those "Tell me about a time . . ." questions, you must be ready with examples that are recent, relevant, and impressive. At your level, they will be expecting you to come in with expertise in the key job competencies, including leadership and people management.

Be ready with stories about your top accomplishments and your biggest wins.

>> **Why are you interested in this opportunity? (Chapter 7):** Experienced candidates sometimes forget that it's not just about whether you could do the job, but also about whether you *really* want the job. Managers know that motivated employees perform better.

When interviewing for a leadership role, it's even more important to demonstrate that you're motivated. There will be a learning curve, so they need someone with the hunger to hit the ground running.

Putting it all together

If all this sounds a bit daunting, don't worry. You don't have to work on all these elements separately. You can make impressive improvements in all aspects of your executive presence simply by preparing and practicing properly.

The preparation will help you choose your most impressive examples and qualifications to highlight — leading to more confidence. You won't be distracted by worrying about what to say and this is the number-one reason people fall back on nervous habits in the interview.

Conscious practice is sure to refine your delivery. By *conscious*, I mean being aware of any body language or vocal habits that could undercut your gravitas.

You can consciously work on better eye contact, pacing yourself, and injecting more energy into your presentation.

If you follow these steps, you can ensure you're serving executive presence in your senior-level interviews.

"I'm Changing Careers"

Career changers face an added level of difficulty when it comes to interviewing. Whether you're planning a slight shift in direction or a more dramatic change, you'd be smart to put extra time into your interview preparation.

It's always easier to interview for a position that seems like an obvious next step from what you're doing now. You're more of a proven commodity, and a quick resume review makes it clear where your interests and abilities lie.

When you're seeking a change, you must make the case for why you want to change and why you'll be a superstar if they take a chance on you.

It's imperative for your interviewers to recognize that you're serious about making the change (and are thus motivated to succeed even if there's a learning curve). You also need to convince them that you have the right transferable skills to succeed in the new job.

As a career changer, even if you've been successful at interviewing in the past, you have to change your approach to address the new requirements and challenges of your career shift.

REMEMBER

It's difficult enough to get in the door to interview for a career change opportunity. Recruiters are quick to toss aside resumes that don't show an obvious fit within a 6-second scan. Career changers work hard to network, hustle, and develop the new skills they need, just to be seriously considered.

So, when you do get the chance to interview, you need to make it count.

Career changers can benefit from all the advice in this book. Becoming a strong interviewer will open doors for you now and in the future. However, I want to call out the key areas to focus on.

With my coaching clients, I have seen how these techniques can be game changers when it comes to persuading interviewers to take a chance on a candidate with an unusual background.

Grab them with "Tell me about yourself"

This common opening question can make or break the interview within the first minute. As a career changer, you have to find a way to grab them with your career story if you want to compete with more traditional candidates.

The goal is to start strong by showcasing your transferable skills and experience and highlighting your commitment to making the change.

TIP

The work you do on your answer to this question also helps you with networking and informational interviews. A shorter version works well for elevator pitches and introducing yourself at networking events or in email or LinkedIn outreach.

As a career changer, your "Tell me about yourself" story requires some creativity. You certainly can't get by with just reciting your resume.

It's always difficult to tell one's whole career story in 1 to 2 minutes. For you, there's an added challenge because you need to cover the highlights of your career while also discussing the career change — what inspired it and what transferable skills and knowledge you can bring to the new role.

TIP

One useful approach is to use my 3-part model to lead with what's most compelling and grab their attention. (Get the full tutorial on the 3-part model in Chapter 6.)

Then, in Part 3 of the answer, when you talk about "why I'm here," you can briefly address the reasons for the career change and your commitment to this new path. You don't have to cover every detail, because they will almost certainly ask follow-up questions.

However, this is a good way to positively frame the transition right at the beginning of the interview — and maybe even head off awkward questions or unspoken doubts.

Inspire them with "Why do you want to work here?"

For career changers, this is probably the most important question. Check Chapter 7 for the best practices for addressing all the angles on this question, including these:

>> Why this role?

>> Why this organization?

>> Why this career path?

That last one isn't often an issue for traditional candidates — the position is a logical next step for them. You, on the other hand, have to sell them on why this is the perfect next step for you even if it's not the logical next step based on your resume.

REMEMBER

Approach this topic in a positive, purposeful, and enthusiastic manner. By *positive*, I mean that you should emphasize how you're moving toward something that's a better fit, not running away from your previous career. By *purposeful*, I mean that it's important to show that you've thought long and hard about this and are fully committed. You're not just exploring. *Enthusiastic* probably requires no further explanation. Any career change requires a learning curve. In this case, they would be taking a chance on hiring you over a more traditional candidate. Help them see that your passion and determination will easily give you an edge — along with the other useful transferable skills and strengths you'll also tell them about.

Become an expert on the job description

Take extra time to thoroughly analyze the job description and identify where you're a great fit (and why) and where they might have doubts. This is a helpful activity for everybody (see Chapter 4 for detailed instructions on how to analyze a job description), but especially for career changers.

First, the hiring team needs to feel confident that you fully understand the job and its requirements if you're coming from a different background. A thorough understanding of the job description will also help you anticipate the difficult questions and proactively prepare how to sell your strengths and play down any perceived weaknesses.

Sell your strengths

You're likely to get at least one question about your strengths. What are your greatest strengths? Why are you a good fit? What would you bring to the role? What sets you apart from other candidates?

This is an opportunity to sell yourself for the position. The problem is that most people are terrible at it. See Chapter 8 for my best practices for selling your strengths in any interview scenario.

Beyond best practices, you'll want to put in extra effort if you're an unconventional candidate coming from a different field. Your interviewers won't necessarily "get" what you can bring to the role. They may not even fully understand what you did in your previous career. You can't rest on your resume and some general positives like *team player* and *hard worker.*

As a career changer, you may need to spoon-feed some of this information with extra examples if your interviewers aren't experts on your previous career path.

Play defense on weaknesses

Unfortunately, it's still quite common for interviewers to ask you to talk about your greatest weaknesses. Nobody likes this question. See Chapter 8 for the best way to address this awkward subject and some sample answers to spark ideas.

On the plus side, as a career changer, questions about weaknesses offer opportunities to address the elephant in the room and reframe your nontypical background.

You can acknowledge that some might see your background as a weakness, but then use the opening to detail all of the ways your past has prepared you for the role and all the strengths that will empower you to conquer the learning curve quickly.

The key is to strike a balance between acknowledging that you're not a conventional candidate and confidently assuring them that you're ready to dive in and do a great job. Don't be too self-deprecating, but don't claim that you're already an expert or else you risk coming across as delusional.

The bonus to this approach is that it allows you to avoid being forced to share additional weaknesses.

They can see clearly from your resume that you're a career changer, so you're not risking anything by bringing it up. In fact, you're seizing the chance to reframe their perception of you.

Show, don't tell

Those "Tell me about a time . . ." questions are quite common, especially at mid-size to large firms where the interview process is highly structured. They're looking to develop an understanding of how you've demonstrated key competencies in the past. (If you haven't already read Chapter 11 for my tutorial on behavioral questions and using the STAR format, you might want to read it now.)

The techniques I highlight in Chapter 11 are a huge help, but as a career changer, you have to put extra work into coming up with relevant examples for responding to behavioral questions. A traditional candidate will have more experiences that are comparable to what the interviewers are familiar with.

You may be short on obvious apples-to-apples comparisons between your past projects and the desired job competencies. That's why it's vital to analyze that job description — and do additional research — to understand the most important competencies for the role at hand. After completing those tasks, you can brainstorm to identify which of your past accomplishments best demonstrate your fit. From there, use that STAR format to outline stories that show your transferable competencies and strengths.

These stories can be used for answering formal behavioral questions but will also come in handy in other ways. Look for opportunities to tell your stories so that you can show them what you've accomplished and what you're like to work with. For career changers, it's important for them to be able to picture you in the job. Stories help you paint the picture.

Show that you're committed

Be prepared with a descriptive answer to that old-fashioned and maddening question: Where do you see yourself in five years? (And all the more reasonable variations like "What are your long-term career goals?")

Listen: Nobody truly knows where they'll be in five years. However, this is still a common question. It's most common from interviewers who prioritize retention and are looking for someone to stay and grow with the organization over years.

This is an important question for career changers because it gives you the opening to establish that you're serious about this career change and committed for the long haul.

You may be seen as a risky hire. Your interviewers don't have a lot of evidence of your commitment to the career path. They don't want to hire someone who will change their mind and flake out.

That's why you need to make it absolutely clear that you've thought this career change through and are excited about a long-term career in the field.

TIP

Look for any opportunity to bring up how excited you are about your new career path — this question is the most obvious opportunity, but you can also talk about it when discussing your interest in the position or what you're looking for in your next role, for example.

Make it stick with practice

Once you have outlined your responses to the key questions, it's time to practice. I realize that interview practice can feel tedious, but it absolutely makes a huge difference when it comes to feeling (and sounding) confident.

For career changers, it's especially important. Even if you were great in your past interviews, you were interviewing for different types of jobs. Compared to now, you were operating in Easy mode. You need to reprogram your approach and break any habits that are counterproductive.

REMEMBER

It's more important to convey confidence and inspire trust in career change interviews than in any other interview setting. Practice is the secret weapon to help you feel comfortable with your answers and fine-tune your nonverbal communications.

"I Don't Have Much Real Experience"

If you're just starting out in your field, I strongly recommend that you review this entire book so that you can take full advantage of each and every interview opportunity you're offered.

I've worked with a lot of students and new graduates, in my coaching practice and at Big Interview, which is licensed by more than 600 schools and universities in the United States and internationally. I regularly speak with the counselors in our clients' career services centers. All this is to say that I have a thorough understanding of what you're dealing with if you're just launching your career.

Read the chapters, follow the techniques for outlining your answers, and then practice until you feel like a pro.

There are a few additional pieces of advice to keep in mind to guide your preparation for your career launch.

Show your potential

For entry-level roles, hiring managers know you won't have much (if any) direct experience in the duties of the role.

Instead, they're likely to focus on evaluating the competencies you'll need to thrive in the key aspects of the job. For example, they're likely to ask you behavioral questions about teamwork, work ethic, problem-solving, communication, and other core competencies.

TIP

Because you lack any real demonstrated experience in a full-time work environment, there will also be more focus on assessing your ability to behave professionally and get along well with others. Talk about any background you have in working with others and meeting deadlines in internships, extracurricular activities, volunteer work, or academic projects.

Interest and enthusiasm are also strong indicators of your potential to excel in the position. Engaged employees are more productive. I often see students and new grads make the mistake of flubbing the answer to the question "Why are you interested in this opportunity?"

They're new to this process and assume that they've communicated their interest by just showing up for the interview. However, if you don't seem excited about being there, it can hurt your chances. Describe in detail why you're interested in the position, the organization, and the career path.

Get creative with your examples

Even if you have no work experience, you need sample stories for behavioral questions. You'll just have to pull your examples from internships, school, hobbies, and volunteer work.

Remember that it's mostly about potential here. If you have examples that are similar to the work you'd be doing, by all means use them. If not, get creative.

Think about the competencies required for the job and then find examples that speak to your potential in those areas. These are some of the most common competencies required in entry-level work:

>> **Teamwork:** You may have good teamwork examples from internship experiences, team sports (school or intramural teams), academic projects (a go-to for many recent college grads), part-time jobs like retail or food service, and extracurricular activities such as school clubs or charity work.

>> **Work ethic:** You can demonstrate work ethic by talking about accomplishments such as exceling with a demanding course load, balancing school with work and/or other commitments, or mastery of a skill that requires strong commitment and practice (athletic, artistic, or otherwise).

>> **Dealing with difficult people:** Good examples can come from challenging team experiences (see the first bullet entry), working in a public-facing job, working with kids (and their helicopter parents), or working for a demanding boss of any kind.

>> **Leadership:** Though most entry-level jobs don't require leadership, many companies like to hire people with leadership potential. Brainstorm for stories that show you stepping up to take the lead, even in a minor sense. For example, you may have led the team in a group class project. Perhaps you were a captain on a team, whether in athletics or another extracurricular activity (think debate club, school magazine, or neighborhood clean-up).

Practice

Again with the recommendation to practice. I know I've gotten pretty predictable with my obsession with practice, but I can't wrap up this topic without mentioning it.

When you're just starting out in your career, good interview skills will take you a long way in demonstrating your potential and establishing rapport with your interviewers.

At this stage, confident interviewing can really set you apart from the competition. Most of those other applicants will not have the knowledge you have, and they won't prepare as effectively.

Embrace this advantage to start your career on the right note.

"I Just Got Laid Off!"

If you picked up this book because you recently got laid off and unexpectedly forced into Job Search mode, I'm here for you. I know how painful layoffs can be. I've been laid off myself three times, and I have worked with hundreds of coaching clients in the same situation.

You may be feeling shock, betrayal, anger, sadness, and anxiety about the future (and maybe a few other emotions as well — maybe even a little relief). These are all normal reactions, especially if you thought things were going well and were blindsided by the news.

Give yourself a little time to process the news if you haven't already. Then, as soon as you can, it's time to develop a game plan to get you gainfully employed again.

Evaluate your options

The first step is to explore your current options. The idea of having to interview again can be overwhelming, especially if it's been a while.

Sometimes, it helps to take a step back and do some self-reflection about what you want to do next (and what you want to avoid). This analysis will make your follow-up steps much easier because you'll be able to focus your efforts on targeting the right opportunities. Here are some questions that could spur some useful self-reflection:

>> Is now a good time to make a career change? What are some interesting directions to explore?

>> Are you interested in a position similar to your last one?

>> Is now a good time to apply for a bigger job with more responsibilities? What does the next step on the career ladder look like for you?

>> What is your ideal company size?

>> Do you prefer in-person work, a remote arrangement, or some kind of hybrid?

>> Are you willing to relocate?

Answering these questions should give you a broad outline to help with your next step.

WARNING

Getting laid off can take a toll on your confidence if you let it. You didn't lose your job because of poor performance or lack of skill or even bad karma. It was an economic decision. Don't take it personally and don't let it cause self-doubt. Remember that layoffs are now just a part of life.

Identify your resources

Take the time to evaluate your resources. Your company may have provided you with a severance package that includes some career help (resume writing, career coaching, or interview prep tools, for example). Take advantage of it — it's the least they could do.

Your network is also a valuable resource. Start thinking about who can help you. Let people know you're looking and accept assistance in whatever form it comes in (a referral, an introduction, a mentorship opportunity, a course discount).

Update your resume and start your job search

Once you've identified your target job type(s), it's time to update your resume and your LinkedIn profile to attract the right opportunities and launch your job search in earnest.

This isn't a book about resume writing or job search strategies, so I'll leave it at that for now. For more advice on these topics, see Laura deCarlo's *Resumes For Dummies* and Max Messmer's *Job Hunting For Dummies* (published by Wiley).

Work on your interview skills

Once you've put the job search wheels in motion, get started with your interview prep so that you'll be ready when the invitations start coming in.

Prepare answers for all the key questions. One of the most important for post-layoff interviews is "Why are you looking for a new opportunity now?" (see Chapter 10). This is where you can address the layoff and proactively counter any concerns about why you're not currently employed.

TIP

If you're still feeling emotional or sensitive about the layoff, it's especially important to outline your speaking points and practice. This helps ensure that you don't come across as defensive or looking like you're hiding something that might be a red flag.

Other priorities are to update your "Tell me about yourself" answer (see Chapter 6), become comfortable selling your strengths (see Chapter 8), and make sure you have at least three to five recent greatest-hits stories to demonstrate the key competencies your target roles require (see Chapter 11).

I also recommend reviewing all the chapters in this book on interview best practices, especially if it's been while since you interviewed last. If you prepare and practice the right way before you start interviewing, you'll be able to speed up your transition from layoff to new job.

"English Isn't My First Language"

Job interviews are challenging enough when everybody's speaking their first language. They're even trickier for international candidates — and anyone who was raised with a different primary language than English.

REMEMBER

The American job interview is different from an interview in China or Brazil or the UK. Some differences are minor, and others are more daunting.

I have worked with hundreds of international students and job candidates — and coached hundreds of them to land jobs and internships at prestigious US-based firms. During that process, I have seen similar challenges come up over and over again.

Here are my top recommendations for overcoming these challenges.

Challenge 1: Self promotion

Let's start with the biggest challenge for many international and ESL job seekers (and for many native US job seekers as well!): self-promotion, or "selling" yourself as a candidate.

Why is this harder for some people than for others? It's partly a matter of personality — if you're shy or introverted or humble by nature, you will probably struggle more than your extroverted buddy.

However, culture also plays a role in your ability to sell your achievements and strengths in a job interview. In his book *Beyond Culture*, the anthropologist Edward T. Hall presented the theory of high-context cultures and low-context cultures.

In *high-context cultures* (including countries in Asia, the Middle East, and South America, among others), social trust must be earned first, and situations and relationships are more important than the actual words spoken.

Low-context cultures (including the United States, the United Kingdom, Germany, and Australia), on the other hand, place more emphasis on the individual and a preference to get down to business quickly (instead of spending more time on establishing trust).

You can imagine why someone raised in a high-context culture would struggle with a US job interview, even putting language aside.

REMEMBER

When interviewing for positions in the United States (and other low-context cultures), it's important to be able to articulate your value to prospective employers and what sets you apart from other candidates. This prospect will be uncomfortable (or even terrifying) for someone raised to blend in and/or to avoid bragging.

However, it's a skill that can be learned. In Chapter 14, I outline a number of techniques to help you learn to sell yourself in interviews, even if you're humble by nature and hate the very idea of it.

Challenge 2: Speaking the same language

Some candidates worry about being fluent in American "interview speak." A lot of this lingo isn't taught in English classes.

Luckily, you can take some simple steps to ensure that you and your interviewer will be able to understand each other:

First, know the job description. Read it thoroughly and translate any buzzwords, industry jargon, or obscure terminology. Google and ChatGPT can help you interpret if you get stuck. This pre-work greatly reduces the chances that your interviewer will toss out a word you don't understand.

Next, research interview questions to get comfortable with common question phrasing so that you won't be caught off-guard in the interview. Start with the questions in Part 3 of this book.

Finally, try to get more comfortable thinking on your feet. Practice will help with that. With your free trial of Big Interview (https://www.dummies.com/go/bigInterview/), you can check out the Interview Roulette tool, which helps you with this skill by quizzing you with randomized questions.

If you do hear a word that you don't fully understand in the interview, do your best to interpret it based on context and tone. If you're still stuck, it's okay to ask your interviewer to clarify the question.

TIP

Sometimes, if you ask the interviewer to repeat the question, they might rephrase it as well and give you some additional context to figure it out.

Challenge 3: Accent

Many international candidates have accents — ranging from barely noticeable to very heavy. Most of my international coaching clients worry too much about their accents. In fact, worrying about their accents tends to distract them from giving great answers and establishing strong rapport.

It's perfectly okay to have an accent. Accents are often lovely and charming to American interviewers. The only real problem with an accent is if it makes your answers difficult to understand.

To minimize problems, make sure you're speaking slowly and clearly. Because interviews are nerve-wracking, candidates often grow anxious and start speaking more rapidly than usual. This can make them much harder to understand. Slow down and your messages are more likely to be received.

If you're uncertain whether you're speaking slowly enough or whether your accent could otherwise be distracting from your message, gather some candid feedback from someone you can trust.

If you get trustworthy feedback that your accent could be an issue, you can find accent-neutralization resources out there. However, I've found that practice and the proper pacing often make accent neutralization measures unnecessary.

Challenge 4: Nonverbal communications

Everybody knows that your nonverbal communications are critical to your first impression and to establishing the right rapport. (See Chapter 15 if you need more evidence.) However, there's a difference in how nonverbal communications are perceived in high-context versus low-context cultures.

In high-context cultures, prolonged eye contact can be seen as aggressive or disrespectful. In low-context cultures, lack of eye contact can be perceived as shifty or uninterested.

Chapter 15 provides an overview of how body language is interpreted US job interviews and techniques to help you refine your nonverbal communications to make a great impression.

Challenge 5: Confidence

In my experience, lack of confidence is the most common reason for bombing a job interview — and this is particularly true for international and ESL job seekers.

Lack of confidence can be exacerbated by any or all of the other challenges I've covered. International candidates also struggle with typical insecurities and nervousness when seeking a new opportunity.

The most effective cure for lack of confidence is interviewing: preparation and practice. Understand interview best practices (see Chapters 1-5), outline strong answers (see Chapters 6-13), and practice until you feel confident and ready.

TIP

Always accentuate the positive. Your unique strengths, personality, and cultural background can help you stand out. Think about the positive aspects of your background as well as the challenges as you prepare for your next interview.

5

The Part of Tens

IN THIS PART . . .

Learn interview tips from hiring managers

Spot red flags when interviewing at a toxic workplace

Land more interviews

Chapter **17**

Ten Interview Tips from Hiring Managers

I spend a lot of time talking to hiring managers and recruiters. I conduct training workshops for hiring managers at lots of different organizations, including startups, large corporations, government agencies, academic institutions, and nonprofits. I also rely on a network of trusted recruiters and hiring managers to make sure I stay up to date on hiring trends and shifting attitudes.

The advice throughout this book is based on real-life perspectives from the people with the power to hire you. However, I wanted to include a chapter that highlights the most common statements I hear whenever I ask hiring managers, "What interview advice would you give to your best friends?"

"Never Lie to Me in An Interview!"

This one comes up a lot. Hiring managers want to believe in you, but many are cynical, based on past experience. If they sense even a hint of dishonesty, the red flags start waving.

It may be tempting to exaggerate some responsibilities or results to make an impression, but it's truly not worth the risk. Most liars get busted eventually. They forget their own fibs, can't lie convincingly, or get caught during reference or background checks.

Think about it from the hiring manager's perspective. Falling for a deceptive candidate can lead to disaster. They end up hiring someone who can't do the job well and/or can't be trusted. That means they look bad as a manager and probably have to waste time and money cleaning up the mess (trying to fix the issue or replacing the dishonest employee).

If they catch you in a lie in the interview process, they will likely move on to someone who inspires more trust.

REMEMBER

That doesn't mean you have to share every little detail about yourself. Telling your story your way is fine as long as you don't present fiction as fact.

Getting caught in a lie can also affect your long-term reputation as a candidate. Most companies use internal applicant tracking systems and note those candidates that shouldn't be considered for future roles. I just heard a story from a friend in HR about rescinding a job offer because of a significant lie. They then had to mark the applicant as a "Do not hire" because they started applying for other roles at the company. This was particularly unfortunate because the candidate probably would have been hired based on their true qualifications if they hadn't lied, and now they've burned their bridges with one of the biggest employers in their field.

TIP

Honesty is always the best policy. If you know you have shortcomings (real or perceived) for the role, work on your resume and interview speaking points to address them and redirect to your strengths.

Let's say you're tempted to fib in an interview because you don't have all the must-have qualities. If you submitted a truthful resume and were still invited to interview, they think you have strong potential despite any gaps. When interview time comes around, be prepared to answer questions about your experience in the missing must-have item. Outline bullet points to sell any related experience and skills but own your limitations and then highlight how you're a fast learner and are committed to working on improving your skill set.

I speak with hiring managers every day, and I can assure you that most would rather hire someone authentic and trustworthy, even if they face a little learning curve.

"Showing Up Is Not Enough"

Another common hiring manager complaint: "Candidates just don't seem that 'into' the job."

They describe applicants who don't bother to research the company or supply detailed answers to questions like "Why are you interested in this opportunity?" or who act bored or distracted when the interviewer is speaking.

You may be thinking, "Well, I applied and I showed up, so I'm obviously interested." However, in a competitive hiring process, you need to show them some enthusiasm.

When considering multiple qualified candidates, enthusiasm is often the deciding factor. Hiring managers know that engaged employees are better performers.

TIP

You don't have to force delighted enthusiasm in every answer. Reinforcing your interest four or five times during the interview process should be enough to let them know you really want the job.

See Chapter 7 for advice on answering questions about why you're interested in the position and why you would want to work for the organization. You can also make your interest clear by doing your research thoroughly (see Chapter 4), asking relevant questions at the end of the interview (see Chapter 13), and following up within 24 hours (see Chapter 2).

"Don't Trash-Talk Your Previous Boss"

Even if your last manager was an evil sadist, avoid getting real about it in job interviews. Unfortunately, most hiring managers see negativity as a red flag. They don't have time to run an independent investigation, so they label you as a possible complainer and move forward with someone less risky.

Also, you want to keep the interview focused on your positive accomplishments. Don't spend that precious and limited time complaining about someone who's already stolen too much of your energy.

WARNING

Avoid negative comments about your former coworkers and clients as well. These will make the interviewer wonder about your attitude and ability to collaborate.

Sometimes you have to talk about a negative experience because it explains why you left a job or why you're looking for a new role now. In those cases, your best bet is to address the situation with neutral language (as best you can) and then shift the conversation in a positive direction. Emphasize what you learned, the positive aspects of the experience, and how it shaped you professionally.

See Chapter 12 for advice on answering tricky questions about past work experience and examples to help you find the right neutral wording.

TIP

Sometimes, if you faced challenges such as a lack of essential resources (staff, technology, budget), you can highlight how this was a growth opportunity and how you managed to find creative solutions. Just frame it as a win instead of as a complaint.

"Tell Me What You (and You Alone) Actually Did"

Some applicants unintentionally bury their accomplishments in generalities and "we" statements.

Yes, using "we" shows that you value teamwork and that you give credit where credit is due. But too much "we" can make the interviewer wonder about your part in the play.

The hiring manager wants to hear about your individual role to evaluate your skills. If "we" landed a big new client, how does the hiring manager know whether you led the charge or just picked up coffee for the rest of the team?

You can demonstrate your team skills while still owning your accomplishments. For example: "The team booked the meeting, and I negotiated the final offer."

WARNING

Strike a balance between "we" and "I." Too much "I" and credit-grabbing can make you sound arrogant and self-centered.

I know this is easier said than done at times. You probably get used to talking about "we" internally, where the focus is on the team and not on promoting yourself. It will feel uncomfortable to put the emphasis on you, but it's necessary if you want to close that job offer.

See Chapter 14 for more advice on learning to "sell" yourself in interviews, even if you're modest by nature.

"Always Follow Up"

Hiring managers want you to send a thank-you email and follow up after the interview.

Of course, some interviewers will ignore your nice thank-you email. That's okay. It's about playing the odds here. Many hiring managers have told me that they see a thank-you email and respectful follow-up as signs of interest and professionalism.

REMEMBER

Good follow-up can help you reinforce a positive interview impression or even boost your image after a mediocre performance.

After the thank-you note, check in periodically if you don't hear back in a timely fashion. Use every opportunity you have to reinforce the idea that you're excited about the role; it will help you stand out from other candidates and increase your chances of landing the job. Just be respectful. Don't stalk or complain.

I often get the question, "How many times is too many for follow-ups?" In my opinion, three is a reasonable number of attempts. However, you should always ask in the interview what the next steps look like for the role you're applying for.

Also, three times is a good limit if you're not getting any positive responses. If your contact provides encouragement or offers a reasonable explanation for a delayed decision, you may want to keep in touch longer (while continuing to explore other opportunities).

For executive roles, the interview process can take up to three months, and that means more follow-ups will be needed. In other cases, they may inform you of their timeline so that you can plan when to check in. For example, they may tell you that they will need at least two weeks to conduct all the first-round interviews before choosing who moves on. Or they may tell you they're in a rush and need to make a decision by the end of the week.

WARNING

If, after three follow-up attempts, you're feeling completely ghosted, it's probably best to move on. If it's your dream job and you've had encouraging feedback, you could make another attempt, especially if you've been informed that there may be delays (hiring manager on vacation or changes to the job description, for example). Just always keep pursuing other options in the meantime.

"Don't Stop Looking"

I asked hiring managers for the advice they would give their best friends. Although they may like the idea of applicants being 100 percent committed to their opportunity only, they will tell their friends to always keep their options open.

To use an old-fashioned, but still appropriate, expression, "Don't put all your eggs in one basket." Hiring managers and recruiters know that an offer isn't guaranteed, even when a candidate is the clear front runner.

This is, unfortunately, one of the most common mistakes I see with my coaching clients. They see a job they love, they apply, they ace the interview, and then they stop looking and cancel other pending interviews because they're *certain* that they found The One. Then they never receive the offer, or it gets rescinded, and they must start over from square one. Don't fall into this trap, no matter how tempting it is to think about never interviewing again.

Keep your options open until you're onboarding. If this past year has proved anything, it's that job security isn't what it used to be, and even if something is in writing, it's not 100 percent certain. (Don't get me started on how much I hate hearing about these situations.)

It's better to be strategic and keep nurturing other leads. It's okay to withdraw your candidacy later if the dream job becomes a reality.

Who knows? You may end up with multiple job offers and a stronger negotiating position for the one you like best.

WARNING

Some companies try to "lock in" candidates by allowing them only 24 to 48 hours to reply to an offer. If that happens to you and you're in the middle of the interviewing process for other opportunities, try asking respectfully for an extension. The average hiring process takes 42 days on average, according to the Society for Human Resources Management (SHRM), so they should be able to give you a bit more time to make this major life decision. If they can't give you at least another day or two to decide, especially without a good reason, that tells you a lot about their culture.

"It's Okay to Negotiate"

On a similar note, hiring managers may not want you to negotiate with *them*, but they would tell their friends to ask for what they deserve. The recruiters I know say they always make a fair initial offer based on their research and internal salary guidelines, but there is usually room for some negotiation for the right candidate.

Once they've made you an offer, you're in a prime position to get what you want. You have leverage because they want to hire you and have invested in the relationship.

Just put some thought into your counteroffer and make sure it's reasonable, given the current job market and what you know about trends in your industry and location. Generally, the expectation is you can ask for a salary 15 to 20 percent higher than the initial offer. You may not get your top number, but it should be considered a reasonable counteroffer to discuss. If you're asking for more than that, you'll need to sell your return on investment (ROI) and rare skills to win the deal.

WARNING

If you receive a lowball offer that's more than 20 percent below your minimum expectation, it's a red flag that the company either doesn't value employees or lacks realistic expectations for the job. You may be better off walking away than trying to negotiate a fair salary.

Most people don't negotiate. The primary reason is fear of offending their future boss or even jeopardizing the offer by asking for too much. Don't let this fear hold you back. If you negotiate in the right way, hiring managers are typically happy to consider your request. Just don't make delusional demands, deliver ultimatums, or flash attitude.

If your manager is offended by a reasonable negotiation, you don't want to work for them. It's one thing to say no and give a good reason for not being able to budge (even if it's the old cliché answer of "budget limitations"). However, anyone who's offended by a candidate merely having the "audacity" to question their offer is a toxic manager.

REMEMBER

If the company can't budge on salary, there may be other benefits you can negotiate. Think about performance bonuses, flexible work schedules, additional paid time off, relocation packages, or education or transportation stipends. You get the idea. Sometimes, HR can get creative to land the perfect hire, but you need to ask for what you need, because no one will give it to you proactively.

"It's Okay to Be Quiet"

Hiring managers complain about candidates who ramble on and on without actually answering the questions (or take so long to answer the question that the interviewer has already tuned out).

Rambling is common. Trust me. I have conducted thousands of practice interviews at this point, and I have heard a lot of long, drawn-out responses.

Sometimes I stop them and redirect, but sometimes I let them keep going to their natural conclusion so that I can advise them on exactly how to cut the fluff. Often, they know they have a habit of rambling when they get nervous, but they don't realize the full extent of how it comes across to interviewers.

REMEMBER

Attention spans are short, and you need to get to the good stuff as quickly as possible. Hiring managers want to hear what you have to say, but they also want you to get to the point.

Another common habit is continuing to talk just to fill the silence, waiting for some sign from the interviewer that you've answered correctly.

You can avoid rambling by following my advice on preparing your bullet points and practicing out loud. You'll know the key topics you want to cover, so you'll also know when to stop talking — and how to circle back to the point if you wander off into the weeds.

Overall, it's important to learn how to embrace silence. It's a mistake to think that awkward pauses must be avoided at all costs. In real life, you sometimes need a moment to think when a friend or colleague asks you a question. It's the same in an interview and you won't be judged for brief pauses.

TIP

If you're caught off-guard by an unexpected question, it's better to take a moment to organize your thoughts than to desperately fill the silence with whatever comes to mind first. A short pause will sound thoughtful and will greatly improve your odds of coming up with a good answer.

"Interview Them While They Interview You"

Organizations tend to have more power in the job interview dynamic. After all, they're the ones with the paying job and multiple candidates lining up to apply.

However, it's also important for you to do your due diligence during the process. Once they've made an offer, you'll need to decide whether it's the right fit for you. The hiring manager wants you to feel good about taking the job, out of consideration for you but also for purely selfish reasons. If you're a poor fit, you won't last long.

REMEMBER

According to the Bureau of Labor Statistics, you'll spend most of your time, Monday to Friday, every week for probably 4.1 years on average at your new place of employment. If you want to stay sane, you should actually enjoy being there.

You can gather the data you need by listening, observing, and asking smart questions during the hiring process. Hiring managers will tell you that some companies excel at painting a rosy picture of a supposedly ideal work environment. As applicants, we want to believe and sometimes fail to follow up on potential red flags.

This is a mistake I see a lot and have made myself, when I was younger: You're excited about a role, and something feels off, but you dismiss it and decide to move forward.

It's tough to walk away from a job offer, especially if you've been chasing it for months or have been out of work for some time. However, if you have any concerns about the fit, don't be afraid to take a step back and do some more research. You can ask the recruiter or hiring manager additional questions or talk to a trusted mentor to get an objective opinion on anything that's giving you pause.

"Be Prepared, but Not Too Prepared"

I hate when hiring managers complain to me that a candidate seemed "too prepared." There is a common misconception that being prepared is equivalent to being inauthentic.

So, if someone tells you not to prepare, keep this in mind and ignore the misguided advice. Trust me. If you go in there without preparing, they'll complain that you were unpolished or didn't answer the questions well.

Preparation will always serve you well. However, sounding scripted or robotic can make the wrong impression. That's where the "too prepared" complaint usually comes from.

As discussed in previous chapters, preparation and practice will make you sound more authentic because it gives you the opportunity to organize your thoughts in advance and develop the confidence to project your best self.

Just don't fall into the traps of scripting fake answers, memorizing your bullet points word-for-word, or relying on generalities about what you think they want to hear.

Be yourself but prepare to be the most professional and articulate possible version of yourself.

Chapter **18**

Ten Red Flags You're Interviewing at a Toxic Workplace

share a lot of tips in this book on how to avoid raising red flags with hiring managers. Now let's discuss how you can spot red flags on the other side of the interview.

It's important to look for clues about what it would be like to actually work for an organization from day to day. If you pay attention, you'll notice positive indicators when you're interviewing at a great place to work. You will also see clues when an organization is dysfunctional or even toxic.

There are a lot of toxic workplaces out there. Working in a toxic environment (and working for toxic people) long-term can cause true psychological damage — leading to burnout, self-doubt, anxiety, and even depression.

So, how do you know when to run screaming from a job offer? It's not always obvious. Part of the challenge is that you always want to believe in the dream. Usually, some parts of the offer are attractive. It's tempting to overlook clues, take the job, and just stop having to interview already.

I made this mistake early in my career. I was bored and ready for a change, so I believed the recruiter, ignored the clues, and took the role. My punishment was to suffer through months with a toxic manager before I could escape.

If you know the red flags to look for and how to investigate them, you'll be able to avoid making a similar mistake.

They Say They're "Like a Family"

Families are not exactly for-profit institutions (okay, maybe the Kardashians). Sure, some families are dysfunctional and toxic, but we don't get to choose our families of origin.

When hiring managers and HR contacts make this comparison, it's usually a lie or a way of rationalizing inappropriate boundaries. Don't allow yourself to be charmed by this buzzword, especially if they can't provide some examples of how exactly they're like a family (in a good way).

Sometimes, this phrase isn't a sign of a toxic environment; it's just the poorly chosen words of a delusional interviewer who wants to woo you. However, in other workplaces, it's a clue that you'll be overworked and underpaid because blind loyalty and sacrifice are part of being a family. Even worse, sometimes it means that your boss will want to hang out with you every day after work.

WARNING

Do yourself a favor if this phrase comes up during the interview process: Probe for more information.

You Notice a "This Is Just How We Do It" Mentality

Look for signs that your manager is fixated on their current way of doing things and not open to ideas or collaboration. This attitude might start from the top of the organization and filter down, or it might just be a problem within the team. Either way, you can expect a nightmare of micromanagement if you accept the job.

REMEMBER

This job won't be a good fit for you if you value growth, flexibility, or autonomy. If you like structure and predictability and you're okay with a bit of micromanagement, maybe you can make it work. Personally, I would run screaming from the room.

They Avoid Questions about Company Turnover

Avoiding questions about turnover is a huge red flag. If people keep leaving, there's a reason, and it might be the job, the team, or the company.

Be wary if the interviewer refuses to answer questions about this topic or if the answers set off your BS meter. They may be trying to hide issues that have scared off many valiant employees before you.

Ask why the position is open. Ask how the team has changed in the past year. Listen carefully to the answers. Check Glassdoor.com to see whether disgruntled former employees have posted warnings.

This was the clue I foolishly ignored when I accepted a job in a toxic work environment. I believed the recruiter when she said the last person in the role had personal issues, even though I knew it sounded fishy. I *wanted* to believe.

They're Confusing Company Culture with Benefits

You ask, "What is the company culture like?" They reply, "We have Pizza Fridays and a 401(k) match."

I love pizza, but it is not a cultural value. Certain benefits may reflect corporate values — for example, the 401(k) match may be representative of a culture that values long-term growth and retention.

Culture is about the values and shared vision that drive behavior within the organization. *Benefits* are the extra perks that come with the job. Benefits are important, too, but they're different.

It's a bad sign if your potential employer doesn't seem to understand the difference between culture and benefits. Also, be wary if the "cultural values" are so vague that they are meaningless or if various interviewers have different descriptions of the company culture.

TIP

Most organizations post official corporate values and descriptions of the collaborative culture in the Careers section of their website. Make note of whether the interviewers' behaviors and attitudes reflect those claimed values.

It's important to understand the culture before accepting a new job. If their values don't align with yours, you're likely to struggle in your new working environment.

They Immediately Dismiss Any Negotiation Attempts

Most job offers assume some wiggle room up to 15 percent or 20 percent for the right candidate. Hiring managers expect candidates to negotiate.

Not every offer is negotiable. Sometimes, the first offer is already more than fair because they love you so much (nice job of interviewing, in that case). In other cases, they face budget restrictions that limit what the hiring manager can offer.

However, if you respectfully counter an initial offer, they should at least hear you out and see what they can do. If the salary isn't negotiable because of company policies, they should be willing to consider other ideas to sweeten the deal for you (a better title, more paid time off, schedule flexibility, or stock options, for example).

If any and all attempts to negotiate are met with a firm refusal, it's a bad sign. If they seem offended that you would even try to ask for more, it's a worse sign.

A healthy organization will respect your needs and expertise and want to offer you a fair amount. They will want you to feel good about accepting the offer and feel valued as an employee.

WARNING

An unwillingness to accommodate reasonable requests is a sign that they don't care about employee satisfaction. This is a cultural value you want to avoid at all costs.

They Ask Inappropriate Interview Questions

Interviewers should not ask you questions about personal details that can be used to discriminate against you. These include age, marital status, gender, religion, country of origin, health status, and others. (See Chapter 2 for a detailed overview of your rights during the hiring process and antidiscrimination laws.)

It isn't illegal to ask questions about these topics, but it *is* illegal to discriminate against a candidate based on their answers. Ethical companies train interviewers to avoid these questions and evaluate all candidates solely on their ability to do the job.

If interviewers ask inappropriate questions, take note. Sometimes it's an innocent mistake. They're new to interviewing or they skipped the training workshop and were just trying to make conversation when they asked whether you have kids.

Give them the benefit of the doubt if it seems warranted. Gracefully avoid the question (see the section in Chapter 2 on knowing your rights for how to do this) and redirect to a more relevant topic. If they continue pushing for information or you notice a pattern of repeated inappropriate questions, that's a big red flag.

REMEMBER

If bias is permitted in the organization, you don't want to work there.

Your Future Manager Is "a Character"

You've probably heard this code phrase used when discussing someone who's a major jerk. In the corporate world, "character" is rarely a compliment. If they meant it in a positive way, they would follow up with "funny" or "brilliant" or "creative."

Pay attention to all clues to your future manager's personality and reputation. You can learn a lot from your direct interactions with them. However, some managers are good at sticking to their best behavior during the interview phase.

Make note of how others speak about them and interact with them. You won't get honesty here. It's not appropriate for other interviewers to trash-talk your boss or tell you to get out while you can. You'll have to read between the lines.

Your relationship with your manager is a primary determinant of your job satisfaction. A good manager can make a tough job more rewarding. However, a toxic boss can turn a dream job into a nightmare.

You will spend a lot of time with this person. They will have significant control over your quality of work life and your future prospects. Do you trust them?

If you have a bad feeling, pay attention to that instinct. Don't jump to conclusions — instead, follow up. Try to get more information about your manager's reputation and management style. Ask other interviewers about your manager in a neutral, open-ended way — for example, "How long have you worked with Mr. Manager?" or "How would you describe Mr. Manager's leadership style?" (for direct reports). Pay attention to what they say *and* what they don't say.

No manager is perfect, but you want to do what you can to avoid getting stuck with a toxic boss.

They Trash-Talk Former Employees

If your interviewers feel comfortable making rude comments about others (not just former employees but also current employees or clients), it doesn't bode well for being treated with respect if you join the team.

I love a bit of harmless snark about a difficult client, but there's a line that shouldn't be crossed. If managers feel comfortable openly criticizing and mocking people in front of a complete stranger (you), they are unprofessional at best and probably just plain mean.

Do you want to work with these people? Do you want to put the fate of your career in the hands of these people?

TIP

Pay attention to how people in the company talk about each other in general. This is a reflection of the culture.

They Don't Care to Answer Your Questions

You should always have the opportunity to ask questions during an interview. If the interviewer doesn't give you time to ask questions, or if they scoff at your questions and avoid answering them, see it as a bad omen of the future.

During the interview phase, they're supposed to be trying to impress you. If they can't make time to explain the job or address your concerns now, just imagine how open they'll be once you're hired.

Choosing a new job is a life-altering decision. No matter how great the job description is (and let's face it, most of them stink), you'll have questions.

At best, this manager has zero social awareness. More likely, it's a sign that they don't care about your needs or about having a dialogue. Do you want to work with or for this person?

They Take Pride in Their "Fast-Paced" and "Demanding" Environment

Get ready to compete with your colleagues over who's the busiest and most stressed-out employee. If a demanding environment is a point of pride, it's important to find out why.

Certain fields are demanding by nature (medicine, stock trading, undercover espionage). You need to be able to stay calm under pressure.

I'm talking here about companies that purposely encourage a high-stress culture that rewards face time and discourages work-life balance.

Sometimes, it's a matter of degree and work preferences. A fast pace can be exciting and fun to a certain degree. High pressure and late nights are tolerable every now and then, but not every day. Pushing yourself to keep up will inevitably lead to burnout.

To determine whether "demanding" is code for "toxic," ask questions about the culture. Ask what a typical day looks like on the job. Inquire about the most challenging projects or initiatives they're working on right now.

If you're hearing a lot about "long nights," "working weekends," and "drinking to numb the anxiety" during the interviews, beware. In the interview, the person is supposed to be making the job sound attractive. The truth is probably even worse than what you're hearing about.

Chapter **19**

Ten Tips for Landing More Interviews

Though this book is about interviewing, I wanted to include a few job-search tips to help you increase your number of interview invitations (and therefore your odds of landing a fantastic job).

Endlessly applying to job boards isn't the only strategy that can help you land your next role. It's the most popular one, for sure, but popular can also mean overused.

Don't rely solely on the same methods everyone else is using. You can also find appealing opportunities through more creative strategies.

Invest Time in Analysis

Directions are useless if you don't know the destination. It's true for road trips, and it's true for career success.

The first and most important step in any successful job search is to get clarity about what you want and define your target jobs.

If you're still in the exploration stage, narrow it to a few specific destinations to investigate. You can always reroute later.

For each destination, define the industry, title (a general description is fine), and most desirable companies.

"I want to be a customer success manager at X company in Z industry."

Once you know where you want to go, you can ask for help on how to get there. You can also search for job openings in a more focused way.

TIP

Informational interviews can be a useful strategy during the exploration stage. Reach out to people who are where you want to be and prepare a list with questions to get the information you need. This will help you gain insights into the role and future growth opportunities. If the conversation goes well, you might end up with some excellent advice or even a referral.

Use a Targeted Strategy

Being intentional and having a clearly defined target is far more effective than a spray-and-pray strategy.

Create a target list of companies that you'd like to work for (with good values, an excellent salary, meaningful benefits, or anything else that makes your heart skip a beat). If you don't have a long wish list of companies, you can do additional targeting based on other parameters, such as title, key responsibilities, or size or type of company.

REMEMBER

You can always adjust your targeting strategy later if you're not getting the results you want.

Treat Your Job Search Like a Marketing Challenge

Marketers adjust their copywriting style to make their products stand out in a sea of other products. Similarly, you should adjust your job search strategy to stand out in a sea of other applicants.

The key is to highlight your unique value proposition and the benefits of hiring you, just like a marketer highlights the problems their product solves.

Here are some examples:

[Product] is life-changing ⇨ Doesn't tell you anything.

[Product] will help you sleep better ⇨ Tells you what you'll gain.

[Product] will help you sleep better in 30 days ⇨ Tells you what you'll gain by when.

Now adjust them for job-seeking:

"Exceeded quota" ⇨ Vague.

"Exceeded quota by 30 percent" ⇨ Getting there — I'm more interested now.

"Exceeded quota by 30 percent in 2 weeks by incorporating cold calling" ⇨ Great! Now I want to hire you.

This is called *positioning,* and the more you work on yours, the faster your "product" will sell.

TIP

I realize that some people don't like the idea of being self-promotional, and if you're struggling with that issue, please visit Chapters 14 and 16.

Pay Attention to Your Application Materials

You'll get better results if you take the time to modify your resume, cover letter, and maybe even your portfolio to match the must-have requirements of the role at hand. Even if you've narrowed your search to one job type, every company has different priorities, and addressing those can help you stand out.

Recruiters will scan your resume for just 6–8 seconds on average, and you can make the most of that attention by prominently featuring the skills they prioritized in the job description.

It doesn't have to be time-consuming. The most common resume sections to customize include the Professional Summary section, Skills list, and most recent position descriptions. (Make sure you're emphasizing the most relevant duties and successes.)

Even if you've targeted a few types of jobs, you can create standard resumes and cover letters for each type. Then you'll just need to compare these templates with each new job description, making a few minor edits to ensure you're highlighting the top qualifications.

REMEMBER

You'll get better results with quality than quantity. In other words, you can send a boilerplate resume to 50 roles and log more applications in less time. However, you'll likely nail down more interview invitations if you apply to fewer openings but spend a bit of time customizing your resume to move it past the gatekeepers.

Get Active on LinkedIn

If you're looking for a job, you can't afford to *not* be on LinkedIn. Your LinkedIn profile can be your job-search landing page.

Even better, as a social network, LinkedIn can be a valuable source of job leads and connections.

The best part is that you don't have to post to be active. You can engage with posts from connections, recruiters, and interesting people in your industry, and this can help you expand your network.

TIP

Optimize your profile before you start engaging. When people start checking out your profile, you want them to be impressed.

If you don't know where to start when it comes to optimizing your profile, follow this simple checklist:

>> **Update your profile picture:** Choose a clear and professional headshot. It doesn't have to be a professional shot but avoid cropped images or images with other people in them.

>> **Update your profile's URL:** Use your name. You don't want "user823" to pop up when someone shares your profile via messages.

>> **Update your profile headline:** This is the text that appears right below your name and the first thing a potential connection will read about you. Try to communicate your unique value proposition as an employee. This can be a job title, a career summary, or a more creative description of how you add value in your career. However, keep it concise and *don't* use all available characters. Consider what it will look like on mobile devices.

- » **Write a strong summary:** After the headline, the "About" section is the most commonly read. Tell your career story and highlight how you can help companies achieve their goals. Use the first person (*I*, not *he* or *she*). Incorporate keywords common in target job descriptions where you can.

- » **Start connecting with people you know:** You'll find that you know a lot of people, and most will be pleased to connect with you. Reach out to coworkers, friends, clients, vendors, university professors, and fellow alumni.

After you've covered the profile basics, it's time for some LinkedIn etiquette:

- » **Add value when you participate.** Commenting on others' posts is useful, but make sure that your comment adds something to the discussion. In other words, adding vague comments such as "Great post!" or the Clapping Hands emoji won't cut it. You don't need to be brilliant. Just include a few words about what you liked about the comment or add a related point.

- » **Being negative or critical on LinkedIn can have the same effect as being negative or critical in an interview.** Avoid venting and bad behavior, especially in a place where potential employers might be watching.

- » **When you're sending connection requests, provide the reason that you want to connect with that person.** Empty requests may be perceived negatively (as in "spammy"), and you want to start off on the right foot. You can mention what it is that brought you to their profile (similar career path, expertise, awards) and go from there. If you know the person (even slightly), mention how you've crossed paths. It's also fine to just say you read and enjoyed their recent posts or comments.

Being on LinkedIn increases your visibility as a candidate, thus increasing your chances of getting hired. And you'll probably meet some cool people that you wouldn't have met otherwise.

WARNING

You'll also encounter some not-so-cool people on LinkedIn, just as on any other social media platform. Some are there to spam, sell, build clout, make themselves sound important, or just share embarrassing selfies. Fortunately, it's easy to unfollow annoying posters or remove a connection if you get spammed.

Invest Time in Networking

You've probably heard the expression that "your network is your net worth," and there's definitely some truth to it despite the lack of real rhyming.

Early in my career, I went out of my way to avoid networking events until a mentor convinced me it was worth stepping out of my comfort zone to meet interesting people in my field. These days, networking is even easier because you don't even have to leave your home.

Although networking is often viewed as transactional, it doesn't have to be like that. You can customize your approach to fit your style and preferences.

For example, if you're someone who doesn't like in-person events or groups, you can stick to LinkedIn or Zoom events.

If you're new to networking, start by taking inventory of your current network

Make a list of every person you can think of in your various circles.

Once that's done, rate each one on a scale from 1 to 5 in terms of how likely they are to be a resource in your job search.

A *resource* isn't just someone who might refer you for a job. Think about those who can offer advice, ideas, or moral support. Think about those natural connectors, who love to make introductions. Think about those who have appreciated your work and might endorse you or be a future reference.

If you're unsure of someone, skip them and go back later.

Once your list is done and the ratings are complete, make a goal to contact five people daily, starting with the highest-rated.

You don't have to ask for help yet — just refresh the connection and catch up. Simply reconnecting with interesting people from your past may energize you and give you some new confidence.

By doing this, you'll also start to feel more comfortable about networking. You'll see that most people are happy to help when they can (and when asked respectfully).

And, by expanding your network, you will expand your opportunities significantly.

Start Doing Cold Outreach

Cold outreach is a tactic used by salespeople to close more deals. They pick up the phone or email their targets. It's called cold because they've never had an interaction with that person.

This strategy can work in your job search as well. Create a list of people with hiring power from your target companies — recruiters, HR reps, and hiring managers at larger companies, or maybe more senior executives at smaller companies.

Search for who's on LinkedIn and reach out to inquire about job opportunities. If you've already identified an open role at their company, ask for advice on whom to contact to apply.

Avoid long paragraphs, excessive details, irrelevant personal information, and desperation ("I need a job today" or similar wording).

Keep in mind that cold outreach is a numbers game. Many won't respond. Don't take it personally and don't spam them with follow-up.

When you get a response, analyze what worked and refine your strategy accordingly.

Always Follow Up

Fortune favors the bold and those who follow up thoughtfully.

>> Follow up after interviews.

>> Follow up with recruiters who reach out.

>> Follow up on all offers of help and advice.

>> Follow up with the people who told you, "Let me know if I can help with anything" when you identify something they could help you with.

>> Follow up on all non-creepy and non-spammy connection requests.

As the job seeker, it's your responsibility to keep the leads flowing.

REMEMBER

Don't spam or harass anyone. Time your follow-up to avoid coming across as pushy or inconsiderate.

Make Your Search Visible (If Possible)

If you can do it without jeopardizing your current job, be open about publicizing that you're looking for your next opportunity. Tell those closest to you (so that they can refer you to someone who's hiring) and post on social media where appropriate (the green banner on LinkedIn is a helpful resource for this task).

REMEMBER

If you're still employed and don't want your employer to know about your job search, you'll have to be more selective about whom you share your job search status with.

In my experience, people love helping when they can. However, your advocates can't know you need help if you don't tell them.

Also, if you discover that an acquaintance has a connection to an opportunity you're interested in, reach out to ask for a referral. Be respectful and appreciative but don't let shyness hold you back. A referral typically gets results four times faster than applying traditionally.

Rather than ask, "Can you refer me?" ask something like this: "Would you feel comfortable referring me for Position X? I think I'd be a great fit, and I'd be happy to answer any questions you have about my background."

Make Your Social Media Profiles Private

According to recent surveys, 67 percent of hiring managers use social media platforms to research potential hires.

Maintain control over your online presence and make your personal profiles private during your job search. You never know what can rub someone the wrong way and cause you to lose an opportunity.

WARNING

Even if you've made your profiles private, be cautious about the content you share online. Nothing is truly secure when it comes to the Internet.

Index

A

About Us section, of company website, 99–100
accent, 300
accessibility, 71–72
accomplishments
    bringing up, 7
    failing to promote, 14
adaptability, 20
after the interview
    etiquette rules, 48–52
    sending thank-you note, 49
age
    asking about, 318
    discrimination, 30, 31
Age Discrimination in Employment Act, 30
AI Resume tool, 27
Amazon, 61
Americans with Disabilities Act, 30
analytical skills, 181–182
Answer Builder tools, 239
antidiscrimination laws, 30–31
anxiety, interview
    curing, 243–246
    managing nerves during interview, 242
    positive thinking to reduce, 244
    practicing to reduce, 243
    psyching yourself up to reduce, 244
    recognizing reasons for, 242
    reducing, 241–248
    relaxation/confidence-boosting techniques for, 244–246
    unexpected questions and, 246–248
applicant tracking system (ATS), 27, 34
arms, crossing, 264
arrogance, avoiding, 8
artificial intelligence (AI)
    candidate communication with, 26
    candidate screening with, 26–27
    hiring for skills in, 19

interview analysis with, 27
jobs affected by, 19
job search with, 20
opportunities in, 20
overview, 19–20
resume screening with, 26
sourcing candidates with, 26
assessments
    interview/hiring cycle, 35–36
    purpose of, 35–36
    skill-based, 25, 35–36
asynchronous video interviews. *See* prerecorded video interviews
AsyncInterview, 72
ATS (applicant tracking system), 27
attention span, 312
authentic, being, 9–10
autism, 258

B

background checks, 38–39
badmouthing, 15, 44
bad posture, 262–263
bag, 252
Bain Interviewing (website), 81
ban-the-box laws, 30
bar raisers, 60–62
behavioral questions
    about, 177
    analyzing, 179–184
    bullet points for, 229
    definition of, 178
    examples by competency area, 179–183
    executive presence in answering, 287–288
    as opportunities, 178–179
    predicting, 107–108
    preparing for, 184–187
    reasons for asking, 178
    remote work experience/competencies, 22–24

About the Author

Pamela Skillings is a certified career and interview coach who has helped thousands of clients land their dream jobs.

She has more than 15 years of coaching experience and is the cofounder and chief coach for Big Interview, the top interview training platform, trusted by more than 700 colleges and universities, ten state workforce agencies, and millions of job seekers each year.

After starting her career in the corporate world and then working in senior-level roles at Mastercard, Citigroup, and other top firms, Pamela discovered her passion for career coaching after experiencing her own midcareer crisis. She walked away from a six-figure corporate job to start her career-coaching practice. Her first book, *Escape from Corporate America* (Random House), was inspired by her career change and a desire to help others looking for more fulfilling work.

Pamela cofounded Big Interview as part of her mission to help as many job seekers as possible and level the playing field for those without connections or access to a personal career coach.

Since then, Big Interview has taught millions of job seekers to ace their interviews and win job offers. Pamela's clients have landed jobs at top organizations, including Google, Goldman Sachs, Disney, Amazon, JPMorgan Chase, and the United Nations.

Pamela has been described as "a guru in the world of job interviews" by the *Wall Street Journal* and has been featured as a career expert by the *New York Times*, CNN, ABC News, and many other media outlets.

In addition to her work with job seekers, Pamela provides consulting and training to organizations committed to fair hiring practices. She has served as an adjunct professor at New York University, teaching future career counselors and coaches. She also provides advice on LinkedIn and loves to connect with readers — follow her at www.linkedin.com/in/skillful.

Pamela lives in New York City with her husband and son.

Dedication

To the amazing Big Interview team: You have created something much bigger than I ever dreamed.

To all my coaching clients over the years, who helped me become an interview expert and create a career that I love.

Author's Acknowledgments

Thanks to all the people who supported me in being able to write this book while managing a busy full-time job and life: my husband, Alex Andrei, and son, Benjamin Andrei, who made sure I took breaks to have fun; the team at Big Interview, especially Cristina Iancu and Maja Stojanovich, who helped with research and proofreading; Tatiana Mulry, who hosted a much-needed writing retreat; and all the wonderful people in my network who shared their insights and challenges for the book.

I also want to thank the dedicated team at Wiley for guiding me through the process and being such a pleasure to work with: acquisitions editor Jennifer Yee, project editor Paul Levesque, copyeditor Becky Whitney, and proofreader Susan Hobbs. Additionally, Wiley hires an outside technical editor to validate the book's content. This book's TE was Maryse Williams, the founder of JobMorph and a former career services director for The Art Institutes and ECPI University.

Finally, a sincere thanks to my parents: Wesley Skillings, who inspired me to write books and always makes me laugh; and Mary Skillings, who showed me the joy that comes from teaching and helping others succeed.

Publisher's Acknowledgments

Acquisitions Editor: Jennifer Yee
Senior Project Editor: Paul Levesque
Copy Editor: Becky Whitney
Technical Editor: Maryse Williams

Production Editor: Pradesh Kumar
Cover Image: © laflor/Getty Images

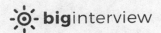
biginterview

Crush Your Interview and Land Your Next Job — Months Faster

All the tips, tools, and practice lessons you need to land your job 4 months faster than the national average

4 WAYS YOU CAN DO THIS

1 Learn How To Answer The Hardest Questions

2 Practice Your Responses Via Video

3 Get AI Answer Feedback

4 Correct Any Of Your Mistakes

LEARN HOW TO OVERCOME TYPICAL OBJECTIONS

MUST-KNOW TACTICS YOU CAN MASTER IN 2 HOURS

CREATE ORIGINAL ANSWERS FOR EVERY QUESTION

READY TO ACE YOUR INTERVIEW? → *Go to **dummies.com/go/bigInterview/** to get your free access*

Big Interview has helped millions of people land jobs at companies like: